WOMEN IN THE WORKPLACE

WOMEN IN THE WORKPLACE:
EFFECTS ON FAMILIES

edited by

Kathryn M. Borman
Daisy Quarm
Sarah Gideonse

University of Cincinnati

ABLEX PUBLISHING CORPORATION
NORWOOD, NEW JERSEY 07648

Printed in the United States of America.

Library of Congress Cataloging in Publication Data
Main entry under title:

Women in the workplace.

   "Developed from a conference held at the University
of Cincinnati in May 1981"—Pref.
   Includes bibliographies and indexes.
   1. Mothers—Employment—United States—Congresses.
2. Children of working parents—United States—
Congresses. I. Borman, Kathryn M. II. Quarm, Daisy.
III. Gideonse, Sarah. IV. University of Cincinnati.
V. Title: Women in the work place.
HD6055.2.U6W65 1984   306.8'5'0973   84-2941
ISBN 0-89391-166-6

Ablex Publishing Corporation
355 Chestnut Street
Norwood, New Jersey 07648

Contents

Dedication

This book is dedicated to our parents:
Edward J. and Eleanor Ficzere Matey
Gordon Lea and Sue Baird Quarm
Theodore and Eila Karwoski

Preface

Women with young children have become an increasingly large and important presence in the workplace. This book focuses on the consequences of women's labor force participation for child care arrangements, family roles, and government policy.

The book's contents are organized into three sections, each composed of chapters with common themes. The Introduction examines the role of the government in responding to the inequities and stresses associated with women's changing economic role. It discusses how government action is constrained by the social context, and in particular by societal values and ideologies. Mythologies surrounding the place of the family in society, appropriate sex roles, the work ethic, the relationship between work and family, and even government's responsibility for the family have hobbled government action. An analysis of the use of scientific information in the policy-making process serves to illustrate problems in producing government reform beneficial to women and their families.

Following the Introduction, the first group of chapters examines childhood socialization. The authors explore effects of maternal employment and other family changes on children's development and socialization as well as the relationship of childhood socialization to adult work roles. Drawing heavily on Sroufe's research on the "kind of care infants and young children require to thrive," Sroufe and Ward (Chapter 1) argue that information about quality care should be considered in making decisions about employment and out-of-home childcare. In Chapter 2, Michael Lamb reviews the available research evidence about "new" forms of family and childcare arrangements. Lamb considers the impact of maternal employment, increased involvement of fathers, and single parenthood on the development of young children. Alice Honig (Chapter 3) uses statistics on working mothers, family configurations, teen parenting, child abuse and neglect, and divorce and remarriage to describe the world in which children are now growing up. Honig goes on to report research on working mothers, childcare arrangements and child adjustment, and innovations in daycare practices. The final chapter in this section, by Borman and Frankel, argues that a major barrier to women's effectiveness in organizational life is the very structure of the workplace. Drawing on Borman's research on children's games, the authors suggest that girls' exclusion from complex games on the playground precludes their preparation for the complex male "games" of the organization.

The chapters in the second section focus on paid and unpaid work, the reciprocal relationships of work and family, sex roles, and inequality. Mortimer and Sorensen provide a comprehensive overview of the linkages between work and family life. Work is not only the source of economic resources but also is a constraint on family life through the psychological impact of work experience on parents. In separate chapters, Glazer and Quarm both highlight the role ideology plays in the persistence of gender inequality. Tying family and gender role ideology closely to the needs of monopoly capitalism, Glazer emphasizes that women's new freedoms— to work, leave marriages, and raise children alone—exist alongside old and new burdens and inequalities. Quarm maintains that the costs of inequality far outweigh the benefits. Consequences of inequality for women include poverty, mental illness, abuse, and burdensome responsibilities.

The two chapters in the final section of the book examine the implications of research for future government policy. Farber reports research investigating the impact of recent historical events on kinship orientations and reproductive cycles. He suggests that current shifts in family norms may be a function of cohort differences in values, and adds the caution that effects of policies may vary according to family orientations. Grubb and Lazerson also use a historical perspective to illuminate connections between the American family and its childrearing responsibilities. They illustrate the contrary effects on families of capitalism, male dominance, and work and childrearing roles, all of which are exacerbated by the ambiguous role taken by the state.

This volume developed from a conference held at the University of Cincinnati in May 1981. The conference assembled the scholars whose work is included here. Their perspectives are taken from the disciplines of psychology, sociology, history, anthropology, and public policy. Partially funded by the Ohio Humanities Council, the conference was an effort to share scholarly analyses with the university community and others.

The major theme was the social significance of maternal employment. A secondary purpose was to generate thought and discussion concerning how the workplace, family services, and public policy should respond to changes resulting from employment shifts. We acknowledge the help and support of all who participated in these discussions, and wish especially to thank the Ohio Humanities Council for its important role in providing funds.

Kathryn Borman
Daisy Quarm
Sarah Gideonse

Introduction.
Government Response to Working Women and Their Families: Values, the Policy-Making Process, and Research Utilization*

Sarah Gideonse

University of Cincinnati

This chapter addresses the federal government's responsibility toward working women and their families, a burden it has been reluctant to assume. A majority of women in the United States are now engaged in paid work outside their homes. This demographic change, which began during World War II, has affected the relationships and roles of family members, employers, and government policy makers. While employment has benefited women and their families in many ways, a number of serious inequities and stresses are associated with women's changing economic role. The demands and characteristics of the workplace can interfere with optimal parenting and family functioning, while family responsibilities can interfere with work effectiveness and mobility. Working women are disadvantaged in pay, job and training opportunities, social security, and the tax code. These problems, together with other societal trends that make many women household heads and sole breadwinners, result in special economic and psychological stress for women and their families. The consequences for children's development is a particular concern.

Reformers and family advocates have called for a variety of government actions for dealing with these problems. Although some progress has been made in this long agenda, notably in ending overt job discrim-

* The author wishes to thank Kathryn Borman and Daisy Quarm, her coauthors, and Pam Maxfield, Susan Fish, and Hendrik Gideonse, for their criticisms and suggestions in preparing this chapter.

1

ination, obtaining politically acceptable solutions has been difficult. Government response has been minimal and characterized by conflict about the appropriateness, feasibility, and thrust of government action. Tension about what is properly public and what is essentially private, and the myriad conflicts inherent in our pluralistic society, have made public action in this area problematic. Indeed, there is uncertainty in the policy-making community about whether federal intervention can or should promote either the health of the family (Steiner, 1981; Wallach, 1981) or greater economic equity (Glazer, Chap. 6; Grubb & Lazerson, Chap. 9, this volume). This chapter takes the position that, although the family and most workplaces are private institutions, their complex interrelationships and the constraints of the social structure make public action necessary and inevitable, if the stresses and inequities affecting working women and their families are to be alleviated.

An initial examination of the social context in which families, employers, and government operate provides a perspective for the chapter's analysis of these problems. The record of federal policy in behalf of working women and their families is then reviewed. The discussion which follows focuses on one particular tool for achieving reform—the application to public policy of the type of scientific knowledge represented in this volume and the barriers to its effective use. Other approaches and impediments to government action are addressed in subsequent chapters.

Some preliminary definitions are in order. *Social context* refers to the social structure—the historical conditions, culture, values, and ideologies and conflicts among them; social, educational, economic, and political institutions and organizations; laws; system of stratification; and role definitions and expectations for different groups—ethnic, age, sex, and classes.

Public policy has a variety of referents. Policy can signify overarching goals or perspectives that serve as criteria for action by a decision making unit—a presidential administration, departmental bureau, or political party, for example. Instances are Carter's announced intention to promote policies that strengthen the family, or Reagan's goal to reduce government spending and interference in the private sector. Such policies for the family can be explicit and coherent, or more implicit, to be inferred from a pattern of decisions over time in a number of policy areas (taxes, social services, welfare, housing, economic regulations, etc.), as in the United States (Kamerman & Kahn, 1978). Policy can also mean strategies for solving problems, such as the "new Federalism," "benign neglect," or programs for educating young children as a way of combatting intergenerational poverty. Finally, policies are evidenced in a wide variety of actions through all phases of the policy process, in formulation, implementation, and evaluation. Government actions include decisions to initiate legislation or ex- and or terminate a program, enacted laws, regulations, budgets and ap- propriations, presidential vetoes, or court decisions.

Research utilization is used in this chapter to mean reference in the policy process to outcomes of research and the application of scientific tools. Research includes basic and applied research, development, his- torical analyses, ethnography, surveys, experiments, evaluations, de- mography, statistical analysis, and other systematic inquiry and analysis.

THE SOCIAL CONTEXT

Our society has expected families and individuals to work out their own destinies with their own resources and to be responsible for their own successes and failures. Americans see work, in which individual family members spend much of their lives, as a world separate from the family and do not adequately recognize either the consequences of work for in- dividual and family lives or the contribution of the family to the workplace (Mortimer & Sorensen, Chap. 5, this volume). Government has largely refrained from concerning itself directly with the family's well-being until it has overtly failed in its responsibilities (see Glazer, Chap. 6; Grubb & Lazerson, Chap. 9 this volume).

To help suggest the range and complexities of influences on employed mothers and their families I draw on two perspectives: (a) Bronfenbren- ner's (1979) view of the environment as a set of nested dolls that affect the developing person at the innermost level, and (b) life course theory that looks at the complex relationships among personality, behavior, and situation within historical contexts (e.g., Runyan, 1982). A brief application of these perspectives to the topic at hand precedes a closer look at a few areas of the social context most salient to understanding the public re- sponsibility for the situation of women in the workplace.

The Perspectives

At the outermost level of the environment, according to Bronfenbrenner, is the "macrosystem," cultural consistencies and belief systems, at least of the majority. In our society these would include:

1. the work ethic and beliefs about individual responsibility for eco- nomic success and failure;
2. differentiated expectations about the abilities, appropriate levels of aspiration, and family and work roles for sexes, ethnic groups, and classes; and patterns of socialization, opportunity, and dis- crimination reflected by these expectations;

3. belief in the family as separate from the workplace, a haven in a heartless world;
4. beliefs about the government's limited role and function in relation to working women and their families.

Next is the "exosystem," settings and events in which the family is not participating directly but which affect it. Individual and family exosystems vary and may be characterized by:

1. economic, labor, and educational policies affecting employment and training, as well as the decision-making processes through which these policies are established;
2. characteristics of the economic system as they affect work, status, income and other life conditions of breadwinners and their families, such as:
   a. opportunities, methods, and bases for job recruitment and promotion;
   b. amount of hierarchy, power or status differential in jobs;
   c. pay scales;
   d. "the amount of variety, autonomy, and meaningful responsibility"

(Special Task force, 1973, p. 270) versus the amount of required obedience, routine, and repetition inherent in jobs.

The "mesosystem" or relationships between settings in which particular families or individuals participate refers particularly to the interconnections of work and home and linkages between family and other caretaking settings for children.

The "microsystem" is a "pattern of activities, roles and interpersonal relations experienced by the developing person in a given setting" (Bronfenbrenner, 1979, p. 22). For our purposes the microsystem is the family, where the influences of the social context, as they affect parental employment, are worked out in interactions among family members. These influences affect both tangible and less tangible aspects of family life. Relatively evident is the impact on family members and the overall health and stability of family life of the family's economic security and social status; the amount of parent accessibility; and the resources available to family members both to purchase the goods, services, and environment necessary for individual well-being and achievement (proper nutrition, health care, education, etc.) and to maximize noneconomic cultural values (Levine, 1974). Less obvious, perhaps, are the effects on family life of the amount of pressure and degree of self-esteem, satisfaction, and personal growth permitted by parents' working conditions (Piotrkowski, 1979); parental goals and values for themselves and their children (Kohn, 1977);

and the modes of adapting to life's circumstances that parents teach their children (Maccoby, 1980). Of course these influences vary with the ontological history, personal strengths, adaptive resources, and maturational levels of individual family members, family structure, and the tasks and stresses inherent in a family's particular stage in a life cycle.

Life course theory is helpful in understanding individuals' interactions with the social context. In this view, individuals move through historical time and the social structure interacting with situations to produce particular behaviors, feelings, and experiences. Behavior in turn affects the individual's personal states and the situations next encountered, part of which the individual can select, create, or influence. The course of experience then is partly a function of individual goals, plans, and choices. The individual can be said to bear some responsibility for many of life's choices and the quality of family relationships. Previous experiences (in the family, education, employment, for example) set individuals on particular life courses, however, and affect the situations they encounter. These experiences, in combination with constraints in the social structure, may limit choice, the perception that a range of choice exists, the clarity of consequences, and the extent to which goals are seen as attainable (Borman & Frankel, Chap. 4, this volume; deLone, 1979; Runyan, 1982).

Placing the family and its members in this broad context does not mean that family life and what happens to individual family members can only be explained in terms of external variables, or that government alone can intervene to manipulate these variables for the benefit of family life and the life progress of individuals in families. It does assert that predicting outcomes for family members requires reference to these factors and that reformers and government leaders ignore the impact of the social system in which families work out their destinies at the risk of great societal stress.[1]

Certain aspects of the macro- and exosystems are particularly relevant to understanding the record of government action on behalf of working women, as well as the barriers to completing the agenda of societal supports. The following section discusses four of these: (a) the relationships between sex-role definitions and work, (b) the work ethic and working conditions, (c) belief in the privacy of the family, and (d) conflicting views about government action. These topics of course do not exhaust the list of pertinent social structure influences on the policy-making process, but, together with other chapters in this volume, should provide an adequate context for viewing the task ahead.

---

[1] The social context variables also do not have a unidirectional affect. Changes in the family structure and sex roles, for example, have influenced ideology and laws (Hayes, 1982). See Mortimer and Sorensen, Chap. 5, this volume, for discussion of the reciprocal influences of family and work.

Sex-Role Identification and Work

Historians can trace the American ideal of different male and female family and work roles to colonial days. However, it was industrialization and urbanization, which separated male and female roles geographically and experientially, that permitted this ideal to approach reality. The male as family head and breadwinner whose paid employment was necessary for family survival and the female as supported wife, mother, household manager, and facilitator of consumption were thus divisions of labor based on economic and historical circumstances. The division became normative, particularly for native stock, middle-class women for whom not working was consistent with their social status and reflective of their husbands' capacity as providers (Chafe, 1976).[2] Many minority, immigrant, and low-income women, large proportions of whom held jobs, probably also ascribed to the ideal of the good husband's responsibility to support his family financially. To them, the good woman's obligation was to nurture her children, defer to her husband, and care for the home, while the good man's duty was to support his family (Komarovsky, 1940; Liebow, 1967; Rainwater, 1970; Rubin, 1976).

Despite the discrepancy between reality and the norm for this latter group and increasingly since the Depression, for middle-class wives and mothers also, this ideal has been remarkably persistent. Adlai Stevenson's injunction to the graduating women of Smith College in 1955 that their role was to "influence man and boy" through the "humble role of house-wife" expressed widely held beliefs (Chafe, 1976, p. 7). In a study of occupational status in 1973, respondents ranked "housewife" higher than 70% of other female dominated occupations (Acker, 1978).

The ideal as normative belief has also been pervasive. It has affected socialization, employment, and training opportunities available for each sex, individual values, occupational choices and achievement, and government policy. Paid work for women has usually required traits and skills isomorphic to those of homemaker mothers, and has been sex-segregated, subordinate, and low paid (Barrett, 1979; Berch, 1982; Ferber, 1982b). The assumption that women were not supporting a family or that their pay represented nonessential income was used as a justification to pay women lower wages (Chafe, 1976).

The effects on women's economic choices of their commitment to the maternal role in particular contradicted classic economic theories. These predict, for example, that better educated women, like better educated men, would spend more time in paid work than less educated

---

[2] Ironically, while these attitudes persisted, since the Depression it was the fact of wives' working that allowed many familes to attain middle-class status (Chafe, 1976).

women, because of their relatively greater productivity level, i.e., their ability to obtain higher wages and the cost of not being in the labor market. Actually, better educated women during the childrearing years spent no more time than other women in the labor market; in fact they spent less. Even controlling for family income, educated women invested more time in the educational and social development of their children, not only because they could afford to, but also because they were more "productive" or "better" at it than lesser educated women. They were more effective in imparting knowledge and skills. Potentially greater productivity in the work force led women to a different allocation of time from men, specifically to roles and tasks seen by them and society to be more important (Moock, 1974).[3]

Societal sex-role expectations affect individual choices about acquiring human capital (education and training) and about the type of work to pursue. They restrict women's labor market opportunities. Numerous studies and analyses have attempted to sort out the relative importance of individual versus workplace factors on women's achievement of occupational status and income (see, for example, research reported by Borman and Frankel, Chap. 4, this volume; Ferber, 1982a, 1982b; Smith, 1979). In contrast to men, whose achievement is enhanced by family attachment, women's wife and mother roles have had a negative effect on their status and income (Mortimer & Sorensen, Chap. 5, this volume). In addition, the occupational status and income of men is explained by fewer variables and by variables of the demographic type—such as father's occupation and status, education, and first job's status. Explanatory variables for women's achievement are much more numerous and tied into sex role expectations and attitudes. A recent analysis (Acock & Edwards, 1982), for example, identified age of marriage and nontraditional sex-role ideology as the most important variables for predicting achievement, along with the more demographic variables, mother's education and woman's education as indirect effects as well as previous jobs.

The Work Ethic and Work

At the same time the nonpaid homemaker role has been ostensibly honored and women's working outside the home portrayed as a threat to family stability and optimal development of children, society has valued paid work much more highly than homemaking: "Earning a living is virtually synonymous with being defined as an adequate person" (Keniston, 1977, p. 84). Work is seen as providing money, self-respect, status, and meaning

---

[3] These findings, reported by Moock (1974), came from studies by Arleen Liebowitz, reported in several unpublished and published papers in the early seventies.

to life (Goodwin, 1972, p. 1). People are identified by what they do, what they make, how they perform—by their achievements rather than by their ascriptive status, as in the family (Rainwater, 1970). Work in fact provides experiences that relate to basic needs of human beings: structure, social experiences beyond the home, participation in "collective purposes," status and identity, and "regular activity" (Jahoda, 1982, pp. 83-84).

Commitment to paid work is a central value in our society. The work ethic of the modern industrial world stresses individual "achievement . . . and universalism [e.g., merit] as a mode for selection for occupational placement" (Rossi & Blum, 1969, p. 49) and extols economic individualism and independence. A majority views success as a result of a person's own initiative and talent and other personality traits. Lack of success, in contrast, is an individual's own fault, rather than the fault of circumstances and birth, exigencies of the labor market, or factors beyond one's control. It reveals lack of effort and other character defects (Feagin, 1975, p. 92). In addition to financial stress, not being employed, particularly for men and increasingly for women, has a number of psychological and social consequences—feelings of inadequacy and failure, social isolation, disorganization, purposelessness, loss of status and identity, family authority, and community respect, even when lack of jobs is widespread (Elder, 1974; Jahoda, 1982; Jahoda, Lazarsfeld & Zeisel, 1933; Komarovsky, 1940; Stone & Schlamp, 1971).

Commitment to the work ethic appears to be accompanied by general satisfaction with one's work. Various research findings point to the conclusion "that most people find their work important and derive satisfaction from it" (Anthony, 1977, p. 274). A great majority of people, including women and those faced with the most menial job opportunities, say they would continue to work even if they did not have to (Goodwin, 1972; Hoffman, 1979; Quinn & Shepard, 1974).[4]

The commitment to work is generally maintained, despite the fact that for the majority of workers in our society the requirements of work are in many ways antithetical to both personhood and parenthood. Workers most want jobs with "variety, autonomy, and meaningful responsibility" and opportunity "to become masters of their immediate environment and ...[gain] feelings that their work and they themselves are important" (Special Task Force, 1973, pp. 269–270). However, such job characteristics are generally associated with managerial and professional work (as is the greatest job satisfaction), rather than with lower level jobs which are far more numerous (Katz & Kahn, 1978). Even those jobs considered "good"

---

[4] Commentators have noted the methodological weakness of much research on worker satisfaction but also the consistency of its findings (Anthony, 1977; Katz & Kahn, 1978; Special Task Force, 1973).

by our society—primary sector employment, which offers job security, formal channels of advancement and employment relations "governed by a more or less explicit system of industrial jurisprudence" (i.e., unionization) (Doeringer & Piore, 1975, p. 70), are often routine, scheduled, and repetitive; many demand a narrow range of skills with inadequate opportunity for workers to use complex mental and physical skills or the development of new skills. They require conformity to external authority and close supervision, even coercion, rather than self-direction, responsibility, or a chance to affect the work environment (Kohn, 1977), to have control over how and when an output is produced and the use to which it is put. The increase in specialization, technology, and bureaucratization in the workplace is endangering those occupations that have been traditionally autonomous (Piotrkowski, 1979; Special Task Force, 1973). Even these are becoming "jobs that are too small for our spirit" (Terkel, 1972, p. xxix).

Moreover, for a significant segment of the working population, particularly for women and minority group members, such "good" jobs are not readily available. They must find jobs in what has been called the "secondary market sector"—services, seasonal work, nonunionized manufacturing, many of which are pink collar ghettos. Here jobs are characterized by lower wages and fewer benefits, poor working conditions, insecurity of tenure, and little chance for advancement or on-the-job training (Doeringer & Piore, 1975; Baker, 1978). Even more than jobs in the primary sector, many of these jobs offer little intrinsic satisfaction, little in terms of "prestige, pride, and self-respect" (Liebow, 1967, p. 60).

In both types of work women (as well as minorities) must face discrimination in types of job opportunities, pay scale, and chances for training and promotion. They also experience sexual harassment, as well as subtle interpersonal rebuffs, and lack of cooperation in the on-the-job training necessary for success (Doeringer & Piore, 1975; Ferber, 1982a). In addition, employers' personnel policies, scheduling, and other procedures often conflict with parenting responsibilities. There is with all these problems some reduced commitment to working and reduced staying power in jobs (particularly among those employed in the secondary sector), as well as some unknown degree of psychological alienation (Anderson, 1980; AuClaire, 1979; Baker, 1978; Liebow, 1967; Katz & Kahn, 1978). But for most workers the work ethic is maintained, even though the conditions of work are problematical.

Many societal institutions have a stake in enforcing these work norms. Although preparation for adult economic self-maintenance is part of any society's socialization program (Inkeles, 1968; LeVine, 1974), people in Western industrialized societies are socialized to believe that not taking work seriously is delinquent (Anthony, 1977). Unemployment and poverty, particularly when widespread, endanger social control by breaking down the reward and penalty bond between individuals and social institutions. Without work people may not conform to communal and family roles, begin to question the legitimacy of the social order and rules, and threaten political unrest. Providing family income gives the breadwinner authority and control within the family, stabilizes a basic institution, and enhances societal stability. In addition, the economic system depends on a dedicated work force and cheap labor supply.

Government ties economic survival to work in many ways. Although authorities have fluctuated in their response to pauperism, relief has frequently been given only in return for work, even for women with young children. Disincentives in addition to work requirements have been used to minimize relief rolls, legally, by strict eligibility requirements, or more informally by intrusive and condescending treatment of applicants by social service agencies. Individuals only become eligible for old age pensions and unemployment benefits when not needed in the work force (Piven & Cloward, 1971).

Belief in the Privacy of the Family

Belief in the privacy of the family includes at least two ideas: (a) that the workplace is a world separate from the family; and (b) that government should involve itself minimally in the family. The belief in the separation of work and family is common, despite the large amount of time individual family members spend at work and the number of reciprocal influences between work and family. The perception is not just a result of the obvious discontinuities of work and home, i.e., that children can no longer follow their parents around at their work as they could on a family farm or business, that housewives' work does not contribute directly to family income, that domestic and commercial relationships have different bases, or even that the routine, segmented nature of many jobs requires the workers' minimal involvement—although all these circumstances are factors. Family breadwinners themselves often see the worlds as separate. They, in fact, value the separation, using it as a way of disengaging from stress or absorptiveness of work, protecting themselves and their families from negative or conflicting emotions generated by their work lives (Piotrkowski, 1979). One consequence of this belief is that employers have not, for the most part, felt it necessary to make adjustments for their employees' family lives.

Government reluctance to involve itself in the family has been traditional, at least in terms of explicit policy to strengthen and support the family. Reflecting American individualistic ideology, policy has generally focused on individuals, who may, of course, be family members, or on alleviating or remediating, rather than forestalling, severe family dysfunction and economic weakness (impoverishment, mental illness, family breakup, etc.). Just as prevalent has been concern that this important institution and its functions be preserved, that government intervention might have negative impact or effectively endorse particular family patterns. Such concerns were expressed in President Nixon's 1971 veto message about comprehensive day care legislation, which argued against committing "the vast moral authority of the National Government to the side of communal approaches to child rearing and against the family-centered approach" (Kamerman & Kahn, 1978, p. 430).

Conflicting Views About Government Action

In recent years the views just discussed have been challenged, and considerable controversy has erupted. This challenge occurs at a time of increasing disquiet about the survival of the family in its traditional form, a heightened understanding of the importance of families for children's development and later achievements, a concern about the implications for families of large numbers of mothers in the workforce, and a determination to achieve equity for women and minorities. The history of recent efforts to engage governmental resources and authority to strengthen families has been well documented elsewhere. These have included proposals to improve families' stability and economic security, alleviate special family problems, such as teenage parenting, redistribute income, enhance the development of children, and alleviate stresses and inequities for working women (e.g., Hayes, 1982; Steiner, 1981; Wallach, 1981). Conflict has surrounded these policy debates about what constitutes a family problem, about what its causes and solutions are, and the appropriate role of government, if any. Policy deliberations have had to deal with such issues as the appropriate sex roles for men and women in the family; how, where, by whom, and with whom children should be raised; what constitutes equity in employment; and the locations of responsibility for educational and economic success and failure (the individual, the family, the culture, the environment).

Public officials, interest groups, and constituencies may occasionally agree on what constitutes an important goal for women, children, and families, such as high quality care for children. At the same time they may still disagree on the extent to which that goal is not being met (see, for example, Bruce-Briggs, 1977; Kamerman, 1980), the most effective solutions and whom they should benefit (e.g., tax credits for day care of individual choice, public support of group day care settings, disincentives to working mothers), the relative priority of the problem given limited resources, and whether the problem should be best left in the private sector.

Family and child policy issues tend to coalesce along liberal and conservative lines. There is, of course, considerable controversy on each side, depending on the issue and the interests being served. Liberals are more willing to risk government action to prevent, rather than remediate, family problems, but are well within the tradition of protecting pluralism and privacy. Their goals are to enhance the capacity of families to function and parents to be in control, to promote the development of children, and to prevent the perpetuation of inequalities. Recent liberal thinking views gross income discrepancies as the main barrier to good parenting. Income buys security, relief from stress, decent housing and neighborhoods, the prerogative to choose quality services and to take advantage of available educational and cultural opportunities. It enables parents to have higher aspirations for their children. Although liberals place much of the responsibility for current social problems within the environment, the purpose of their proposed reforms is to restore to private families effective responsibility for their own destinies by giving them adequate resources and choices (Lichtman, 1981; also deLone, 1979; Keniston, 1979). Weak families mean more government (President Carter, quoted by Steiner, 1981). Liberal proposals include different methods of income redistribution and ways to end sex and ethnic group discrimination, promote job equity and full employment, and remove barriers to effective family functioning and optimal child development.

In general, conservatives advocate little government action to assist families except the most unlucky and dysfunctional. They believe that parents should take more responsibility for their economic lives and private behavior and for developing their children's characters. As such, they oppose government's supplying funds that may support life styles they see as immoral (e.g., having illegitimate children, communal living, homosexual unions). They doubt that income has much to do with happy stable families or bringing up children to be responsible adults (Lichtman, 1981). They point out that family instability (i.e., divorce, illegitimacy, etc.) has accelerated since 1960, at the same time that the federal government's efforts at income redistribution and economic prosperity have increased real family income (Carlson, 1980; Finn, 1978). Conservatives are less sanguine than liberals about the potential for damaging families with government programs. They decry the effects of welfare dependency on individual initiative and children's socialization for adult economic roles and the potential government interference in parental control of child-rearing and traditional family functions (McCathren, 1981).

A major inconsistency in the conservative stance is their support of legislation that interposes government into the privacy of women's lives and families. For example, their efforts to limit women's access to abortions interfere with individual and family choice about reproduction. The attempt to require that parents be informed when minors obtain prescription birth control devices at federally funded clinics infringed on relationships between parents and their children, mainly daughters. This inconsistency suggests conservatives have a more fundamental agenda than reducing government interference. Certainly part of it is the maintenance of women's traditional roles and relationships (see, e.g., Gelb & Palley, 1982).

Summary

Working women and their families are operating in a world with strongly held values and value conflicts about appropriate sex roles for women; relationships between and among individuals, families, the workplace, and the government; the work ethic; theories about the causes and cures of social problems; and how government should intervene, if at all. These belief systems are reflected in the structure of work and other institutions affecting economic opportunity. There are also the realities of workplace, over which individuals and families have little control, and the requirements of society for good workers, stable families, conformity to societal norms, and new generations of workers. As the next section will document, values and realities have had a profound influence on the record of government action in behalf of working women and their families.

RECORD OF GOVERNMENT ACTION

Historically, the United States government's posture toward workers and their families has been generally consistent in reflecting traditional societal attitudes about sex roles, families, work, and the proper role of government. Policies which have enforced the work ethic by tying survival with work, for example, are consistent with a belief in economic individualism, as are social security and manpower programs, which have differential benefits for men and women and reinforce normative sex role definitions. During the last 50 years, however, unprecedented events, as well as major societal trends, have led to departures from what might be called normative policies. The Great Depression is one historical event that led the government to change its hands-off policy with regard to work and social security. The greatly increased numbers of women in the workplace represent a recent and important trend that has been associated with policies promoting sexual equity at work and financial relief for child care, replacing a number of policies that discouraged women from working.

Government policies can be divided into those that are directed to work and training, which have largely benefited men, since they, as traditional breadwinners, have usually been given preference, and those that are mainly directed to women's financial support and employment.

Government and Men's Work

Until the Depression, breadwinners, mainly men, were expected to find work in the "free market" economy and to rely on private institutional or family charity when unable to support themselves and their families. Government had no obligation to assure jobs, income or training or to regulate the economy to prevent wide economic fluctuations. Although a distinction was made between the deserving and undeserving poor, official responses to poverty reflected the belief that poverty was a failure of personal initiative and character. Alms houses, which emerged with urbanization and industrialization and required work in exchange for minimal support, were essentially punitive in intention. Progressive Era reforms assumed that the poor were dependent children and that the state should act as a parent. Widows were required to demonstrate moral worthiness in order to receive pensions (Goodwin & Milius, 1978; Piven & Cloward, 1971; Rothman, 1978).

The recognition that the unemployed were "your friends and mine, . . . [not] unemployables and chronic dependents" during the unprecedented crisis of the Great Depression resulted in an expanded federal role in protecting economic and personal security that included providing work and work training. During the Depression years, the government sponsored a variety of job creation and work relief projects as part of its effort to keep people from starving, to "maintain the morale, skills, and physical condition" of workers, and to provide jobs to those who wanted them and who were normally hard workers. Men were the beneficiaries of the great bulk of these programs, although a women's division existed for a few years to plan "special projects for women and to see that they got equal consideration for jobs in other agencies when *suitable* opportunities existed." Suitable opportunities were such traditional tasks as sewing, canning, nursing, and the like (Goodwin & Milius, 1978, pp. 7–12).

The federal involvement in economic security was a precedent; after World War II, Congress committed itself to full employment but waited until the early sixties, when unemployment rose, to enact a variety of manpower programs. Their thrust has been to increase human capital in keeping with the view that individuals' characteristics are responsible for their unemployment. Programs were designed to rehabilitate workers, to compensate for deficits in education, skills, and other characteristics seen as necessary for employability (e.g., promptness, dress, job-seeking skills) and for obsolete skills caused by changes in technology. Intermittently, the government has created and/or subsidized jobs, mostly in the public sector, and authorized tax credits to employers who hire certain categories of workers. The emphasis in recent years has been on the hard-to-employ, the cyclically and structurally unemployed, and youth.

Many of these programs have provided temporary income and, in some cases, have helped participants obtain secure well-paid employment. In general, however, they have not significantly reduced the employment problems of their target groups. One reason for this failure is the continued assumption that it is the characteristics of the individual rather than of the economic system and the labor market that need changing. A second reason has been the worsening of the economy and changes in technology, which have brought about significant reductions in traditional working class jobs as well as requirements for specialized training and skills for available jobs. Third, the programs have often not emphasized necessary remedial education or rigorous training in marketable job skills (Ginzberg, 1980; Levitan & Marwick, 1973)

Government and Women's Work

Government actions have both reflected prevailing societal attitudes about women's role and supported the labor requirements of the economic system. At the turn of the century, beliefs about women's proper place were reflected in regulatory legislation that limited hours and conditions in which women could work. Lawmakers justified the regulations as protecting mothers' childbearing and rearing, housekeeping, and other family functions. Historical evidence suggests, however, that the laws' enactment may have also been motivated by an interest in preventing women from competing for scarce jobs in a labor surplus economy (Berch, 1982). In contrast, during World War II when women's labor was necessary for the national defense, married women were encouraged to take jobs previously viewed as appropriate only for men, and some federal funds for day care facilities were allocated. Even then, the monies were minimal, and those facilities supervised by the Children's Bureau "were encouraged to locate away from factories in order not to make working too convenient for mothers" (Hayes, 1982, pp. 153–154). Aid to Dependent Children (ADC), authorized in 1934 as part of the Social Security Act, aimed to eliminate or reduce the need for mothers in families without a working husband to leave their children and go to work. Such mothers were, of course, assumed to be among the deserving poor, their impoverishment a result of husbands' death or disability.

The fact that increasing proportions of women of all backgrounds and marital statuses entered the work force after World War II did not initially result in changes in federal policy. Policymakers were still reluctant to put the force of government behind nontraditional roles for married women—to create incentives for mothers to give up primary care responsibility for their children. Typically, the policy made exceptions for poor women, many of whom had always worked. In 1954 Congress amended the tax code to permit itemized deductions as a business expense of child care costs up to $600, limiting them essentially to the population covered by ADC, adding single fathers and dual-worker families with low income. Congress would not encourage women who did not have to work or who would in their opinion just work for money to spend on themselves, to leave their roles as "sentinels of home and family" (Hayes, 1982, p. 217).

Since the sixties, as the welfare-supported population increased sharply and policymakers became aware that only a small percentage of supported children received aid through the death of a parent (that is, their mothers were divorced, separated, abandoned, or never married), many no longer viewed these families as part of the deserving poor. The suspicion grew (largely unsupported by research) that many of these women brought on their own problems or could support themselves if they wished (Goodwin & Moen, 1980); the prospect of intergenerational welfare dependency was an increasing concern. The result was a return to traditional approaches that tied work with relief. The Work Incentive Program (WIN), established in the late sixties, required eligible recipients to register for employment services (counseling, training in job skills and job-seeking skills, and job placement). In a number of states, families with unemployed fathers not covered by other unemployment benefits became eligible, but they have always been, until the recent economic depression, a small percentage of total recipients. The ages of children which allowed the parent to be exempt from WIN registration were gradually lowered to include preschool children, if their parent was separated from them part of the day (e.g., children in Head Start or day care, or in full-time school). These requirements were enforced despite the fact that few poor women had the experience, skills, or education to qualify for jobs beyond the poverty level with the benefits equivalent to those that welfare status provided (particularly Medicaid) and that the costs of subsidized child care and the WIN program may have exceeded savings in welfare expenditure (Garvin, Smith, & Reid, 1978). At the same time, as in other manpower programs, male breadwinners frequently had greater access to preferred training and placement, either because of official priorities, as in WIN, or because of regulations such as those permitting only one job per family (Berch, 1982; U.S. Dept. of Labor, 1979).

The civil rights and women's liberation movements both advocated an end to discrimination and promoted equity in employment. The sixties saw the passage of the Equal Pay Act, the Civil Rights Act, as well as executive orders for affirmative action.[5] Previously enacted protective laws for women were overturned and discrimination in pay, hiring, firing, promotion, training, and benefits because of sex, parental, or marital status prohibited by federal law, judicial decisions, and administrative regulations. In addition, federal contractors are required to have plans for overcoming sexual and racial discrimination in employment. Although *overt* discrimination on the basis of sex is now difficult, and the principle of equal employment opportunity for all women clearly established (Barrett, 1979, p. 55), the enforcement arms have had limited effectiveness; their inadequate power and funds, as well as the enormous complexity of the problem, contribute. There is, in addition, evidence that employers often only comply to the letter rather than the spirit of the laws (e.g., Berch, 1982; see also Glazer, Chap. 6, this volume).

During the seventies federal policymakers, with a majority of women in the work force, found that "maintaining disincentives against [middle-class] working women was no longer an acceptable social policy" (Hayes, 1982, p. 32). The restrictions on tax relief for employment-necessitated child care were eliminated. Presently, all taxpayers may claim a 20% credit on child care expenses up to $2,000 for one child and $4,000 for two or more, regardless of family income. The form of tax relief also better allows poor families to participate and benefit. The infamous marriage penalty that taxed working married couples more highly than single workers has undergone some reform. Pregnancy is no longer grounds for forced unpaid leave, dismissal, or loss of seniority, and its costs can now be covered by disability insurance.

A number of important inequities affecting working women and families persist. In addition, there continues to be an inadequate support structure for combining parenting with employment. The problems include differential treatment by social security and unemployment compensation, segmented labor markets (pink collar ghettos, barriers to higher paid jobs and skills acquisition), marked and increasing disparity between women's and men's wages, even in jobs of comparable worth, inadequate child care facilities, and employer unwillingness to adopt practices more supportive of family life. These and other problems are discussed elsewhere in this volume and by other analysts (Berch, 1982; Ferber, 1982a, 1982b; Kamerman, 1980; Smith, 1979; and Stromberg & Harkess, 1978).

As we have seen, government response to the problems of working women has been slow and incomplete. The reasons are many and vary with different issues. While many are practical, many involve values and beliefs, such as I have discussed. Cultural lag, in which institutions take

---

[5] Lawmakers opposed to its provision originally included women in the provisions of the Civil Rights Act in order to assure its defeat (Smith, 1979).

time to adjust to societal change, may be a factor. Expensive social programs and employment benefits seem unfeasible in a time of high unemployment, an ailing economy, skyrocketing deficits, and many competing priorities. Solutions to remaining economic and employment inequities, particularly those associated with the secondary labor market and sex segregation of jobs, are not obvious, but would probably require greater intervention in the economy than is currently acceptable politically. Policymakers hesitate to enact legislation that is either controversial, appears to ally government with particular family structures, or promotes changes in sex roles—in other words, to become involved in essentially private concerns. Finally, our political system has an enormously complex policy-making process, particularly where there is no widespread consensus, inadequate information about optimal courses of action and their consequences, and many competing interests which stand to lose or gain by policy changes (Ferber, 1982a; Hayes, 1982; Steiner, 1981). Many of the proposed policies are a threat to those "invested in the status quo" and perceived as "broadly redistributive of traditional values, . . . resources" and "existing power configurations" (Gelb & Palley, 1982, p. 11). An analysis of the use of scientific information in the policy-making process for families and children will serve to illustrate some of the problems in bringing about more effective government action, since barriers to research use are in many ways similar to barriers to reform in general.

RESEARCH AND GOVERNMENT POLICY

As this and other volumes testify, scholars have much to say about improving the lives of working women and their families. There are many points in the government policy-making process at which different types of social science research should be useful, even essential. Indeed, government invests much effort and expense in informing itself through research obstensibly to improve its decisions.[6] "The modern state is distinguished by the extent and number of its activities, most of which are planned, monitored, evaluated, and recorded" (Abt, 1979, p. 89).

Yet those who wish to improve the lives of working women and their families, believing that policy should be based whenever possible on scientifically derived information, perceive the impact of research about

---

[6] Although the last 20 years saw large expenditures for extramural research, the Reagan administration has sharply reduced the resources available for behavioral and social inquiry and, in the opinion of many scientists, inserted ideological considerations in the choice of research priorities.

families and children on social policy as limited and disappointing. They are concerned about its effect on *whether* action is taken and *how* action is taken. One national committee on child development observed that 90% of the recommendations about actions for children by a White House conference in 1909 remained to be acted on in the mid-seventies (Butler, 1981). "Those who carry out the research and those who commission it . . . [feel] research does not really serve to guide policy, or is misused, or lies on a shelf unused" (Rein & White, 1977, p. 120). In the current administration, economic and ideological considerations seem to dominate policy choices. The "experimenting society" called for by Donald Campbell (1969) over a decade ago, in which alternative social programs would be thoroughly evaluated and appropriately modified or discarded for potentially better solutions to important problems, has failed to materialize (see also H. Gideonse, 1980).

The actual extent to which government policymakers use research is unclear (Rein & White, 1977). A recent study of the federal policy-making process for children found instances where research and analysis played a role, sometimes an important and even crucial one, but only as one of many factors responsible for instigating policy concerns and shaping the substance of policy (Hayes, 1982). Its influence was mediated by political requirements, constituency pressures, ideology, leadership, and other contextual factors. In some cases findings were ignored or dismissed. It is likely that many affects of research have been indirect, such as when research information becomes part of the decision-makers' overall perspective "integrated . . . with their own values and experiences" (Rein & White, 1977, p. 121), or when it sensitizes decision-makers to issues, useful approaches, objectives and criteria for their choice, or the benefits of evaluation. Research information can help defuse controversy by allowing technical issues to become the focus (Gelb & Palley, 1982). Research plays a greater direct part in decision-making the less political or value laden the issues are, important interests threatened, and the smaller the cast of characters involved (Hayes, 1982). Such is seldom the case with issues about families, children, sex roles, and work.

Research has different uses at different points in the policy process, and the nature of these uses affects the particular difficulties in application at each point. Policy functions can be divided into three processes: formation, implementation, and evaluation. These are not usually simple stages but overlapping and cyclical policy functions (Nakamura & Smallwood, 1980). A closer look at each policy function, its characteristic uses of research, and the typical problems and issues that arise should illuminate the potential of, and barriers to, research use. The issues discussed tend to pervade all functions but are more problematic for the one with which it is discussed.

Policy Formation

The Policy Function.   Policy can be initiated by legal authorities (departments, Congress, etc.) or by interested groups and individuals in response to particular concerns, crises, or "general public concern" (Nakamura & Smallwood, 1980, p. 22). The formal government decisions that result "set the strategic framework of rules" for policy implementation and range from "vague exhortations" to highly specific goals and strategies for problem solution (Nakamura & Smallwood, 1980, p. 31–2).

One may distinguish among different levels of federal policy formation. The highest, usually involving top officials in the three branches of government, concerns problem identification and consideration about *whether* and *how* government action is appropriate. It occurs when a policy initiative significantly expands or alters existing government involvement in terms of goals, target groups, strategies, and resource commitments, when consensus is lacking or potential conflict among values or interests exists. The middle level of policy formation occurs when what is at question is not government action per se, but rather *what types* of action, by what means and by whom, and the extent of resource commitment: "The debate is about the results of alternative government actions—i.e., their effectiveness and efficiency, their fairness, costs, and distributional effects, and the administrative competence of alternative agencies" (Hayes, 1982, p. 62). Secondary actors are responsible—the president's appointees and Congressmen and their staffs (Hayes, 1982). The last level of policy formation overlaps with the implementation function and concerns technical issues of carrying out an agreed upon approach to problem solution— preparation of regulations and criteria and procedures for monitoring the program, etc. Persons responsible are lower level staff of elected officials.

The wide range of actors, government units, and types of activities in the policy formation process potentially permits a number of entry points for contributions of social scientists and other scholars, within and outside government, through such means as Congressional and public hearings, reports and recommendations of advisory committees and panels, in-house feasibility studies and literature reviews, interest group lobbying, and the media. In fact, the decline in the role of political parties in policy formation has extended the influence of interest and constituency groups, which can introduce research information and research based proposals from outside the official policy-making apparatus (Gelb & Palley, 1982).

Types of Research Relevant to Policy Formation.   Knowledge building research on "social and behavioral processes" and human development can identify problems and suggest strategies (Hayes, 1982, p. 50). An example is research on critical periods in children's development which identified optimal ages or life stages for intervention and influenced the initiation of Head Start and other programs for preschool children.

A second type of research is "problem exploring" (Hayes, 1982, p. 50), or more specifically, in our area of interest, "research for family policy" (Nye & McDonald, 1979). This type of research looks into the possibility that particular social, economic, and environmental conditions, life styles, family structures, etc., may present problems requiring social action. Such research might include the questions posed by Bronfenbrenner (1978) in his "call for first priority . . . to rigorous research on the conditions in which families live, the way these conditions affect the capacity of the family to function, and how these conditions might be altered (by policy inventions or other means) to enhance that capacity" (p. 785). Although more applied in intention than knowledge building research, policy exploring research may not always have direct policy implications or lead to concrete proposals. It may only be "a step toward putting issues on the agenda" (Rein & White, 1977, p. 120). Or it may contribute to a growing understanding of an issue or a way of looking at a problem (Rein & White, 1977).

A third category of research is directed explicitly at policy formation. One type is prospective family impact analysis (Hubbell, 1981; Kamerman and Kahn, 1978; Nye & McDonald, 1979). Such research projects the intended and unintended consequences of alternative program initiatives on "the family as a social institution, the family as an interacting group, and the individual family members" (Nye & McDonald, 1979, p. 475). This research involves forecasting techniques, simulations, and quasiexperiments with pilot projects and feasibility studies. The extensive research associated with the negative income tax pilot projects is an example.

Another type of policy-forming research clarifies available techniques for achieving a goal and their relative effectiveness, examines whether public action is the most effective or feasible way to approach problem solution, and collects information on public acceptability of certain types of policies (Abt, 1979). Policy formation research may be incorporated into an approach that acknowledges limitations to knowledge about optimal solutions and probable consequences and uses a program initiative to increase understanding of strategies and goals, "simultaneously [as] a step toward a solution and a way of gathering better information for the next step" (Nakamura & Smallwood, 1980, p. 36; Gideonse, 1980). In doing so this type of research overlaps with evaluation.

Problems with Research Utilization. A large part of the frustration of family researchers and advocates stems from the failure of research to influence the earliest stage of the policy formation process–to persuade policy makers that a social problem exists or that a particular type and amount of intervention should occur. Since policy-making takes place within the social context described earlier, value issues are important complications in the formation of policies about work, women, children, and families. The nature and sources of many conflicts that interfere with policy enactment were described in an earlier section. Value issues show up in other ways, in the role research can play in policy decisions, in different views about how social research should be conducted, and in the role of the scholar-as-advocate in influencing policy decisions.

One problem is the traditional dichotomization of political decision-making and the scientific endeavor, which places the former in the realm of values, the latter in the realm of objective fact. In this traditional paradigm the function of research is to provide "a body of theory or a body of research results [which] may show the consequences of alternative actions; but those consequences must be evaluated on grounds that are outside of the realm of knowledge—that is, on grounds of comparing alternative values" (Cohen, 1980, p. 269). Research is seen as a process characterized by rules of evidence and reasoning to obtain unbiased and reliable knowledge that is publicly demonstrable. It strives "to maintain a rigorous scientific objectivity throughout the research endeavor," using objective criteria for choosing research topics, and avoiding preconceptions about, for example, "ideal family structures and family relationships, good and bad public policies and the like [which] can cloud the formulation of research questions and taint policy research reports to the point of making them useless" (Nye & McDonald, 1979, p. 480).

In contrast, public policy formation is a political process in which ways are found to reconcile values and other differences and weight various needs and interests against each other. Research evidence about problems and consequences is but one source of argument for choosing among different options, and it is public officials, not social scientists, who make these choices. It would be nice to believe that public officials make use of persuasive findings about the environments that are optimally conducive to the development of children, the health of families, and the promotion of economic equity and verified theory of how government can facilitate them. Certainly, robustness of research theory and findings may increase the chances of their use. However, there is a tradition of relying on the personal and political judgment of elected leaders; these leaders are often unwilling to attend to research findings that require them to support controversial legislation or that are antithetical to or challenge deeply held beliefs and folk theories (theirs and their constituents') about families and human development, individual achievement, and the economy. In matters of judgment rather than of fact—so often the case with recommendations for political actions—who is to say whether the scholar or the senator is most wise?

A second problem is that policymakers may not believe that scholarly recommendations are value free and objective. Indeed, despite the scientific ideal just outlined, personal values influence topics chosen for investigation, problem conceptualization, theoretical perspectives, choice of methodology, the collection of data, and their interpretation. Scholars are themselves stakeholders in society and generate knowledge consistent with their values and interests. More obvious to the policymaker is the role of the scholar as advocate, representing interest group organizations and sitting on panels and advisory boards, whose recommendations for actions, as interpretations of research, are influenced by judgment and personal values (Lichtman, 1981). The scholar and his recommendations are thus put on the same footing as any other interest group.

A third problem is with the value perspective inherent in traditional scientific methodolgy. This methodology relies on mathematic and statistical analysis, experiments, and surveys in the service of objectivity and generalizability which, in the opinion of many analysts, are inadequate to the subject—to understanding the source of problems and to projecting feasible and effective solutions (Gideonse, 1980). The traditional paradigm raises epistemological issues in policy application. Findings that emerge from many recommended research techniques, such as experiments, are limited in their applicability to diverse situations, a particular problem for social programs applied nationwide. Surveys result in probability statements about researcher-defined topics at one point in time and in particular circumstances that may not project into the future. Hypothesis testing— the traditional approach to obtaining support for theory—may be futile, if theories are not grounded in the realities of concrete and actual situations, an understanding of the meanings of the situations to the participants, and how they affect action (Cronbach & associates, 1980; Douglas, 1980; Gideonse, 1980; Guba and Lincoln, 1981; Johnson, 1975; Wax, 1975; Weiss & Rein, 1970). Research findings usually pertain to groups of individuals and may be only partial explanations or predictions for particular individuals within groups, and certainly for individuals in other groups. An individual's characteristics and circumstances may differ in known and unknown ways from those in the research sample and relate to each other in unique ways. For example, policies based on research indicating the desirability of relieving parental stress (caused by work requirements or single parenthood, as instances) would have to contend with a variety of individual motivations, constraints, and circumstances to which the traditional scientific methods might not be sensitive.

Criticisms of the traditional scientific approaches and proposals for alternative methodologies continue to be debated in the research community (e.g., Meyers, 1981; Cook & Reichardt, 1979). (The reader may want to consult these and other sources listed in the preceding paragraph for further discussion and proposed solutions.)

A related but somewhat different problem has to do with what the existing body of research findings has to offer policy formulation. The problem goes beyond the difficulty of the lay policymaker's interpreting inconsistent or ambiguous findings or even disillusionment when programs based on research have had disappointing results. Although the quality and breadth of information available to policymakers (as well as the scholarly resources from which to commission policy-related work) have vastly improved, the "map of social policy knowledge . . . is still . . . incomplete and in many places distorted, resembling, perhaps, Renaissance maps of the New World . . . [There is no] unified theory of social and economic change" (Abt, 1979, pp. 89–90). For example, policy makers could not make a choice between liberal and conservative approaches to family policy by drawing on existing research evidence on how family health is accomplished (Lichtman, 1981; Steiner, 1981). Some actually doubt whether research can in fact provide answers to questions which are essentially issues of value and matters of social conflict or can predict the consequences and benefits of alternative government actions (e.g., Steiner, 1981). On a less global level, we may have excellent research findings on how babies become attached to a parent and the benefits for their development, although these are more controversial (see Maccoby, 1980; Sroufe & Ward, Chap. 1, and Lamb, Chap. 2, this volume); or the types of work settings facilitative to parenting. However, less progress has been made in the social engineering and assessment necessary for translating these findings into feasible and politically acceptable solutions. In fact, research on attachment might well be translated into different applications, depending on the values and political views of the actors—into improved daycare facilities or into disincentives for mothers working, as examples. Research on the problems of work in the past was often distorted, biased, or influenced by either ingnoring women or studying them only in relation to traditional gender role definitions (Acker, 1978; Mortimer & Sorensen, Chap 5, this volume). An understanding of the sources and ramifications of wage and job discrimination is recent and, for proposed solutions such as equal pay for jobs of comparable worth, for example, imcomplete (Ferber, 1982b).

A final problem I will mention is not unrelated to value issues but extends them to include the self-interest of the participants in policy formulation. It is particularly characteristic of the middle level of policy formulation, when specific government actions and potential implementors are being cosidered. The different interest groups, target populations, public and private agencies (federal, state, and local), and individual policymakers are likely to have somewhat different goals and stakes in the outcomes of decision-making. Conflict can scuttle any initiative or result in compromises in which research findings play very little role (Steiner, 1981; Hayes, 1982).

Policy Implementation

The Policy Function and Types of Research. During policy implementation, activities relate to the "mandates legitimized by the policy makers" in policy formation (Nakamura & Smallwood, 1980, p. 23) but depend for their specific content on the degree of specificity the policies provide about goals and strategies. The amount of implementer discretion thus required and permitted, as well as the variety of government levels and groups involved in determining the form of implementation, affect both the type and amount of scientific information and advice drawn upon. Family impact analyses of projected program activities and other types of research useful for policy formation would again be relevant if implementation requires the development and refinement of means.

Problems with Research Utilization. When political actions are non-specific, and many program decisions deferred, implementation is likely to be characterized by value and interest group conflicts. Even the best designed programs can in implementation be confronted by misinterpretation, indifference, resistance, and technical problems on the part of organizations and local power brokers. Implementers may have personal goals, attitudes and skills in conflict with research based policies and may lack the sophistication to understand and apply social science research or to be receptive to its use. Implementing organizations may resist requisite alteration of goals and ways of operating. Further, federal compliance tools are limited because our federal system's dispersed power and control permits evasion and dilution of federal programs and policies. The vast literature on organizational change and program implementation is relevant here (see, for example, Katz & Kahn, 1978, pp. 653ff; Nakamura and Smallwood, 1980).

Policy Evaluation

The Policy Function and Types of Research. The evaluation phase of the policy process can result in program continuation, redesign, expansion, or termination. Evaluation efforts "to understand the functioning and effects" of social programs have increased greatly since the late sixties. Republican and conservative interest in terminating expensive Democratic-sponsored social programs, use of cost-benefit ratios, public demand for government accountability, and concern about needed program reforms appear to have motivated the great expansion of formal policy evaluation (Meyers, 1981).

Evaluation activities may be part of the ongoing program operation, contracted by the policy-making apparatus, an independent audit (such as by the GAO), or independent research. They include traditional evaluation of stated and implied goals and functions as well as impact analysis. Other evaluation concerns are costs and benefits, efficiency, equity, client participation, short- and long-range effects, and satisfaction of constituents (Nakamura & Smallwood, 1980).

Problems with Research Utilization. Social programs have increasingly incorporated evaluation activities, often by mandate. Issues include the type of evaluation to be undertaken (purpose, methodology), the quality or utility of its findings, and the uses made of them by policymakers. Much has been written about these questions, but a few of particular importance should be mentioned here.

One such question concerns the problem of evaluating action programs with diffuse, elusive, or shifting goals, since the conventional approach is measurement of goal accomplishment. The programs are often a product of a political process in which greater precision in goal statements would cause dissension among interest groups and supporters. Sometimes imprecision is a result of uncertainty about how a problem can be alleviated. Sometimes actual goals cannot be stated publicly. Sometimes goals and strategies shift during the complexities of implementation (Meyers, 1981; Weiss & Rein, 1970). As a consequence, evaluation reports are vulnerable to charges that inappropriate or too narrow outcomes were measured or inaccurately weighted.

A related problem is that experimental designs, traditionally the methodology of choice (Campbell & Stanley, 1966), are often not technically feasible or appropriate, because they require controlled treatments and randomized selection and assignment of subjects; yet it is this design that policymakers often believe is essential to acquire reliable information for decision-making. They may reject evaluation findings from nonexperimental designs. Further, evaluation findings are often equivocal, their generalizability to other settings ambiguous, and their implication for policy action open to diverse interpretations.

Finally program administrators do not always have incentives to undertake scientifically sound evaluation and if they do to make optimal use of their findings. Their status, self-esteem, jobs, and even the survival of their organizations are at stake; what they want is information to protect, stabilize, and justify their programs, rather than evidence that might question their effectiveness. Congress, which provides continuing authorization and resources, may be more interested in issues of equity and distribution of program services among their constituents, about whether they are pleased with the service, than in the efficiency of the program (Abt, 1979). "Use of evaluation appears to be easiest when implementation implies only moderate alterations in procedure, staff deployment, or costs, or where few interests are threatened" (Weiss, 1972, p. 320).

Other Problems

Some problems are not typical of any one policy function. They fall into the more technical domain and as such may be more amenable to solution. One problem is timing of research and evaluation; research schedules and report writing often do not coincide with policy timetables. The problem is greater the more thorough and careful the evaluation is—a Catch-22 (Abt, 1979; Rein & White, 1977). Often the form in which it is written is not easily accessible to decision-makers in terms of applicability to policy (Pizzigati, 1981). Scholars and advocates have been insufficiently knowledgeable about appropriate points of access to the policy making process and to necessary political strategies (Hayes, 1982; Gideonse, 1980).

Summary

The potential application of research findings and methods to major policy functions and the circumstances and problems that reduce their influence on decisions were analyzed to illustrate the complexities and difficulties in effecting government action in behalf of working women and their families. Research has a legitimate and potentially powerful role in policy processes and probably has had some impact. Yet its influence is more limited than scholars and advocates would like.

Part of this limitation is the separation of scientific and political functions. Policy choices have many bases other than research—the reconciliation of group and organizational interests and values, availability of resources and competing priorities, precedents, and folk theories and ideologies about sex roles, families, work, and the proper role of government. The conflicts in values and interests can scuttle any initiative or result in compromises that bear minimal relation to scientific knowledge. Organizational constraints and inertia are additional difficulties in the implementation of research based programs and ways of operating.

Other problems relate more to research itself—its methodologies, accomplishments, and how its practitioners function. These include the way values influence the conduct of research and the use of research-based recommendations, the limitations of predominant scientific paradigms in social research, particularly in their application to policy, and the state of the art of research and theory about social and economic change.

CONCLUSION

Many stresses and inequities are associated with the demographic change that is the topic of this volume, the greatly increased proportion of women with families engaged in paid work outside their homes. Although futurists contend we are entering an era of greater reliance on self-help and individual initiative (Naisbitt, 1982), the context of these stresses and inequities requires government action if enough change is to take place. Strongly held belief systems and interests sustain the status quo. As Grubb and Lazerson document in Chap. 9, little reform for women has ever taken place in our country without the benefit of government initiative. Obviously, existing inequities in the *law*—social security being the most egregious example—cannot occur without government action. Other needed reforms, such as equal pay for jobs of comparable worth, the broadening of opportunities for women beyond pink collar ghettos, access to higher-paying positions and acquisition of on-the-job training, and the improvement of work conditions generally, but particularly in the secondary labor market, are recognizably difficult (Doeringer & Piore, 1975; Ferber, 1982a, 1982b), but unlikely to occur without political intervention and incentives. Government action to support the family life and parenting responsibilities of working parents has detractors among those who see these problems best handled by the private sector. However, only a small minority of employers has been responsive to these needs. Government may not want to become involved in mandatory legislation or broad-scale support of group day care, but it can provide incentives and leadership, at least as an employer.

Researchers and their products clearly have a role to play in reform efforts. The interdisciplinary research and analyses represented in this volume are examples of work that could influence policy, either directly or indirectly by sensitizing decision makers to issues or useful approaches and objectives. Some of the barriers to greater research utilization are legitimate, and some are beyond the control of scholars and their work. Fortunately, progress is being make in alleviating the technical, methodological and state-of-the-art limitations. The scholarship represented in this volume is a step in this progress and a useful entry into the policy debate about ways to remediate the stresses and inequities faced by working women and their families.

REFERENCES

Abt, C. C. Social science research and the modern state. *Daedalus,* 1979, *108,* 89–100.

Acker, J. Issues in the sociological study of women's work. In A. H. Stromberg & S. Harkess (Eds.), *Women working: Theories and facts in perspective.* Palo Alto, CA: Mayfield, 1978.

Acock, A. C., & Edwards, J. N. Equalitarian sex-role attitudes and female income. *Journal of Marriage and the Family,* 1982, *44,* 581–589.

Anderson, E. Some observations of black youth unemployment. In American Assembly, Columbia University, *Youth employment and public policy.* Englewood Cliffs, N.J.: Prentice-Hall, 1980.

Anthony, P. D. *The ideology of work.* London: Tavistock, 1977.

AuClaire, P. A. Employment search decisions among AFDC recipients. *Social Work Research and Abstracts,* 1979, *15,* 18–26.

Baker, S. H. Women in blue-collar and service occupations. In A. H. Stromberg & S. Harkess (Eds.), *Women working: Theories and facts in perspective.* Palo Alto, CA: Mayfield, 1978.

Barrett, N. S. Women in the job market: Occupations, earnings, and career opportunities. In R. E. Smith (Ed.), *The subtle revolution: Women at work.* Washington, DC: The Urban Institute, 1979.

Berch, B. *The endless day: The political economy of women and work.* New York: Harcourt Brace Jovanovich, 1982.

Bronfenbrenner, U. Who needs parent education? *Teachers College Record,* 1978, *79,* 767–787.

Bronfenbrenner, U. *The ecology of human development.* Cambridge, MA.: Harvard University Press, 1979.

Bruce-Briggs, B. "Child care": The fiscal time bomb. *The Public Interest,* 1977, *49,* 87–102.

Butler, J. A. Social science and the formation of policy toward children. In H. C. Wallach (Ed.), *Approaches to child and family policy.* Washington, DC: Westview Press, 1981.

Campbell, D. Reforms as experiments. *American Psychologist,* 1969, *24,* 409–429.

Campbell, D. T., & Stanley, J. C. *Experimental and quasi-experimental designs for research.* Boston, MA: Houghton Mifflin, 1966.

Carlson, A. C. Families, sex, and the liberal agenda. *The Public Interest,* 1980, *58,* 62–79.

Chafe, W. H. Looking backward in order to look forward: Women, work, and social values in America. In American Assembly, Columbia University, *Women and the American economy: A look to the 1980s.* Englewood Cliffs, NJ: Prentice-Hall, 1976.

Cohen, B. P. *Developing sociological knowledge: Theory and method.* Englewood Cliffs, NJ: Prentice-Hall, 1980.

Cook, T. D., & Reichardt, C. S. (Eds.). *Qualitative and quantitative methods in evaluation research.* Beverly Hills, CA: Sage, 1979.

Cronbach, L. J., and associates. *Toward reform of program evaluation: Aims, methods, and institutional arrangements.* San Francisco, CA: Jossey-Bass, 1980.

deLone, R. H. *Small futures: Children, inequality, and the limits of liberal reform.* New York: Harcourt Brace Jovanovich, 1979.

Doeringer, P. B., & Piore, M. J. Unemployment and the "dual labor market." *The Public Interest,* 1975, *38,* 67–79.

Douglas, J. D., Adler, P. A., Adler, P., Fontana, A., Freeman, C. R., & Kotraba, J. A. *Introduction to the sociologies of everyday life.* Boston, MA: Allyn & Bacon, 1980.

Elder, G. H., Jr. *Children of the Great Depression: Social change in life experience.* Chicago, IL: University of Chicago Press, 1974.

Feagin, J. R. *Subordinating the poor: Welfare and American beliefs.* Englewood Cliffs, N.J: Prentice-Hall, 1975.

Ferber, M. A. Why are women paid less than men? In *Equal Pay and Comparable Worth, Third Annual Symposium on Women and Public Policy Proceedings.* Cincinnati, OH: University of Cincinnati, 1982. (a)

Ferber, M. A. Women and work: Issues of the 1980s. *Signs, Journal of Women in Culture and Society,* 1982, *8,* 273–295. *(b)*

Finn, C. E., Jr. The family under fire. *The Public Interest,* 1978, *50,* 146–151.

Garvin, C. D., Smith, A. D., & Reid, W. J. (Eds.). *The work incentive experience.* Montclair, N.J: Allanheld, Osmun, 1978.

Gelb, J., & Palley, M. L. *Women and public policies.* Princeton, NJ: Princeton University Press, 1982.

Gideonse, H. D. Improving the federal administration of education programs. *Educational Evaluation and Policy Analysis,* 1980, *2,* 61–70.

Ginzberg, E. (Ed.). *Employing the unemployed.* New York: Basic Books, 1980.

Goodwin, L. *Do the poor want to work? A social-psychological study of work orientation.* Washington, DC: The Brookings Institution, 1972.

Goodwin, L., & Milius, P. Forty years of work training. In C. D. Garvin, Smith, A. D., & Reid, W. J. (Eds.). *The work incentive experience.* Montclair, NJ: Allanheld, Osmun, 1978.

Goodwin, L., & Moen, P. Evaluation and implementation of family welfare policy. *Policy Studies Journal,* 1980, *8,* 633–651.

Guba, E., & Lincoln, Y. *Effective evaluation.* San Francisco, CA: Jossey-Bass, 1981.

Hayes, C. D. (Ed.) *Making policies for children: A study of the federal process.* Washington, DC: National Academy Press, 1982.

Hoffman, L. W. Maternal employment: 1979. *American Psychologist,* 1979, *34,* 859–865.

Hubbell, R. The family impact seminar: A new approach to policy analysis. In H. C. Wallach (Ed.), *Approaches to child and family policy.* Washington, DC: Westview Press, 1980.

Inkeles, A. Society, social structure, and child socialization. In J. A. Clausen (Ed.), *Socialization and society.* Boston, MA: Little, Brown, 1968.

Jahoda, M. *Employment and unemployment: A social-psychological analysis.* Cambridge, England: Cambridge University Press, 1982.

Jahoda, M., Lazarsfeld, P. F., & Zeisel, H. *Mariethal: The sociography of an unemployed community.* Chicago, IL: Aldine-Atherton, 1971 (first published in German, 1933).

Johnson, J. M. *Doing field research.* New York: Free Press, 1975.

Kamerman, S. B. *Parenting in an unresponsive society: Managing work and family life.* New York: Free Press, 1980.

Kamerman, S. B., & Kahn, A. J. (Eds.). *Family policy: Government and families in fourteen countries.* New York: Columbia University Press, 1978.

Katz, D., & Kahn, R. L. *The social psychology of organizations,* Second Edition. New York: Wiley & Sons, 1978.

Keniston, K. *All our children: The American family under pressure.* New York: Harcourt Brace Jovanovich, 1977.

Kohn, M. L. *Class and conformity: A study in values,* Second Edition. Chicago, IL: University of Chicago Press, 1977.

Komarovsky, M. *The unemployed man and his family.* New York: Octagon Books, 1971 (originally published in 1940).

Levine, R. A. Parental goals: A cross-cultural view. In H. J. Leichter (Ed.), *The family as educator.* New York: Teachers College Press, 1974.

Levitan, S. A., & Marwick, D. Working and training for welfare recipients. *Journal of Human Resources,* Supplement 1973, *8,* 5–18.

Lichtman, A. J. Language games, social science, and public policy: The case of the family. In H. C. Wallach (Ed.), *Approahes to child and family policy.* Washington, DC: Westview Press, 1981.

Liebow, E. *Tally's corner: A study of Negro street corner men.* Boston, MA: Little, Brown, 1967.

Longwood, R., & Simmel, A. Organizational resistance to innovation. In C. H. Weiss (Ed.), *Evaluating action programs: Readings in social action and education.* Boston, MA: Allyn & Bacon, 1972.

McCathren, R. R. The demise of federal categorical child care legislation: Lessons for the '80s from the failures of the '70s. In H. C. Wallach (Ed.), *Approaches to child and family policy.* Washington, DC: Westview Press, 1981.

Maccoby, E. E. *Social development: Psychological growth and the parent–child relationship.* New York: Harcourt Brace Jovanovich, 1980.

Meyers, W. R. *The evaluation enterprise: A realistic appraisal of evaluation careers, methods, and applications.* San Francisco, CA: Jossey-Bass, 1981.

Moock, P. R. Economic aspects of the family as educator. In H. J. Leichter (Ed.), *The family as educator.* New York: Teachers College Press, 1974.

Naisbitt, J. *Megatrends: Ten new directions transforming our lives.* New York: Warner Books, 1982.

Nakamura, R. T., & Smallwood, F. *The politics of policy implementation.* New York: St. Martin's Press, 1980.

Nye, F. I., & McDonald, G. W. Family policy research: Emergent models and some theoretical issues. *Journal of Marriage and the Family,* 1979, *41,* 473–485.

Piotrkowski, C. S. *Work and the family system: A naturalistic study of working-class and lower-middle-class families.* New York: Free Press, 1979.

Piven, F. F., & Cloward, R. A. *Regulating the poor: The functions of public welfare.* New York: Vintage Books, 1971.

Pizzigati, K. A. L. Social science research and social policy: Legislative perspectives of a congressional science fellow. In H. C. Wallach (Ed.), *Approaches to child and family policy.* Washington, DC: Westview Press, 1981.

Quinn, R. P., & Shepard, L. *The 1972-1973 quality of employment survey.* Ann Arbor, MI: Survey Research Center, University of Michigan, 1974.

Rainwater, L. *Behind ghetto walls: Black families in a federal slum.* Chicago, IL: Aldine, 1970.

Rein, M., & White, S. H. Can policy research help policy? *The Public Interest,* 1977, *49,* 119–136.

Rossi, P., & Blum, Z. D. Class, status, and poverty. In D. P. Moynihan (Ed.), *On understanding poverty: Perspectives from the social sciences.* New York: Basic Books, 1969.

Rothman, D. J. The state as parent: Social policy in the progressive era. In W. Gaylin, I. Glasser, S. Marcus, & D. J. Rothman, *Doing good: The limits of benevolence.* New York: Pantheon Books, 1978.

Rubin, L. *Worlds of pain.* New York: Basic Books, 1976.

Runyan, W. McK. *Life histories and psychobiography: Explorations in theory and method.* New York: Oxford University Press, 1982.

Smith, R. E. (Ed.) *The subtle revolution: Women at work.* Washington, DC: The Urban Institute, 1979.

Special Task Force to the Secretary of Health, Education and Welfare. *Work in America.* Cambridge, MA: MIT Press, 1973. Excerpted in R. C. Edwards, M. Reich, & T. E. Weisskopf, *The capitalist system,* Second Edition. Englewood Cliffs, NJ: Prentice-Hall, 1978.

Steiner, G. Y. *The futility of family policy.* Washington, DC: The Brookings Institution, 1981.

Stone, R. C., & Schlamp, F. T. *Welfare and working fathers: Low income family life styles.* Lexington, MA: Heath Lexington Books, 1971.

Stromberg, A. H., & Harkess, S. (Eds.). *Women working: Theories and facts in perspective.* Palo Alto, CA: Mayfield, 1978.

Terkel, S. *Working.* New York: Avon Books, 1975 (originally published 1972).

Wallach, H. C. (Ed.). *Approaches to child and family policy.* Washington, DC: Westview Press, 1981.

Wax, R. *Doing fieldwork: Warnings and advice.* Chicago, IL: University of Chicago Press, 1975.

Weiss, C. H. Utilization of evaluation: Toward comparative study. In C. H. Weiss (Ed.), *Evaluating action programs: Readings in social action and education.* Boston, MA: Allyn & Bacon, 1972.

Weiss, R. S., & Rein, M. The evaluation of broad-aim programs: Experimental design, its difficulties, and an alternative. *Administrative Science Quarterly,* 1970, *15,* 97–109.

U.S. Department of Labor. *WIN: 1968–1978. A Report at 10 Years.* Washington, DC: US Department of Labor, 1979.

I
CARING FOR CONTEMPORARY CHILDREN

Chapter 1
*The Importance of Early Care**

L. Alan Sroufe
Mary J. Ward

Institute of Child Development
University of Minnesota

Very important issues are considered in this book, issues concerning who should care for children and how this care should be arranged. Our society is changing rapidly, and with these societal changes it is inevitable that there be changes in childrearing practices. In current times, these changes include changes in the care of infants and toddlers, as more mothers work outside the home and as both two-worker families and single-parent families rely on out-of-home care for their children. Whatever our philosophical views about such changes, all of us are concerned about the consequences of such changing patterns of care for our children.

In this chapter our attention will be focused on another issue, that is, not on who should take care of young children and how this care should be arranged, but on the *kind* of care infants and young children require to thrive. We will approach the matter from a developmental perspective by examining the nature of the developing infant. We will illustrate the capacities for social engagement in the newborn and will consider environmental factors that influence the unfolding of these capacities. We will trace the development of the infant's social capacities through the first two years and, along the way, point out the role of the quality of care in promoting healthy psychological development. During this time period, incredible growth and change take place, as the infant moves from rather

---

* Preparation of this paper was aided by Grant No. HD05027, National Institute of Child Health and Human Development and Grant No. MH15755, National Institute of Mental Health.

total dependency to an active role in a dyadic relationship, toward what John Bowlby (1969) calls a "goal corrected partnership" with its care givers and the beginning of relationships with peers.

Much is now known about infant social and emotional development and it seems prudent to consider this information in making decisions at a national policy level and at a personal, individual level. In large part, there are no simple answers to questions about the benefit or harm of day care, the appropriate time for mothers to return to work, the appropriateness of fathers staying home half-time, and so forth. Day care, in and of itself, cannot simply be viewed as good or bad. Whether out-of-home care interferes with, or promotes, healthy development will depend upon a host of factors. We believe that day care policy should be informed by a knowledge of infant development, and we believe that such knowledge as currently exists has clear implications for policy. We also believe that individual decisions should be based on accurate information about development. Different families will work out different solutions, depending on their particular needs and circumstances. However, we suspect that these decisions would, in fact, be influenced by knowledge about the kind of care infants require were this information available. It is to this end that this chapter was written.

THE COURSE OF EARLY DEVELOPMENT

The Social Capacities of the Newborn

In many ways the newborn infant is a rather helpless and primitive creature. Not only is it entirely dependent on its caregivers for sustenance and basic care, but it has relatively little capacity to organize its behavior or make sense out of the world. Its cortex—that part of the brain which serves reasoning, thought, and integration of experience—is virtually nonfunctional. That is, while the basic anatomical structures are in place, the rich interconnections between the cortex and other parts of the brain are not yet established (Tanner, 1970). The normal newborn is largely a reflexive organism and in some essential ways is not different from an infant born without a cortex (Harmon & Emde, 1972). Over the first few months of life many of the inborn reflexes drop out and are replaced by more voluntary capacities as the cortex matures (Oppenheim, 1981).

On the other hand, newborns are equipped with some basic capacities which serve them well in the typical environment into which they are born. They hear and can discriminate sounds characteristic of those represented by human speech, and they are attracted by human voices (Eimas, Siqueland, Jusczyk, & Vigorito, 1971). They are able to follow movement with their eyes, and they are especially attracted to visual contrasts (shadings of light and dark) which are well represented in the human face (Fantz, Fagan, & Miranda, 1975). They grasp objects placed in their hands, and they can mold their bodies to another body. The significance of all of this is that if someone is available to talk to an infant and be visually present and hold it, then the infant will listen, watch, and mold its body to that person. The infant is well equipped to respond to human stimulation.

The reflexes of the infant also provide a built-in signal system which, while simple, is nonetheless effective. In particular, the infant will cry when distressed, much the way we shiver when we are cold. And, when the distress is alleviated, usually through some kind of ministration from the caregiver, the infant will settle down. It is also the case that many of the behaviors exhibited by the newborn—frowns and simple smiles while asleep, wide-eyed following of the moving face, and gurgling vocalization— are endearing to caregivers, promoting their further engagement with the infant. Moreover, despite its lack of cognitive understanding, the newborn is responsive to (becomes familiar with) the particular patterns of care of a particular caregiver (Sander, 1975).

A further capacity of the newborn deserves special mention. Developmentalists refer to this capacity as detection of contingency (Papousek, 1961; Watson, 1972). Despite the newborn's primitive memory capacities and the great difficulty of establishing associations (e.g., with classical conditioning), the young infant has a remarkable capacity to detect contingent responsiveness in the environment. In a series of fundamentally important studies, Papousek (1961) has shown that very young infants may learn complex sequences of head turns in order to receive the opportunity to obtain milk. For example, infants have learned to turn their heads twice to the right, then twice to the left. To be sure, head turning and sucking are responses well within the capacity of the newborn, but what is important to us here is that the infant is able to learn to organize these behaviors in terms of an outcome in the environment. Even in the early weeks of life, infants are responsive to a responsive environment. While the newborn is a primitive creature, it can be competent within a responsive caregiver–infant system (Ainsworth & Bell, 1974).

All of these capacities converge in the early months of life in normal circumstances to move the infant toward social participation. At first, for example, infants' smiles are largely due to attainment of a certain physiological state. In the first days of life they smile primarily when they are sleeping lightly (Emde & Harmon, 1972). These REM smiles (which may also occur when they are awake but drowsy) seem to be a function of fluctuations in nervous system excitation (Sroufe & Waters, 1976). The infant's arousal rises above then falls below some threshold. For example, when one gently rouses a sleeping infant, chains of these tiny smiles appear and evaporate. Soon, one can elicit these early smiles by gently stimulating a drowsy baby. Within a few weeks, one can readily produce smiles in an alert infant through gentle rhythmic stimulation (e.g., baby talk) and soon after even larger smiles can be produced by more vigorous play (e.g., clapping the infant's hands together).

By eight weeks or so a dramatic development unfolds. By this time the infant's own cognitive efforts may play a large role in smiling. Through nature's design, infants smile when, following extensive cognitive effort, they are able to "recognize" a visual event (Kagan, 1971). Apparently the infant's effort, followed by the relaxation which occurs when the event can be "assimilated," produces the arousal fluctuation that is associated with the smile. It is at this time that reliable smiles to the human face occur. The human face, because of its initial attractiveness and continued presence, becomes the first visual object for the infant. In the following two months these smiles become more selective, being much more readily elicited by the caregiver than by faces in general. The infant in a new sense "knows" the caregiver, and the caregiver senses this new social recognition.

The Development of the Signaling System

By the end of the first half year the infant has developed much more elaborate capacities to organize and direct behavior and to signal its wishes to the environment. The infant has developed considerably its ability to modulate arousal—to control the input of stimulation from the environment and to maintain focused and organized behavior even in the face of moderate excitement. For example, in the course of face-to-face interaction, the level of arousal or excitation at times exceeds the infant's management capacities. If the excitement continued, the infant would become distressed. By 4–6 months, however, the infant can deliberately turn away from the source of the stimulation and thereby lower the level of arousal. Distress is averted and, shortly, engagement of the event may be resumed.

In general terms, by 4–6 months the infant is capable of an early form of social partnership—a coordinated signaling and responding system which leads to even more complex patterns of organized behavior (Brazelton, Koslowski, & Main, 1974; Stern, 1974, 1977). The infant attends to the caregiver and with changes in the caregiver's facial expression and voice, the excitement builds, sometimes punctuated by movements of the infant's arms and legs and brief looks away. The caregiver waits and responds again, and soon the infant smiles and vocalizes, to the caregiver's delight. In fact, Stern (1974) has argued that this "goal"—the infant's positive affective response—structures the interaction between the partners.

The most important thing for our consideration here is that this coordinated behavior is heavily dependent upon the caregiver's sensitivity. The infant signals its openness to stimulation, its continued interest in the interaction and its comfort with the pacing of stimulation by its attention and looks away and, ultimately, by its smiling and cooing. But the caregiver must "read" the signals accurately and adjust behavior accordingly, if the infant's participation is to be maintained and the outcome of a given interaction is to be positive. The infant cannot participate at all, if the caregiver fails to provide the appropriately varied and modulated stimulation. Inappropriately timed or intrusive stimulation will lead to distress. For example, if, when the infant turns away, the caregiver persists with intensified efforts to force attention, the infant likely will become over-aroused and will cry. On the other hand, if the pacing and timing (what Ainsworth calls "cooperativeness," e.g., Ainsworth, Bell, & Stayton, 1971) of such interactions is appropriate, the infant can play its part well. Through countless interactive experiences, he or she learns to sustain attention and to maintain organized activity in the face of increasing amounts of excitation (Brazelton et al., 1974; Sroufe, 1977). In time, the infant learns to play a more active role in initiating interactions, in guiding and altering them, and even in responding to the caregiver's leads. The interaction becomes more mutual; it is as in teaching a child to play ping-pong. At first, the adult hits a ball directly to the child's stationary paddle and adjusts returning balls so that they continue to bounce off of the un-moving paddle in the child's hands. Eventually, the child can hit back the ball and can be given increasing responsibility for fielding balls that are slightly offcenter. In time, the child can take full responsibility for fielding off-target balls, and can control the direction of the game.

One might reasonably ask how the caregiver learns these complex managerial skills, this finely tuned responsivity. She or he learns it from the infant. Through hours of routine interaction in caring for and playing with the infant, there is ample opportunity to learn about the particular mood and nature of the particular infant and to read the infant's signals. Generally, infants are quite clear in communicating their needs and desires, and they are certainly clear in communicating their distress and pleasure. All that is required is sufficient experience with them. In short, this important learning commonly occurs as a matter of course.

The Formation of a Secure Attachment

As a product of cognitive developmental changes and interactional experience, infants in all cultures form what are referred to as *specific attachments* before the end of the first year (Ainsworth, 1967; Bowlby, 1969; Kagan, Kearsley, & Zelazo, 1978; Schaffer & Emerson, 1964). That is, they discriminate caregivers from all other individuals and recognize them as coherent, integrated objects (persons). They know that various sights, sounds, smells, and behaviors are all associated with the same source, and they know that the caregiver continues to exist even when not in sight (Piaget, 1952).

In our view we emphasize the caregiver's centrality in the infant's behavioral organization. By the end of the first year, the infant follows the caregiver's movements, calls for the caregiver when separated, and seeks out the caregiver (in particular when injured, distressed, or wanting to be picked up; see Tracy, Lamb, & Ainsworth, 1976). In general, the infant's exploration of the world is "centered" around the caregiver. The infant explores and plays with novel objects at a distance from the caregiver, occasionally looking, smiling, or vocalizing from a distance, and occasionally bringing toys to share. Returns to the caregiver typically are brief, as the infant again ventures away to explore. If the infant approaches something quite novel, such as a stranger, he or she immediately follows this by retreating to the caregiver (Bretherton & Ainsworth, 1974). In a novel setting, infants commonly sit facing the caregiver as they play. When experimenters block the infant's view of the caregiver with a partition, infants increase their vocalizations and keep track of the caregiver in that way (Carr, Dabbs, & Carr, 1975). Even a blind infant, when equipped with a sonar device, played so as to keep the caregiver centrally located (Bower, personal communication). All of this is aptly described by Ainsworth as the "attachment–exploration balance," the infant using its relationship with the caregiver to support exploration (Ainsworth, Blehar, Waters, & Wall, 1978).

Virtually all infants, however reared and however treated, form specific attachments. Given our primate heritage and the social basis of our adaptation, the tendency to form such important ties to caregivers is built in strongly (Bowlby, 1969; Breger, 1974). All that is required is that someone be present and interact with the infant over a period of months and, inevitably, the infant will form an attachment.

The quality of the attachment relationship, like any other relationship, may vary, however. For most infants, attachment and exploration are well balanced; the infant separates readily when stress is minimal and explores freely, yet quickly returns to or signals to the caregiver when threatened or distressed. Infants are active and effective in seeking physical contact when they need it, and they maintain the contact until comforted. Commonly, this settling with the caregiver is readily achieved and thereby enables a rapid return to play and exploration. The quality of the affective bond of such infants is also seen in their positive greetings of the caregiver (when not distressed) and in their natural tendency to share their delight with the caregiver when playing.

Ainsworth refers to this group of infants whose attachment is so effective in serving their development as "securely attached" (Ainsworth et al., 1978). By this, she refers to the confident expectations that these infants have with regard to the caregiver. They have learned to signal their needs and desires *purposefully* to the caregiver and to anticipate the caregiver's response. They separate readily to explore, Ainsworth argues, because they are confident that, *should* a threat or difficulty arise, the caregiver will be accessible (physically and psychologically) and will take prompt action to address the problem. They need not be concerned about this in advance. The caregiver has routinely been responsive before. Similarly, they seek contact with their caregivers when distressed, because they are confident that such contact will alleviate the distress. Moreover, the contact may be relatively brief and the settling rapid, because the infant is so experienced with the effectiveness of such contact. By 12 months, there have been countless opportunities for the infant to learn that contact with the caregiver is followed quickly by a restoration of equanimity.

Ainsworth has described other infants whose attachment relationships are not so effective in promoting development. These "anxiously attached" infants do not show a favorable attachment/exploration balance and, especially, are not able to use the caregiver as a secure base for exploration. In Ainsworth's laboratory procedure these infants show one of two basic patterns:

Anxious/Resistant Attachment. These infants may have difficulty separating from the caregiver in a novel playroom and may need contact and reassurance prior to any further stress. Their exploration is limited and they tend to be wary of a stranger. They are upset by brief separations from the caregiver but, more importantly, they have difficulty settling when the caregiver returns after a separation. They may squirm to get down only to want back up again. They may push away or kick their feet or angrily reject toys offered by the caregiver. In short, they mix contact seeking with the contact resistance and thus fail to be settled.

Anxious/Avoidant Attachment. These infants separate readily enough in a novel situation, and they accept a stranger's advances. They often are not upset when left with the stranger. However, they do not seek contact or even interaction when mothers return from the 3-minute separation, and such avoidance (looking away, turning away, starting to approach, then veering off, or simply totally ignoring) is more pointed after the second separation (when the infant is left alone and most babies, including these, are distressed). In this situation, the more they need contact, the less they seek it, with a subsequent impact on exploration behavior.

Based on Ainsworth's work and now on others' (e.g., Farber & Egeland, 1980; Grossmann & Grossmann, 1982), something is known about what leads to secure or anxious patterns of attachment. The factor that has been isolated is generally referred to as *caregiver sensitivity*. Longitudinal studies in which infant and caregiver interaction is observed early in the first year and pattern of attachment is examined at 12 months show that if there is a history of reliable and effective responding to the infant's signals, the infant is likely to be secure in its attachment. This result is especially interesting when one considers the case of crying. When caregivers responded promptly and effectively to infants' cries early in the first year, by 12 months the infants cried *less* and were assessed to be securely attached (Bell & Ainsworth, 1972). The infants did not learn to cry in reaction to the caregivers' responsiveness; rather they learned that the caregiver would respond to their signals. This confident expectation promotes their use of more mature signaling modes (e.g., calling), and makes it unnecessary for the infant to signal unless the need is clear-cut. One need not cry at the slightest threat, for if the threat becomes more serious a quick response on the part of the caregiver is assured.

One of these predictive studies began when the infants were as young as 6–15 weeks (Blehar, Lieberman, & Ainsworth, 1977). Even at that early age, it was found that caregiver responsiveness predicted later secure attachment. Infant behavior did not. This finding is not surprising, since early in life infant behavior is highly changeable. As our consideration of development suggested, it takes several months for the infant to become a stable partner in the interaction. Nonetheless, the responsiveness of the caregiver forecast the quality of this incipient partnership even before it was formed. (To date, there is no evidence that temperamental differences influence whether the attachment will be secure or anxious. It should be noted that securely attached infants can be quite different temperamentally, high or low on activity, cuddly or not cuddly, etc. Even an easily frightened infant would be considered securely attached, if he or she sought contact when frightened and if the contact were effective.) As one might suspect, several factors influence the quality of care. Studies have now shown that quality of attachment is influenced by the social support system available to the caregiver (Crockenberg, 1981), life stress experiences (Vaughn, Egeland, Waters, & Sroufe, 1979), and family history (Morris, 1982).

The interaction histories of the two groups of anxiously attached infants are in ways very similar. For both groups, the caregivers (mothers in these studies) are rated low on sensitivity to the infant's signals and low on cooperation. Cooperation involves stimulating the infant when it is open to stimulation and ministering to it in ways that mesh with its ongoing behavior. There was one striking difference in the care of the infants who later were anxious/avoidant. When these infants sought physical contact (i.e., to be picked up) they were routinely rebuffed. Their mothers held them as much as other mothers but when the *infants* sought the contact, the mother turned them away (Ainsworth et al., 1978). It does not seem surprising that these infants learned to avoid their mothers later when their needs for contact were aroused.

The Movement Toward Autonomy

A major developmental issue for the second year centers around what Margaret Mahler calls "separation-individuation" (Mahler, Pine & Bergman, 1975). While from the moment of birth the infant is moving toward being a separate individual, the second year marks an important turning point in this process. Based on advances in cognitive development and nurtured by experiences of separating to explore and engaging the environment on his or her own, the toddler inevitably develops an awareness of separateness from the caregiver. Breger (1974) and Mahler point out how this inevitably leads to a major crisis; namely, how to maintain the previous closeness with the caregiver while moving toward autonomy.

However, this crisis is approached within the foundation provided by the prior relationship and, normally, it is resolved as inevitably as it began (Sroufe, 1977). First, most infants find independent exploration and mastery to be rewarding. They rapidly develop confidence in their own abilities and therefore are less needy of the former kind of closeness (that is, their conflict will be in moderate bounds). Second, the deep-seated belief in the caregivers' availability and responsiveness will continue to serve them as they move farther into the outside world. Third, the affective sharing of play (usually from a distance) that is such a large part of the early toddler period represents a new, more mature way of maintaining psychological contact.

> The security of attachment influences the quality of exploration and play during the "practicing" phase. Similarly, there are at least two ways that the quality of this latter adaptation is important for the infant's handling of the (second year) crisis. First, to the extent that exploration is interesting and gratifying and to the extent that mastery skills, confidence, and competence with objects are developed, the pull of the outer world will be strong. Development is its own impetus. The child will feel strong urges to go on developing new skills and encountering new experiences, and this will more than balance his wishes for the former type of closeness with his caregivers. At the same time, the caregiver's faithfulness in being available for comforting when the infant is distressed and the caregiver's enjoyment of play and sharing experiences with the infant help it to know

that contact will not be lost as it moves away. The bond is intact; it is merely transformed. (Sroufe, 1977, pp. 164–165)

While all healthy toddlers will exhibit a certain amount of willfullness, and even negativism and tantrums, a well-formed caregiver–child relationship provides a basis for dealing with such behavior. If the caregiver's dependability has been established previously, the infant will be likely to wish to comply with parental desires and will accept limits readily when they are imposed: "You have been consistent and dependable before; you probably mean what you say now." Moreover, parental limit-setting and prohibitions are legitimized by the relationship's history. They are not impositions of foreign power. The child knows the caregiver, and the caregiver knows the child. They face complex developmental issues from within their relationship.

There is clear research evidence in support of all this discussion. First, Stayton, Hogan, & Ainsworth (1971) found that when mothers had been sensitively responsive to young infants' signals, the infants were more compliant to maternal requests by the end of the first year. At this age issues of power are only nascent, so this study indicates the natural tendency of infants to comply with parental desires when they have experienced sensitive care. They wish to stay connected and harmonized with the caregiver. Several other studies have shown that even during the "terrible two's," relationship history predicts strongly how well the caregiver–toddler pair will function (Bates, 1982; Main & Londerville, 1978; Matas, Arend, & Sroufe, 1978; Sroufe & Rosenberg, 1980). In all of these studies, infants who had been securely attached were more compliant to parental requests and were more effective in using parental assistance than infants who had been anxiously attached. In our tool problem studies, for example, two-year-olds were faced with increasingly challenging tasks that required them to go beyond their own resources (Gove, 1982; Matas et al., 1978). Toddlers who had been securely attached, having engaged the problems with enthusiasm and persistence, turned to their mothers for help when they were faced with tasks beyond their abilities. They listened to the mothers' clues carefully, cooperated with them, and ultimately solved the problem with great satisfaction. Anxiously attached children were much less effective. The children who had shown resistant attachments became quickly frustrated and upset; they directed this tantrum and frustration behavior at their mothers, and the pair become so embroiled in a power struggle that solving the problem became lost as a goal. Anxious/avoidant children, in contrast, tended to be less involved affectively in the problems and more indirect in expressing anger at their mothers. They tended to ignore her suggestions and to direct anger at the tool problems. Neither group of anxiously attached children complied with their mothers or showed enthusiasm in facing the problems.

DEVELOPMENTAL CONSEQUENCES OF EARLY CARE

In addition to these different outcomes for secure and anxious children during the toddler period, three separate studies have now documented later correlates of these early patterns of attachment in the preschool years.

In the first study, observers who had no knowledge of attachment history watched children for 5 weeks in a preschool (at age 3½ years). The observers' descriptions of the children were summarized into two categories, one pertaining to social competence ("is a peer leader," "is attended to by other children," etc.) and one pertaining to personal competence ("is curious," "sets goals which stretch his abilities," etc.). Securely attached children were found to be significantly higher than insecurely attached children in terms of both competence categories, with 16 of the 24 individual items distinguishing the groups beyond the .05 level of confidence (Waters, Wippman, & Sroufe, 1979).

In the second study, both teacher descriptions and laboratory behavioral observations were used to study another group of children at age v1,25-dihydroxyvitamin $D_3$5 years. Children who had been securely attached were found to be more competent in both the school and laboratory settings (Arend, Gove, & Sroufe, 1979). The secure children were more flexible in engaging opportunities and coping with problems in the environment and, as in the Waters et al. (1979) study, were more curious. Differences in intelligence cannot account for these findings, since the attachment groups were not different on IQ.

The final study was quite comprehensive. Here, two preschool classes were assembled with children having different attachment histories (Sroufe, 1983). The children were observed daily in the range of situations provided by the preschool. In addition, extensive data were obtained from the teachers. The teachers rated the children who had been securely attached as more healthy emotionally ($p < .0001$) and higher on self-esteem ($p < .001$), as more socially competent ($p < .01$) and as more independent ($p < .0001$) than children who had been anxiously attached. Based on teacher Q-sort descriptions (Block, 1961), the securely-attached children were more flexible in managing impulses and more empathic ($p < .01$). All of these judgments were made without knowledge of the child's developmental history.

The teacher judgments were confirmed and extended by the behavioral observations made by coders who had no knowledge of the children's histories. Children who had been anxiously attached as infants required more support, guidance, and discipline from the teachers ($p < .01$), and when observed in a large group setting, were more than 3 times more often ($p < .01$) sitting next to teachers and on teachers' laps than securely attached children (who sat near peers). The anxiously attached children exhibited more negative affect and impulsive, negative behaviors ($p <$

.01) and less often showed positive affect ($p < .01$) in initiating contact or responding to others than did securely attached children. Not surprisingly, the anxiously attached children had significantly fewer friends, and they were significantly less popular than the securely attached children (as assessed through sociometric techniques).

Specific outcomes for the particular attachment histories also became apparent. Children who showed anxious/resistant patterns of attachment tended to be: (a) passive, weak, and ineffectual, commonly hovering near a teacher and waiting for support to engage the environment, or (b) impulsive, hyperactive, anxious, and easily frustrated. On the other hand, children who had been anxious/avoidant tended to be: (a) hostile, devious, and antisocial; (b) emotionally isolated (often expressing their dependency in indirect ways), or (c) disconnected and "out of touch."

Such coherence of behavior over a 3-year time period is quite reasonable. These behavior patterns follow from the expectations that these children have developed concerning themselves and others and from the ways of coping with the environment that they evolved in adapting to their early care. By age 4½ years, securely attached children were confident in their *own* resources. They enjoyed new experiences and could stay flexible in the face of challenges. They expected social encounters with peers to be positive and they expected teachers to be available. The anxious/resistant children, presumably in the face of inconsistent care, continued to need reassurance about adult availability, were doubtful of their ability for self-control, and had not developed skills in dealing with the object (and later social) world. Thus, unremitting dependency concerns or impulsive control issues resulted. The anxious/avoidant children, in the face of chronic emotional unavailability of the caregiver, developed a precocious (and therefore unworkable) self-reliance. At times they appeared to view the world as hostile or turned anger against themselves. Other children responded primarily with emotional isolation. Their unmet needs for nurturance and contact remained in force, as witnessed by dependency rankings as high as those of the anxious/resistant children, but these needs were shown through a desperateness of contact in safe circumstances, or were manifested very indirectly, or became apparent only in time, when they began to feel safe in the situation (Sroufe, Fox & Pancake, 1983).

There are, of course, exceptions to this continuity of behavior. Some anxiously attached children (approximately one quarter) looked reasonably well in the preschool, and some (again, one quarter) secure children showed notable problems. All children have problems and all have strengths. Moreover, we do not mean to imply that early care and attachment patterns directly cause preschool behavior. Early experience does, however, shape the initial personality structure (the attitudes, expectations, and early coping styles that the children bring forward). And with development, children create their own experience (for example, seeking out or avoiding peer experiences). Still, these incipient patterns of personality are influenced by later care as well, and they are subject to change. Commonly, the early patterns are supported by later care. One study showed, for example, that mothers of securely attached children also encouraged and supported peer contacts (Lieberman, 1977). And in our studies we find that mothers of securely attached infants are more sensitive and supportive of their children in the tool problems at age 2 and in teaching tasks at age 3½ years. There is commonly coherence in care as well as coherence in development (Sroufe, 1979).

We would underscore, moreover, that these patterns of functioning are open to change. In one study we found that when life circumstances of the family were highly changeable, the child's pattern of adaptation was also subject to change (Vaughn et al., 1979). In examining children who changed from anxious to secure patterns of attachment between 12 and 18 months of age, it was found that the mothers of these children independently reported significantly greater reduction of life stress (moving, illness, partner changes, job changes, etc.) than did mothers of children changing from secure to anxious attachment. Our interpretation, of course, is that changes in experienced stress influenced the quality of the caregiver–infant interaction and thereby the quality of the attachment manifested. There is no "critical period" for attachment.

Even in the course of our preschool, we noted changes in the children as a function of their changing family circumstances. Moreover, many of the anxiously attached children showed improvements in their adaptation over the course of the school term. While we had no control group, so that conclusions are tentative, many of these changes were dramatic and rather obviously linked to particular goals of the nursery school program. Further research is likely to confirm that the adaptation of children changes as a function of the care they receive.

IMPLICATIONS

While our review of issues surrounding early care and development necessarily has been brief, certain basic points have been illustrated. First and most importantly, adequate care at any one age typically builds upon a history of experience between caretaker and child. Through interaction, the caregiver learns to read the signals and understand the moods and nature of the infant, so that she or he can respond appropriately in subsequent phases. Second, the infant develops over time its capacities for the engagement and organized behavior that are required for increasingly reciprocal participation. What begins as dyadic regulation, heavily influenced by the caregiver, becomes reciprocal dyadic regulation and ultimately, self-regulation as the infant moves forward in development (Sander, 1975). When this process goes well, the infant is prepared to engage the larger world with both confidence and competence.

Established findings from the study of early development have clear implications for a number of contemporary social issues, especially those surrounding arrangements for care of young children. The most general and important of these implications is that *the quality of early care makes a difference,* a profound difference, in the development of children. Issues surrounding out-of-home care and alternative life styles are enormously complex, and decisions in these areas are, and should be, influenced by many factors. But as these decisions are made we should not lose sight of the nature of the process of human development and the factors that influence it. There are more specific implications from research on early development for social policy issues as well. In the following sections we will consider some specific issues.

Who Will Be an Attachment Figure?

From the process view of attachment, it should be clear that the infant will have attachment relationships with whomever is available for interaction in an *ongoing* way. In Bowlby's (1969) terms, infants tend to have a small hierarchy of such relationships; that is, attachments tend to be ordered in terms of their centrality.[1] The primacy of a relationship would be determined largely by the extensiveness of the infant's interaction with a particular person, and thus could be with biological mother, biological father, adoptive parents, daycare workers, or other caring person. The infant knows only the interaction; it does not know biological status.

An infant can well be attached to mother, father, *and* daycare worker, and each of these relationships would be established in its own right. There is no reason to suspect that, were father the primary caregiver or were caregiving equally divided, this would pose problems for the infant. Nor would there necessarily be problems if some third person were primary caregiver. Studies in Israel of infants who spend a great deal of time with a substitute caregiver show that infants are indeed attached to both the "metapelet" and the parent (Fox, 1977). Moreover, a child's relationship with a caregiver is specific to that person. Recent research by Main and Weston (1981) suggests that infants may have a secure attachment relationship with one parent and an anxious relationship with the other. In other words, a child's attitudes and expectations about a particular person derive from its experiences with that person. Furthermore, it seems that

---

[1] From an evolutionary perspective, this is entirely reasonable. In times of danger, the infant cannot hesitate, but must know immediately where to seek protection.

the child's relationships with *both* parents influence the child's pattern of interaction with others. Children who had secure relationships with both mother and father showed the highest levels of relatedness with a playful adult, and children who had insecure relationships with both parents showed the lowest levels of relatedness. Children who had a secure relationship with one parent but not the other fell in between on level of relatedness. Interestingly, in this sample where mothers were primary caregivers (i.e., spent more than twice as much time with the babies as fathers), secure attachment to mother alone was associated with better outcomes than secure attachment to father alone. Thus, this study suggests that attachments are quite specific and that the centrality of an attachment determines its impact on the child. A positive relationship (a secure attachment) with a daycare worker could complement or enhance secure relationships with parents, though a substitute caregiver cannot fully "make up" for a child's nonoptional attachment relationship with parents.

The Quality of Attachment Relationships

The quality of the infant–mother or other attachment relationship is not strictly dependent on amount of contact with the infant. To be sure, through interaction one has opportunity to learn to coordinate behavior with the infant's needs and signals, but home care and continuous interaction do not guarantee a secure attachment. In Ainsworth's studies, mothers of anxiously attached infants (even in the avoidant group) had as much contact with their infants as did mothers of securely attached infants. The quality of the attachment was dependent upon the quality of the ongoing interaction—the sensitivity and responsiveness of the care (Ainsworth et al., 1978).

Thus, it is not the fact of working or not working that determines the quality of a parent–child relationship:

> It is apparent that maternal employment is not a single condition or a variable of mothering; it is rather a set of conditions which may vary greatly from case to case.
>
> Personal variables which characterize the mother as an individual have generally been ignored in studies of child-rearing . . . (The) mother's gratifications and frustrations in her other adult (non-mother) roles, her achievement needs, and her feelings of self-fulfillment influence her functioning as a mother and affect what is mediated to the child by her child-rearing practices. Employment status may be intimately bound up with the mother's self-attitudes and values. (Yarrow, Scott, deLeeuw, & Heinig, 1962, p. 123)

One could well imagine a case where an infant's mother stayed home with her infant, only to wind up feeling resentful, isolated, and unfulfilled. The chances of a secure attachment between the mother and her child developing in such circumstances might well be less than in another case where mother's activities outside of the home increased her self-esteem, enhanced her social support, and left her feeling rejuvenated. For example, in one study (Yarrow et al., 1962), childrearing patterns were unrelated to employment status among middle-class mothers. However, the way working or not working was combined with other maternal characteristics *was* important in distinguishing the quality of mothers' childrearing. If mothers *preferred* their roles, working or not working made little difference in their childrearing. When mothers were *dissatisfied,* however, working mothers actually showed more adequate mothering, were more confident, and reported less conflict with their children than nonworking mothers. And among nonworking mothers, those who preferred to work, but did not out of a sense of "duty," showed the least favorable childrearing qualities of all mothers. On the other hand, we would suspect that if a mother's job left her with few emotional resources and unable to take up the task of responsive care, any increase in self-esteem would be of little benefit to the infant. In other words, the *meaning* of a mother's working ot nor working is what will affect the development of attachments.

Roles for Fathers

Currently, there is much interest in a reconsideration of the father's place in the childrearing enterprise (Lamb, 1976; Parke, 1978). Most often when people think of an increased role for father, they think of fathers' sharing more equally in the range of childrearing tasks. We have considerable sympathy for this point of view: expanded participation in childrearing by fathers is probably to everyone's benefit. The point we would make, however, is that the father's role is of central importance in several ways, even when families follow the more traditional path of mothers staying home and fathers working during the infancy period.

First, the father can provide essential emotional support for the mother. Emotional support for the primary caregiver appears to be extremely important in fostering that caregiver's sensitivity to the infant. For example, in families where husbands gave emotional support to their wives, the infant–mother relationship was affectionate, involved, and sensitive. On the other hand, the more husbands criticized and were in conflict with their wives, the more negative and stressful were mother–infant interactions (Pedersen, Anderson, & Cain, 1977). In other words, the marital relationship supports the parent–child relationship. As the role of such support in the *child's* development is better recognized, marital partners can come to view the task of infant care as a *joint* responsibility. By making decisions to reduce stress from work, for example, or making adjustments in other aspects of their daily lives, father, can be in a better position to offer emotional support (as well as support with caretaking duties) for their spouses and to have a fuller experience of participating in the child's development. Employers also should become more sensitive to this need.

Second, by fostering their own interaction with the infant, fathers can play an important role in the child's second-year transition. During this time infants are not only moving away from infantile dependence on the primary caregiver, but they are evolving new ways of being in contact with others through play, games, sharing of objects, and so forth. Research has shown that these are the very activities that many fathers naturally enjoy doing with their infants (Lamb, 1977; Clarke-Stewart, 1978). Thus, fathers or other secondary caregivers may be in an ideal position to promote the child's smooth transition from infancy to early childhood, by aiding the child in its growing autonomy from the primary caregiver.

Single parents can, of course, provide care for all of the emotional needs of the infant. They can alter their behavior in keeping with the requirements of each developmental period. It seems clear to us, however, that single parents should be very active in creating social support systems (e.g., family, friends) for themselves. Unless the caregivers' own needs are being met, they will be hard pressed to give emotionally to their infants in the unilateral manner that is required. Infants are ill-prepared to meet the emotional needs of their caregivers, and thus cannot provide needed support for their parents.

Out-of-home Care

Decisions concerning out-of-home care will always be made on the basis of an individual family's needs and frequently depend more on economic factors than on social, philosophical, or child development issues. Nonetheless, when families do have a wide range of choices open to them, some guidance in making a decision is available from knowledge of early development. Those providing out of home care also may receive guidance from child development research.

It seems clear that out of home care per se need not have undesirable consequences for early development or even for the infant–caregiver attachment. Only when the out-of-home care precludes ongoing, good quality parent–child interaction is it likely that day care would be seriously disruptive of the infant–parent attachment. And only when both parent and substitute care are inconsistent and unresponsive would one expect serious developmental disturbances in a child. Some out-of-home care, which itself is characterized by consistency and responsiveness, in the context of ongoing quality care at home, would be expected to have no more than temporary disruptive effects on parent–child interaction. On the other hand, full-time day care, which profoundly disrupts an emergent attachment relationship (perhaps because the parent returns home exhausted and unable to be sufficiently responsive to a child who has received inadequate care all day), may well have consequences for the attachment relationship. And inconsistent, haphazard out-of-home care would be expected to have negative consequences for a child's development, just as would chaotic home care. Let us examine some of these issues more closely.

Timing. Our knowledge of the developmental course of attachment suggests that the period between the sixth and twelfth months of a child's life is not an optimal time to begin full-time out-of-home care. Recall that during this period the specific attachment is "crystallizing." Separation distress is marked; fear of strangers may be intense. Unfortunately, many employers grant maternity leaves for only 6 months and require that mothers return to work full time at the end of that period. Thus the infant is confronted with repeated and extended separations from the person who has been with her or him full time. And these separations take place at a point in development when the infant is especially vulnerable to disruption from separations. A much wiser policy on materntiy leave would be to allow mothers to return to work part-time as late as possible in the child's first year. Another alternative may be to allow caregivers to return to part time work before the child is 6 months old, and to continue part time work for as long as possible.

The disruptiveness of beginning day care between 6 and 12 months would not lead us to encourage earlier full-time day care or to imply that full-time day care after 12 months is without potential risks. The early months are, of course, very important for establishing routines and learning to read signals. It only seems reasonable that the partners who have been fully involved in the early months have a better foundation with which to move toward the specific attachment phase. The secure attachment is a product of the sensitivity and repsonsiveness of the earlier phase, of the opportunity to acquire confident expectations over an extended period of time. Similarly, during the movement toward autonomy in the second year, it is important for the infant to know that the intactness of the relationship is not threatened by its actions (Sander, 1975). The caregiver is taxed during this period to reassure the infant of his or her continued availability, and separations may be stressful. Still, by this time the child has vastly expanded cognitive (and even verbal) abilities and can much better grasp that the caregiver will inevitably return. Moreover, by the second year, there has been considerable opportunity for the child to have established trust in the caregiver's responsiveness to his needs (Erikson, 1963). However threatening daily separations might be, with an older, securely attached child the threat is countered by a deep-seated belief that the care-giver will remain available.

Where there is choice, we would encourage parents to delay onset of day care for as long as possible and, especially, to make the transition to full-time substitute care gradual. For many families, part-time, out-of-home care, begun gradually and leading toward full-time care only in the late preschool years has posed few problems for development and has had many advantages. There are also families, of course, where full-time day care, begun early, has not been seriously disruptive of the child's development. Parents who decide to begin full-time day care early in the child's life need to realize, however, that they must make a strong com-mitment to finding opportunities for quality interaction with their infants when they are home together.

Quality. The quality of the out-of-home care is, of course, the other factor in the equation. If the substitute care is consistently sensitive and responsive, it can provide a further context for the infant to learn that it can have an impact on the environment, that its needs will be met, and that its signals will be acknowledged. There are cases, no doubt, where the substitute care is vastly superior to the home care received and the out-of-home care is of great advantage to the infant or toddler (Belsky & Steinberg, 1978). Excellent substitute care, and home care which does not disrupt parent–child interaction, may be the best of all possible worlds. In high quality, out-of-home care, the infant has experience not only with other caring adults, but with other children, and these experiences may supplement such experiences at home.

Research suggests that high quality day care can ameliorate some of the disadvantages arising from inadequate home care, especially with re-gard to cognitive skills (Belsky & Steinberg, 1978). However, when sub-stitute care is of poor quality, the situation for a child and its family may be very undesirable. In fact, in our opinion, a child who receives inade-quate care at home is better off with no day care experience than with the experience of inferior out-of-home care. For when substitute care is poor, in addition to chaotic, unresponsive, or inconsistent home care, the infant has the added inconsistency of changing patterns of care when he is not at home. Poor-quality substitute care can disrupt a child's devel-opment and the development of the parent–child relationship. As a society we have a responsibility to insure that no child experiences inadequate out-of-home care.

Individualized care. Before we conclude our discussion of substitute care, some comments about the nature of that care is in order. In general, we would advocate arrangements that allow infants and young children to receive individualized out-of-home care. It would be ideal for an infant to be cared for primarily by one or two substitute caregivers, so that child and caregiver can get to know each other well. Through regular and exclusive contact in day care, each partner can learn about the other, and the likelihood of the adult's providing maximally responsive care is increased. For example, the longer substitute caregivers had cared for infants, the more they showed positive affect, play, and responsive caregiving in ways that resembled mothers' styles of caregiving (Rubenstein, Pedersen, & Yarrow, 1977). Furthermore, through regular contact with a substitute caregiver, the infant can acquire the anticipations that become confidence. A secure attachment to a day care worker poses no threat in and of itself to the security of the infant–parent attachment (Fox, 1977), and as we have suggested may enhance a secure infant–parent attachment.

In day care centers, the rate of personnel turnover often is high, precluding the possibility of caregivers and children knowing each other well. Furthermore, it appears that in a group setting with a large number of preschool children (i.e., 20) in one room, little individualized caregiving occurs because of practical constraints (Rutter, 1980). And in other situations, policy dictates that numerous workers care for a particular infant. Sometimes there is an explicit desire to avoid the formation of infant–day care worker attachments, and other times low budgets and other circumstances result in frequent changes in assignments of worker to infant. Whatever the origins of practices that discourage the existence of individualized care for infants, such practices should be changed.

CURRENT STATUS OF RESEARCH ON OUT-OF-HOME CARE

Research on out-of-home care has been discussed in this volume and has been reviewed by others (Belsky & Steinberg, 1978; Rutter, 1980). Our brief review of the status of this research will be in light of the developmental concerns that we have raised.

In general, research on out-of-home care has been seriously inadequate in its attention to developmental issues. First, few studies have examined systematically the impact of the time of onset and of the quality of day care. Most research on day care has focused on high quality, university centers and has not given attention to the age at which day care begins. Furthermore, little research has focused on children younger than 3 years old. Research on substitute care for infants is especially inadequate, both because of the lack of attention to time of onset and because of inadequate measures.

The few studies that have involved infants have not even approached rigorous assessment of the impact of day care. The most frequently used measure of emotional adjustment in infants appears to be separation distress (Rutter, 1980). As we have seen, whether or not an infant cries at separation is by no means an index of the quality of a child's attachment. An anxiously attached infant may cry a lot or not at all (as do some anxious/avoidant infants). Similarly, securely attached infants may be very distressed or not at all distressed when left alone.

Thus, lack of day-care versus home-care group differences in frequency of duration of separation distress provides no basis upon which to judge the impact of day care on attachments. More comprehensive assessments of the infant–caregiver relationship or infant adaptation (e.g., security of attachment) are required. Unfortunately, most of the data that have been used to conclude that day care has no deleterious effects on the development of parent–infant attachment involve such simple group comparisons. For example, Kagan et al. (1978) observed day-care and home-care children's crying and fussing in laboratory separations. They concluded that day care had no negative impact on the formation of attachments on the basis of their findings of no group differences. This is but one example of research that was interpreted from a political rather than an empirical base. In similar ways, those who wish to argue *for* the existence of deleterious effects of day care can use equally inadequate studies to back their arguments. However, when we are dealing with issues involving infants' and young children's lives, it is important that decisions be based on accurate interpretation of adequate data. As of now, data on the impact of day care do not indicate that substitute care has harmful effects, but many of the relevant dimensions have not been studied.

One recent study is an exception to the rule of inadequacy in day care research. Vaughn, Gove, and Egeland (1980) examined infant–mother attachment relationships at 12 and 18 months in three groups of families: (a) infants who began full-time day care before 12 months (early care group); (b) infants who were placed in full-time day care between 12 and 18 months (later care group); and (c) infants who received home care during the first 18 months. The most dramatic finding from this study was that 47% of the early care group showed anxious/avoidant attachments (the pattern associated with maternal unavailability) at 12 months as compared to 28% and 19% of the later care and home care groups (at 18 months, the comparable figures were 41%, 16%, and 13%).

The results of this study were complex and indicated that by the time a child was 18 months old, factors other than home versus day care influenced the quality of the infant–mother attachment. The intactness of the family and the frequency with which the family experienced stressful life events were of importance in deciding the quality of the attachment. For example, at 18 months, children from intact families were likely to be securely attached, even if out-of-home care began early.

The Vaughn study involved the use of careful controls on demographic variables such as mother's age, education, and socioeconomic status, so its results deserve careful consideration. This study is also of crucial importance because of its adequate measures of attachment and consideration of the importance of the timing of day care. This study does not, however, indict day care per se, for a number of reasons. First, many of the children who received out-of-home care maintained secure attachments to their mothers. Second, the quality of out-of-home care in this sample of economically disadvantaged families was often very poor. The substitute care arrangements were highly changeable (from one setting and type of arrangement to another), and caregiving at particular sites was haphazard or unresponsive to the infants' needs.

The results of this study remain to be replicated and studied in more depth. It is not clear, for example, whether there would be such a high frequency of anxious/avoidant attachments in children who received high-quality out-of-home care. Similarly, the impact of early-onset part-time day care remains to be seen. However, given that most urban poor families have available less than adequate arrangements for substitute care, these results suggest the need for attention to the circumstances surrounding day care for infants.

SUMMARY AND CONCLUSION

In the preceding pages, we have considered some issues about substitute care from a developmental perspective. We have discussed the course of human development in the first two years and have tried to point out how our knowledge of development can inform decisions about policy regarding child care.

Research has given us a wealth of information about the social and emotional development of human infants. We know that even the youngest infant has reflexes and behavioral tendencies (e.g., molding its body to others) that adapt it to contact with others. Furthermore, it is clear that these early behaviors increasingly come under the infant's control, so that in several months the infant becomes an increasingly active partner in social exchanges and eventually develops specific relationships (attachments) with people it knows well.

All of this development takes place within the context of the infant's interactions with caregivers. Through countless opportunities to observe an infant, a parent or other caregiver comes to know the infant's signals and learns to be sensitive and responsive to those signals. And the infant's experience of sensitive and responsive care leads it to feel confidence in the caregiver's support and reliability: to have a secure attachment with that person.

A caregiver's provision of adequate care for a child at any one age usually builds on a history of experience with the child. A person who knows a child well can provide developmentally appropriate care. Similarly, establishing a secure attachment with a primary caregiver in the first year aids the infant in its going about further tasks of development. Confidence in the caregiver's responsiveness and trust in the caregiver's availability for support and guidance eventually becomes confidence in self and trust in others. Early experience affects a child's development in profound ways. Though children are responsive to intervention, attitudes and expectations that they acquire early in life color their later experience.

Learning to be responsive to an infant's signals requires that time be spent in ongoing interaction with the infant, but day care does not in and of itself preclude establishing infant–parent attachments. Similarly, establishing attachments with substitute caregivers need not interfere with the development of infant–parent relationships. Routine separations may, however, cause disruptions in parent–infant interaction, especially in the second half-year of the infant's life. And a parent who is separated from his or her infant during the day needs to arrange time to nurture the development of the relationship with the child.

Responsive out-of-home care can enhance experiences of sensitive and responsive care at home, though day care may not fully make up for the consequences of inadequate home care. Furthermore, inadequate day care may have a profound negative impact on the development of the child and of the parent–child relationship. Parents' decisions and social policy should be informed by the importance of high-quality substitute care.

Unfortunately, we have seen that research on day care has provided few clear answers about the impact of day care on social and emotional development. Data do not appear to indicate that day care has harmful effects on children's development, but the interpretation of these data is limited by the general inadequacy of the research. We need studies that consider the impact of the time when day care begins and of the quality of substitute care. And we need studies that use well-established measures of social/emotional adjustment. Careful studies that deal with the crucial dimensions of substitute care can provide parents, educators, and policymakers with guidance for their decisions, and provide infants and children with an optimal environment for development.

REFERENCES

Ainsworth, M.D.S. *Infancy in Uganda: Infant care and the growth of love*. Baltimore, MD: Johns Hopkins University Press, 1967.

Ainsworth, M. D. S., & Bell, S. M. Mother-infant interaction and the development of competence. In K. J. Connelly & J. Bruner (Eds.), *The growth of competence*. New York: Academic Press, 1974.

Ainsworth, M. D. S., Bell, S. M., & Stayton, D. J. Individual differences in strange situation behavior of one-year-olds. In H. R. Schaffer (Ed.), *The origins of human social relations*. New York: Academic Press, 1971.

Ainsworth, M. D. S., Blehar, M. C., Waters, E., & Wall, S. *Patterns of attachment*. Hillsdale, NJ: Erlbaum, 1978.

Arend, R., Gove, F. L., & Sroufe, L. A. Continuity of individual adaptation from infancy to kindergarten: A predictive study of ego-resiliency and curiosity in preschoolers. *Child Development*, 1979, *50*, 950–959.

Bates, J. The concept of difficult temperament. *Merrill-Palmer Quarterly*, 1980, *26*, 299–319.

Bell, S. M., & Ainsworth, M. D. S. Infant crying and maternal responsiveness. *Child Development*, 1972, *43*, 1171–1190.

Belsky, J., & Steinberg, L. D. The effects of day care: A critical review. *Child Development*, 1978, *49*, 929–949.

Blehar, M. C., Lieberman, A. F., & Ainsworth, M. D. S. Early face-to-face interaction and its relation to later infant-mother attachment. *Child Development*, 1977, *48*, 182–194.

Block, J. *The Q-sort method in personality assessment and psychiatric research*. Springfield, IL: C. C. Thomas, 1961.

Bowlby, J. *Attachment and loss*. (Vol. 1). *Attachment*. New York: Basic Books, 1969.

Brazelton, T. B., Koslowski, B., & Main, M. The origins of reciprocity: The early mother–infant interaction. In M. Lewis & L. Rosenblum (Eds.), *The effect of the infant on its caregiver*. New York: Wiley, 1974.

Breger, L. *From instinct to identity*. Englewood Cliffs, NJ: Prentice-Hall, 1974.

Bretherton, I., & Ainsworth, M. D. S. Responses of one-year-olds to a stranger in a strange situation. In M. Lewis & L. Rosenblum (Eds.), *The origins of fear*. New York: Wiley, 1974.

Carr, S. J., Dabbs, J. M., & Carr, T. S. Mother–infant attachment: The importance of the mother's visual field. *Child Development*, 1975, *46*, 331–338.

Clarke-Stewart, K. A. And daddy makes three. *Child Development*, 1978, *49*, 466–478.

Crockenberg, S. B. Infant irritability, mother responsiveness, and social support influences on the security of infant–mother attachment. *Child Development*, 1981, *52*, 857–865.

Doyle, A. Infant development in day care. *Developmental Psychology*, 1975, *11*, 655–656.

Eimas, P. D., Siqueland, E. R., Jusczyk, P., & Vigorito, J. Speech perception in infants. *Science*, 1971, *171*, 303–306.

Emde, R. N., & Harmon, R. J. Endogenous and exogenous smiling systems in early infancy. *Journal of the American Academy of Child Psychiatry*, 1972, *11*, 177–200.

Erikson, E. H. *Childhood and society*. New York: Norton, 1963.

Fantz, R. L., Fagan, J. F., & Miranda, S. B. Early visual selectivity. In L. B. Cohen & P. Salapatek (Eds.), *Infant perception: From sensation to cognition* (Vol. 1). New York: Academic Press, 1975.

Farber, E., & Egeland, B. Maternal, neonatal, and mother–infant antecedents of attachment in urban poor. Paper presented at the meetings of the American Psychological Association, Montreal, September 1980.

Fox, N. Attachment of kibbutz infants to mother and metapelet. *Child Development*, 1977, *48*, 1228–1239.

Gove, F. L. Unpublished doctoral dissertation, University of Minnesota, 1982.

Grossmann, K., & Grossmann, K. E. Maternal sensitivity to infants' signals during the first year as related to the year-olds' behavior in Ainsworth's strange situation in a sample of northern German families. Paper presented at the International Conference on Infant Studies, Austin, TX, March 1982.

Harmon, R. J., & Emde, R. N. Spontaneous REM behaviors in a microcephalic infant. *Perceptual and Motor Skills,* 1972, *34,* 827–833.

Kagan, J. *Change and continuity in infancy.* New York: Wiley, 1971.

Kagan, J., Kearsley, R. B., & Zelazo, P. R. *Infancy: Its place in human development.* Cambridge, MA: Harvard University Press, 1978.

Lamb, M. E. *The role of the father in child development.* New York: Wiley, 1976.

Lamb, M. E. Father–infant and mother–infant interaction in the first year of life. *Child Development,* 1977, *48,* 167–181.

Lieberman, A. F. Preschoolers' competence with a peer: Influence of attachment and social experience. *Child Development,* 1977, *48,* 1277–1287.

Mahler, M. S., Pine, F., & Bergman, A. *The psychological birth of the human infant.* New York: Basic Books, 1975.

Main, M., & Londerville, S. B. Compliance and aggression in toddlerhood: Precursors and correlates. Unpublished manuscript, 1978.

Main, M., & Weston, D. The quality of the toddler's relationship to mother and father: Related to conflict behavior and the readiness to establish new relationships. *Child Development,* 1981, *52,* 932–940.

Matas, L., Arend, R., & Sroufe, L. A. Continuity of adaptation in the second year: The relationship between quality of attachment and later competence. *Child Development,* 1978, *49,* 547–556.

Morris, D. L. Attachment and intimacy. In M. Fisher & G. Stricker (Eds.), *Intimacy.* New York: Plenum, 1982.

Oppenheim, R. W. Ontogenic adaptations and retrogressive processes in the development of the nervous system and behavior: A neuroembryological perspective. In K. J. Connolly and H. F. R. Prechtl (Eds.), *Maturation and development: Biological and psychological perspectives.* London: Heinemann, 1981.

Papousek, H. Conditioned head rotation reflexes in infants in the first months of life. *Acta Paediatrica,* 1961, *50,* 565–576.

Parke, R. D. Perspectives on father–infant interaction. In J. D. Osofsky (Ed.), *Handbook of infancy.* New York: Wiley, 1979.

Pedersen, F., Anderson, B., & Cain, R. An approach to understanding linkages between the parent-infant and spouse relationships. Paper presented at the biennial meetings of the Society for Research in Child Development, New Orleans, LA, March 1977.

Piaget, J. *The origins of intelligence in children* (2nd ed.). New York: International Universities Press, 1952. (Originally published, 1936.)

Rubenstein, J. L., Pedersen, F. A., & Yarrow, L. J. What happens when mother is away: A comparison of mothers and substitute caregivers. *Developmental Psychology,* 1977, *13,* 529–530.

Rutter, M. Social/emotional consequences of day care for preschool children. Donald W. Hastings Lecture, University of Minnesota, Minneapolis, MN, October 1980.

Sander, L. Infant and caretaking environment. In E. J. Anthony (Ed.), *Explorations in child psychiatry.* New York: Plenum, 1975.

Schaffer, H. R., & Emerson, P. E. The development of social attachments in infancy. *Monographs of the Society for Research in Child Development,* 1964, *29,* (Serial No. 94).

Sroufe, L. A. *Knowing and enjoying your baby.* New York: Spectrum, 1977.

Sroufe, L. A. The coherence of individual development. *American Psychologist,* 1979, *34,* 834–841.

Sroufe, L. A. Infant–caregiver attachment and patterns of adaptation in preschool: The roots of maladaptation and competence. In M. A. Perlmutter (Ed.), *Minnesota symposia on child psychology. Vol. 16,* Hillsdale, NJ: Erlbaum, 1983.

Sroufe, L. A., Fox, N., & Pancake, V. Attachment and dependency in developmental perspective. *Child Development*, 1983, *54*, 1615–1627.

Sroufe, L. A., & Rosenberg, D. Continuity in the organization of infant and toddler behavior. Paper presented at the International Conference on Infant Studies, New Haven, CT, April 1980.

Sroufe, L. A., & Waters, E. The ontogenesis of smiling and laughter: A perspective on the organization of development in infancy. *Psychological Review*, 1976, *83*, 173–189.

Stayton, D. J., Hogan, R., & Ainsworth, M. D. S. Infant obedience and maternal behavior: The origins of socialization reconsidered. *Child Development*, 1971, *42*, 1057–1069.

Stern, D. N. Mother and infant at play: The dyadic interaction involving facial, vocal, and gaze behaviors. In M. Lewis & L. Rosenblum (Eds.), *The effect of the infant on its caregiver*. New York: Wiley, 1974.

Stern, D. N. *The first relationship: Infant and mother*. Cambridge, MA: Harvard University Press, 1977.

Tanner, J. M. Physical growth. In P. H. Mussen (Ed.), *Carmichael's manual of child psychology*, Vol. 1 (3rd ed.). New York: Wiley, 1970.

Tracy, R. L., Lamb, M. E., & Ainsworth, M. D. S. Infant approach behavior as related to attachment. *Child Development*, 1976, *47*, 571–578.

Vaughn, B., Egeland, B., Sroufe, L. A., & Waters, E. Individual differences in infant–mother attachment at 12 and 18 months: Stability & change in families under stress. *Child Development*, 1979, *50*, 971–975.

Vaughn, B. E., Gove, F. L., & Egeland, B. The relationship between out-of-home care and the quality of infant-mother attachment in an economically disadvantaged population. *Child Development*, 1980, *51*, 1023–1214.

Waters, E., Wippman, J., & Sroufe, L. A. Attachment, positive affect, and competence in the peer group: Two studies in construct validation. *Child Development*, 1979, *50*, 821–829.

Watson, J. S. Smiling, cooing, & the game. *Merrill-Palmer Quarterly*, 1972, *18*, 323–340.

Yarrow, M. R., Scott, P., de Leeuw, L., & Heinig, C. Child-rearing in families of working and nonworking mothers. *Sociometry*, 1962, *25*, 122–140.

Chapter 2
Fathers, Mothers, and Child Care in the 1980s: Family Influences on Child Development

Michael E. Lamb
University of Utah

In the 1970s, an explosion of interest in the topic of socialization and socioemotional development occurred, returning to prominence an issue that had fallen from favor in the preceding decades. Like the research and theorizing that dominated the earlier era of concern with this topic, most of the attention within the 1970s was on the family, since many of the more important aspects of socialization were believed to take place within the family early in life, when extrafamilial experiences were few. Thus it was with parental—especially maternal—influences that psychologists were concerned.

In order to make their hypotheses testable and their models concise, however, students of socialization made a number of simplifying assumptions about the sorts of families in which children were being raised. Prominent among these was the assumption that "normal" socialization took place in the context of two-parent families, in which fathers assumed responsibility for financial support while mothers eschewed involvement in employment in order to assume responsibility for the care of children, homes, and families. This simplifying assumption was never wholly satisfactory, because it failed to accord attention to the many families which violated the supposed norm. Moreover, this "model" of the family has become increasingly unsatisfactory as the number of deviant families has continued to mount. Mothers are employed outside the home in the majority of American families today, for example, and the continuing rise in divorce rates means that many children spend at least part of their childhood in single-parent homes. Unfortunately, psychologists have only recently recognized that the "normal" American family is no longer statistically normative, and hence that we must consider the effects of various family forms more systematically and carefully than in the past.

My goal in this chapter is to review the available evidence concerning the effects of new forms of family and child care arrangements on the development of young children. To do this, I first review our current understanding of the ways in which socialization proceeds in traditional (mother as caretaker, father as breadwinner) two-parent families. In this section, I attempt to summarize the information without detailed analysis of specific studies and without discussion of many topics regarding which there remains much uncertainty. Then I focus attention on three major deviations from the traditional pattern: maternal employment, increased paternal participation in child care, and divorce/single parenthood. Since we still have only a sketchy understanding of the way in which these deviations affect child development, it is sometimes necessary for me to speculate about the effects of these deviations on the basis of our knowledge concerning socialization in traditional families.

SOCIALIZATION IN TRADITIONAL FAMILIES

In this brief overview, our current understanding of maternal and paternal influences is reviewed. First, I discuss the formation of infant–parent attachments and the evidence suggesting that the security of infant–parent attachment affects later socioemotional behavior. I then review research suggesting that parents influence the development of gender role and gender identity, achievement motivation and cognitive competence, morality, and psychological adjustment. I devote more space to development in infancy and toddlerhood, because the findings concerning this phase of life are clearer and more consistent than are those concerning later childhood and adolescence.

Socioemotional Development in Infancy

To whom do attachments form? The most important factor determining who infants form attachments to appears to be exposure: Infants form attachments to those people who have been available to them extensively and consistently during the first 6–8 months (Ainsworth, 1973; Rajecki, Lamb, & Obmascher, 1978). Presumably, it is also important that the adults interact, responding to the infants' signals appropriately and providing for some of their needs (e.g., for contact comfort) but unfortunately this has not been established empirically (Lamb, 1978a; Rajecki et al., 1978).

In most societies, mothers assume primary, if not sole, responsibility

for infant care. It is their faces that infants are most
they are alert; mothers are likely to pick up and con
they are distressed and feed them when they are hu
their mothers' consistent availability and responsiveness,
infants to form primary attachments to them, as indeed
to do (Lamb, 1980). From around 6–8 months, infants
differentially to separations from their mothers (Stayton, Ainsworth, &
Main, 1973), and they begin to retreat to their mothers when alarmed by
the appearance of strangers or by other stressful circumstances. Mothers
are better able to soothe their infants than other women are (Ainsworth,
1973). Less self-evident, perhaps, is the fact that most infants form attachments to other figures—fathers in traditional Western cultures (Lamb,
1977c, 1980; Schaffer & Emerson, 1964) or consistent substitute caretakers
in others (Fox, 1977)—at about the same time as they form attachments
to their mothers, even though the amount of time infants spend interacting
with their fathers is significantly lower than the amount of time they spend
with their mothers (Lamb & Stevenson, 1978). At least within those families willing to participate in research projects (a somewhat select sample,
one suspects), infants discriminate both mothers and fathers from strangers
(Lamb, 1977a, 1977c, 1980). They seek proximity, contact, and comfort
from their fathers with the same intensity and frequency as from their
mothers, without apparent preference (Lamb, 1976b, 1977a). By the end
of the first year, however, the situation changes somewhat. Although infants continue to show no preference for either parent in familiar or
stressfree situations, they turn to their mothers preferentially when distressed (Lamb, 1976e). This tendency is still evident at 18 months of age
(Lamb, 1976a), but appears to have disappeared by 24 months (Lamb,
1976c).

Sex differences. A rather different shift in preference occurs in the
stressfree home environment during the second year of life. Although parents respond preferentially to neonates of their own sex (Parke & Sawin,
1980), these preferences diminish over the course of the first year. There
are no major sex differences in the behavior of either parents or infants
in the latter part of the first year, but the situation changes during the
second year. Starting around the first birthday, fathers begin to pay greater
attention to sons than to daughters, and apparently as a result, boys start
to focus their attention and proximity/contact-seeking behaviors on their
fathers (Lamb, 1977a, 1977b). By the end of the second year, all but one
of the boys in my small longitudinal study were showing marked and consistent preferences for their fathers on a number of attachment behavior
measures (Lamb, 1977b). Girls were much less consistent: by age two,
some preferred their mothers, some their fathers, and some neither parent.

his finding is consistent with other evidence suggesting that parents are initially less concerned about establishing sex-appropriate behavior in daughters than in sons (cf. Lamb, 1976d, 1981c).

Because attachment figures are by definition sources of protection and comfort (Bowlby, 1969), the preferences for mothers when distressed, alarmed, or frightened are especially pertinent in defining mothers as the primary attachment figures for most infants. However, this does not mean that mothers are preferred in all circumstances and for all types of inter-action. Rather, mothers and fathers engage in different types of interaction with their infants and thus come to represent different types of experiences. Mothers, as primary caretakers, are much more likely to engage in care-taking routines than fathers are; for their part, fathers are relatively more likely than mothers to play with their infants, and the play itself is likely to be more unpredictable and physically stimulating than mothers' play is (Lamb, 1976b, 1977c; Belsky, 1979). Infants respond more positively to play bids from their fathers (Lamb, 1977c) and through 30 months, prefer to play with their fathers when they have a choice (Clarke-Stewart, 1978). Boys continue to show this preference through 4 years of age, whereas girls switch to a preference for their mothers between 2 and 4 years of age (Lynn & Cross, 1974).

The formative significance (if any) of the distinctive behavioral dif-ferences between mothers and fathers remains to be established. I have suggested elsewhere that they may permit infants—especially boys—to establish a sense of gender identity and learn sex-typed behavior (Lamb, 1977b; Lamb & Lamb, 1976).[1] However, this speculation is based on evi-dence that gender identity is established in the first two to three years of life (Money & Ehrhardt, 1972) and that boys may have difficulty estab-lishing masculine sex roles when their fathers are absent early in their lives (Biller, 1981; Lamb, 1981c). Unfortunately, there have yet to be lon-gitudinal studies in which outcome measures are used to determine whether variations in maternal and paternal roles have long-term development im-plications.

Individual differences in parent–infant attachments. Even if respon-siveness may not affect whether or not attachments form, the respon-siveness or unresponsiveness of adults does appear to influence the quality

---

[1] By definition, *gender identity* refers to the individual's awareness of and comfort with his/her gender, whereas *sex role* refers to the extent to which the individual's behavior resembles the socially defined models of "masculine" and/or "feminine" behavior. There is no necessary relationship between these two constructs; individuals with secure gender identities may feel free to violate cultural stereotypes and prescriptions, while those whose gender identities are insecure may conform rigidly to the socially defined sex-appropriate roles.

or security of attachment relationships (Ainsworth, Blehar, Waters, & Wall, 1978), although the evidence on this score is still inconclusive (Lamb, Thompson, Gardner, Charnov, & Estes, 1984). Ainsworth and her colleagues reported that when mothers were sensitively responsive to their infants during the first year of life, their infants formed secure attachments to them. When the mothers were insensitive, insecure relationships resulted. As yet, no one has determined whether the same factors account for individual differences in the security of infant–father attachments, but my colleagues and I are currently investigating this issue by means of longitudinal studies.

In order to assess individual differences in the quality of infant–adult attachments, Ainsworth and Wittig (1969) devised a laboratory procedure, the Strange Situation, which permitted one to determine how infants organize their attachment behaviors around attachment figures when they were distressed. The primary focus in the Strange Situation is on the infant's responses to reunion with the attachment figure following two brief separations. Securely attached infants, by definition, behave in the manner predicted by ethological attachment theory; they use their parents as secure bases from which to explore, especially in the preseparation episodes, and they attempt to reestablish interaction (often by seeking proximity or contact) when reunited with their parents following the brief separations. Some insecurely attached infants are labeled "avoidant" because they actively avoid their parents when reunited: others are called "resistant" because they respond to reunion with angry ambivalence, both seeking contact/interaction and rejecting it when it is offered.

Ainsworth's reports concerning the consistent relationship between early parental behavior and infant behavior in the Strange Situation have elicited a great deal of attention, particularly in light of evidence that the patterns of behavior observed in the Strange Situation are characteristic of the relationship rather than the infant (i.e., the same infants may behave differently with their mothers and fathers: (Lamb, 1978b; Grossmann, Grossmann, Huber, & Wartner, 1980; Main & Weston, 1981) and that the patterns of behavior can be remarkably stable over time (Connell, 1976; Waters, 1978). The theoretical interpretations offered in the paragraphs that follow reflect my confidence in the Strange Situation procedure. Some caveats are in order, however. First, the relationship between parental behavior and behavior in the Strange Situation was established in only one small longitudinal study—the very study from which the hypotheses grew. There is thus a clear need for replication in larger, hypothesis-testing studies and for more serious consideration of the role played by initial differences among infants in determining security of infant–parent attachment. Thus far, researchers have not been able to replicate Ainsworth's findings, but few have followed her observational procedures closely (Lamb et al., 1984). Second, the stability of Strange Situation behavior over time is not always as high as Waters and Connell reported: Vaughn, Egeland, Sroufe, and Waters (1979) and Thompson, Lamb, and Estes (1982) reported substantially lower stability (62% and 53%, respectively) over a comparable period of time. In both cases, temporal instability was systematically related to stress and major changes in family circumstances and caretaking arrangements. These findings suggest that the security of attachment, as assessed in the Strange Situation, reflects the *current* status of the infant–adult relationship. When patterns of interaction change for any reason, the quality of the relationship may change also, and thus we observe changes in the organization of the infant's attachment behavior. Only in especially stable circumstances are we likely to find long-term stability or consistency. Contrary to Sroufe's implicit claims (see Sroufe, in press), there does *not* appear to be a sensitive period during which infants establish relationships that will remain secure or insecure from that point on, but the degree of flexibility and the consequences (if any) of repeated changes in the security of attachment remain to be established.

Individual Differences in Strange Situation Behavior. Adults, of course, differ in their responsiveness to infant signals (e.g., signals of distress) as everyday observation and Ainsworth's longitudinal study confirm. These individual differences among parents probably produce individual differences in infants' expectations regarding their parents' behavior, which may in turn account for differences in the way infants behave in the Strange Situation (Lamb, 1981a, 1981b). Adults may differ along two dimensions—predictability and appropriateness—with deviation along either dimension constituting insensitivity (Ainsworth, Bell, & Stayton, 1974; Lamb & Easterbrooks, 1981). Adults who respond predictably and appropriately should have infants who turn to them unhesitatingly when alarmed or in need of comfort and who are able to use the adults as secure bases from which to explore. This is the secure pattern of behavior described earlier. Adults who are fairly consistent but often behave inappropriately or aversively should have infants who expect inappropriate responses from their parents and who thus turn away from, rather than toward, them when distressed. Such avoidant patterns of behavior are also observed in the Strange Situation. Adults who are unpredictable and who sometimes respond aversively should produce uncertainty and ambivalence in their infants, and angry ambivalent behavior in fact constitutes the third major pattern of behavior ("resistant") observed in the Strange Situation. From the limited data currently available (Ainsworth et al., 1972, 1974), it appears that the major patterns of behavior observed in the Strange Situation may be associated with the styles of parental behavior described here. Of course, we still need to see these associations replicated in independent samples.

Although it is assumed by most researchers that the infant's behavior in the Strange Situation is determined by the adult's prior behavior, there is some evidence that the adult's behavior in the *immediate* situation is at least correlated with the infant's behavior and may provide cues for the infant. For example, Estes, Lamb, Thompson and Dickstein (1981) found that, when mothers and infants were assessed on the same day, the mothers of securely attached 19-month-olds were more expressive and affectively involved than the mothers of insecurely attached infants. It is not yet clear whether the mothers' immediate behavior in the Strange Situation: (a) directly causes the infants' behavior; (b) simply reminds infants of their mothers' typical mode of behavior; or (c) is causally unrelated to the infants' Strange Situation behavior.

At the same time that they are developing specific expectations about the behavioral propensities of attachment figures, infants are also learning about themselves—specifically, about their ability to elicit responses from others, and thus to control, or at least influence, their own experiences (Lamb, 1981a, 1981b). Recognition of one's own efficacy, which I call perceived effectance, is as important developmentally as a sense of trust in others. Once again, I expect individual differences in the perceived effectance of infants to be correlated with variations in their parents' behavioral propensities. When adults respond promptly and consistently to their infants' signals, their infants should develop high perceived effectance. When the adults' responses are less predictable, lower perceived effectance should result.

Predictive Validity of Security of Attachment. Security of attachment is a developmentally interesting construct in large part because it has predictive validity. Several studies have shown that the way infants behave in the Strange Situation can predict how they behave in a variety of situations months and even years later provided there is continuity in family circumstances and caretaking arrangements (Lamb et al., 1984).

In an early study, Main (1973) reported that infants who were securely attached to their mothers at one year of age were more cooperative with and friendly toward an unfamiliar woman 8 months later than were insecurely attached infants. Thompson and Lamb (1983) found that securely attached infants were more sociable with unfamiliar females at both 12½ and 19½ months. Furthermore, sociability was stable over time when the security of attachment was temporally stable, but not when attachment security changed between 12½ and 19½ months. Waters, Wippman, and Sroufe (1979) and Pastor (1981) showed that securely attached infants were later more socially competent in interaction with peers than insecurely attached infants were. Securely attached 18-month-olds later displayed more persistence and enthusiasm in problem-solving situations than insecurely attached infants did (Matas, Arend, & Sroufe, 1978). Finally, Arend, Gove, and Sroufe (1979) reported that securely attached infants demonstrated more ego control and ego resiliency than insecurely attached infants did several years later.

Main and Weston (1981) sought to determine what would happen when infants were securely attached to one parent and were insecurely attached to the other. They found that the nature of the attachment to the mother (primary caretaker) was most highly related to the infants' responses to a strange adult, although the quality of the infant–father attachment was also independently related. (Unfortunately, the assessments of sociability all took place in the mothers' presence, six months before the father–infant attachment was assessed.)

Other studies of predictive validity are reviewed by Lamb et al. (1984), and the conclusion to which their findings consistently point is that security of attachment has predictive validity if, and only if, the sample consists of families in which there are stable family and caretaking arrangements or in which there is stability in the security of attachment. In the absence of such stability, there appears to be no relationship between security of attachment and later child characteristics.

Summary. We still need much more research if we are to understand the long-term formative significance of individual differences in attachment. I am optimistic that the behavior observed in the Strange Situation will prove to have replicable predictive validity, but I doubt that the significance will be as great as some now seem to believe (e.g., Sroufe, 1978, 1979, in press). Infant experiences are formatively significant, but so too are the other experiences that children encounter as they mature. An infant who has established insecure relationships with both of its parents is *more likely* to develop in a suboptimal way than is one who is securely attached to both parents, particularly if the parents' behavior and circumstances remain reasonably consistent over the years. Parents quite frequently do change, however, either because their circumstances change, because they find it easier/harder to relate to infants than to preschoolers, or because they have adjusted to their child's temperament. As their behavior changes, so too may the security of the infant–parent attachments. Evidence concerning the importance of temporal stability in family/caretaking circumstances in assuring predictive validity confirms this view (Lamb et al., 1984). Furthermore, a variety of people other than parents affect the socialization process, and their diverse influences make it highly unlikely that one will find strong linear continuity from infancy.

Parental Influences on Older Children

In comparison with the research on infancy, the research concerning older children is less programmatic and less focused on defining the processes whereby parents affect their children's development. With few exceptions, the studies are correlational rather than experimental in nature, and longitudinal investigations are rare. Consequently, few conclusions can be stated with any confidence.

Processes of Influence. Studies have identified both direct and indirect parental influences on their children. Most directly mediated parental influences on child development are believed to involve either of two processes: behavioral conditioning or observational learning. It is obvious that parents attempt to shape their children's behavior through the discriminating application of punishments and rewards, and these attempts are often successful—at least in the short-term. In addition, children learn by imitating their parents without any effort on their parents' part, although we know that children are most likely to imitate models who are warm, nurturant, and powerful (Bandura, 1977; Mussen, 1967). This, of course, maximizes the tendency to imitate parents rather than other adults.

Whereas psychologists have written about behavioral shaping and imitation for many years, they have only recently come to appreciate the importance of indirect effects (Belsky, 1981). Indirect effects involve influences of one parent on the other, who then behaves differently toward his/her children. The potential for indirect effects is enormous, and we are only beginning to appreciate the diverse ways in which they may affect child development (cf. Lewis & Feiring, 1981; Parke, Power, & Gottman, 1979). Both direct and indirect effects are implicated by the studies discussed in the paragraphs that follow.

Gender Role and Gender Identity.[2] As mentioned earlier, parents (especially fathers) are particularly attentive (and thus salient) to children of the same sex from infancy. This may facilitate the acquisition of gender identity, which seems to occur in the first two to three years of life (Money & Ehrhardt, 1972), and the establishment of sex-typed behavior.

Probably because they are much more concerned about "appropriately" sex-typed behavior than mothers are (Bronfenbrenner, 1961; Goodenough, 1957; Sears, Maccoby, & Levin, 1957; Tasch, 1955), fathers

---

[2] Most of the studies reviewed in this section and other portions of the chapter have measured "masculinity," "femininity," or "androgyny" by comparing the convergence between individual's self-descriptions or actual behavior and culturally defined stereotypes of "masculine" or "feminine" behavior. We do not know whether there is any relationship between the measured masculinity, femininity, or androgyny of an individual's behavior or personality and his/her psychological adjustment or mental health.

emit reinforcements and punishment for sex-typed behavior more consistently than mothers do (Langlois & Downs, 1980). Boys whose fathers
are absent or uninvolved tend to be less stereotypically "masculine" than
those whose fathers are psychologically and physically present (see Biller,
1974, 1981, for reviews). On the other hand, it is not the case that "masculine" fathers have "masculine" sons (e.g., Mussen & Rutherford, 1963;
Payne & Mussen, 1956). Significant correlations between paternal and
filial "masculinity" occur only when the father is also warm: indeed, nurturance is more reliably related to the "masculinity" of sons than the
fathers' "masculinity" is (Mussen & Rutherford, 1963; Payne & Mussen,
1956; Sears et al., 1957). Girls whose fathers are "masculine" tend to be
more "feminine" (Heilbrun, 1965; Johnson, 1963; Mussen & Rutherford,
1963; Sears, Rau, & Alpert, 1965), presumably because these fathers
complement and encourage their daughters' "femininity." Both boys and
girls develop less traditionally sex-stereotyped attitudes about male and
female roles when their mothers work outside the home (see Hoffman,
1974, and Lamb, 1982, for reviews) and when their fathers are highly involved in child care (Radin, 1978; Sagi, 1982). Both of these effects are
probably attributable to the fact that these parents provide less traditional
models for their children to emulate. There is no evidence that the acquisition of a secure gender identity is affected in any way by increased
paternal involvement or maternal employment.

Of course, sex-role acquisition is not only affected by parental behavior.
From the preschool years through adulthood, significant influences are ex-
erted by peers (Fagot, 1977; Fagot & Patterson, 1969; Lamb, Easterbrooks,
& Holden, 1980; Lamb & Roopnarine, 1979; Nash & Feldman, 1981),
teachers (Dweck, 1978; Fagot, 1977; Serbin, Tonick, & Sternglanz, 1977),
and the media. Most of these socializing agents have a similarly tradition-
alizing effect, making it difficult to appraise the relative importance of each.

Achievement and Achievement Motivation. As mentioned earlier, appropriate responsiveness to infant signals and needs appears to foster the
development of a sense of personal effectance, which is a basic component
of achievement motivation (Lamb, 1981a). Other studies show that parents
who provide stimulation that is developmentally appropriate and plentiful
have more cognitively competent children (see Stevenson & Lamb, 1981,
for a review). High achievement motivation develops in boys when parents
are warm, not controlling, and encourage independence (Radin, 1976, 1981;
Rosen & D'Andrade, 1959; Winterbottom, 1958). Girls benefit when they
receive less unconditional nurturance than the average girl does (Baruch
& Barnett, 1978). In traditional families (i.e., when fathers are primary
breadwinners and are the instrumental leaders of their families), the models
fathers provide are especially important. Warm encouragement from fa-

thers was important to many high-achieving women, since there were few female role models for them to emulate (Baruch & Barnett, 1978). This may still be true for women growing up today in traditional families and communities.

Children whose fathers are absent tend to perform more poorly at school than children from two-parent families (Radin, 1981; Shinn, 1978) but these effects are much more consistent in lower-class than in middle-class families (Radin, 1981). Perhaps this is because single mothers in lower-class families are subject to more severe economic and socio-emotional stresses that affect their ability to guide and stimulate their children. Interestingly, Blanchard and Biller (1971) reported that qualitatively similar effects occurred when fathers were nominally present but were uninvolved with their sons. By contrast, children with highly involved, nurturant fathers tend to be more cognitively competent and to manifest the internal locus of control which is one aspect of higher achievement motivation (Radin, 1978; Sagi, 1982).

Recently, conceptualizations of achievement motivation have been influenced by attributional theory (e.g., Dweck, 1978; Weiner, 1974). Individuals can attribute their successes or failures to either controllable or uncontrollable (external) factors and to either effort or ability. Achievement motivation is enhanced when others attribute the child's successes to effort (and failures to the lack of effort) and encourage the child to attribute responsibility in this way. By contrast, achievement motivation is squelched when failures are attributed to a lack of ability and success to the easiness of the task. Although most researchers have studied the ways in which teachers affect the development of attributional styles (Dweck, 1978), it is likely that parents are also influential.

Moral Development. In recent years, the ascendance of Kohlberg's cognitive developmental theory of moral development (Kohlberg, 1969) has provoked a focus on normative issues and a deemphasis of individual differences. Furthermore, to the extent that environmental influences are explicitly considered, Kohlberg has emphasized interactions with peers rather than parents.

A comprehensive review of research on the determinants of moral development a decade ago concluded that parental disciplinary style was indeed influential (Hoffman, 1970). Children develop internalized controls (consciences) most readily when their parents discipline through induction and least when their parents employ a power-assertive strategy. Induction involves encouraging the child to consider the implications of its behavior (notably, its disobedience) for other people. Although some studies show that boys whose fathers are absent display less moral internalization and are more likely to become delinquent than boys whose fathers are present, the preponderance of the evidence indicates that mothers have a much greater influence on moral development than fathers do (Hoffman, 1981).

Psychological Adjustment. Most of the research on this topic has been concerned with the antecedents of psychological maladjustment. As noted below, many studies show that children whose parents are divorced or whose fathers are absent are more likely to manifest signs of psychological maladjustment (see Biller, 1981, for a review) but the mode of influence is unclear. Large-scale epidemiological studies (e.g., Rutter, 1973, 1979) show that marital hostility and discord are among the most reliable causes of psychological maladjustment.

In one of the few studies concerned with parental influences on psychological adjustment, Baumrind (1971, 1975) reported that socially competent children (those who are friendly, independent, and assertive with peers and compliantly nonintrusive with adults) are likely to have authoritative parents—that is, parents who provide firm and articulately reasoned guidance for their children. Both authoritarian parents (those who fail to provide any rationale for their instructions) and permissive parents (those who fail to provide adequate guidance) have less socially competent children.

Summary. It is clear that parents influence their children both by the way they behave toward their children and by the way they interact with one another. Direct and indirect parental influences on the development of sex roles, morality, social competence, effectance, achievement, and psychological adjustment have been demonstrated, although we can only speculate about processes of influence since they have been explored inadequately.

Both mothers and fathers affect their children's development. In cases where parental sex role is important (e.g., the development of sex differences and sex roles), mothers and fathers appear to affect their children differently, but in the main, they influence their children in similar ways. In some areas (e.g., sex role development), fathers exert a disproportionate influence, either because they are especially concerned about the issue, or because their relative novelty increases their salience in the eyes of their children. In other respects (e.g., the predictive validity of attachment security), mothers are more influential. However, in these cases the relative importance of the fathers' influence may increase as their relative involvement in childrearing increases. Finally, the quality of the marital relationship and other indirectly mediated effects may be much more influential than was once believed.

NONTRADITIONAL FAMILY FORMS

In the preceding section, I focused on the processes and outcomes of socialization in traditional two-parent families. As noted earlier, however, such families are becoming increasingly uncommon as novel family forms become more popular. The most recent estimates suggest that only 23% of the households in the United States now fit the traditional pattern, with father as sole breadwinner and mother at home caring for one or more children (Pleck & Rustad, 1980). In this section, we focus on three of the more common deviations from the traditional norm: maternal employment, increased paternal participation, and divorce/single-parenthood. My goal is to describe both the ways in which the processes of socialization may differ in these nontraditional family conditions, as well as their likely or demonstrated effects on child development.

Maternal Employment

Recent statistics demonstrate that an increasing number of women now choose to remain in paid employment after their children are born. By 1978, 50% of the women in the United States and 44% of the married women with husbands present were in the paid labor force, and the number of employed women is expected to rise to 57% by 1995 (Glick, 1979). Employment rates are not substantially lower for married mothers in intact families than for women in general: in 1979, 52% of the mothers of school-aged children (6- to 17-years-old) and 36% of the mothers of infants and preschool-aged children were employed (Glick & Norton, 1979). For obvious reasons, employment rates are even higher among single mothers and Black mothers— both single and married (Glick & Norton, 1979). Clearly, therefore, most American children now grow up in families in which both parents, or the single resident parent, are employed outside the home.

Many studies of maternal employment have examined the effects of maternal employment on the sex-role attitudes of their children—particularly daughters (see Lamb, 1982). The results of these studies are fairly consistent regardless of the children's age or sex, the families' socioeconomic standing, or the measurement technique employed. Girls and boys whose mothers are employed have less stereotyped attitudes and expectations than those whose mothers are not employed (Almquist & Angrist, 1970; Baruch, 1972; Douvan, 1963; Duvall, 1955; Finkelman, 1966; Frieze, Parsons, & Ruble, 1972; Gold & Andres, 1978c; Hartley, 1960; Hoffman, 1963; Hoffman & Nye, 1974; King, McIntyre & Axelson, 1968; Meier, 1972; Peterson, 1958; Romer & Cherry, 1978; Smith, 1969; Vogel, Broverman, Broverman, Clarkson & Rosenkrantz, 1970). In some of the earlier studies, this was viewed as an undesirable effect, due to the assumption that well-adjusted girls should be "feminine" and well-adjusted boys should be "masculine." Today, by contrast, social scientists suggest that androgynous males and females are more mature, moral and best-adapted to the more egalitarian world in which we live: hence these same effects are now considered to be desirable (e.g., Hoffman, 1977, 1979). This interpretive change is an excellent example of the need to be wary of subjective value judgements which color the interpretation of research findings. The results themselves, of course, are not surprising and appear readily explicable. Since the mothers of these children provide less sex-typed models of female behavior, it is reasonable to expect that their children will have more liberal views of the capacities and responsibilities of men and women. Thus one is less likely to hold that mothers should stay home with their children when one's own mother does not do so.

Another of the proposed effects of maternal employment is not as well established. There is some evidence that in lower- and lower-middle class families, maternal employment is associated with strains in the father–son relationships which appear to reduce the extent to which these boys admire their fathers (Douvan, 1963; Gold & Andres, 1978b; Hoffman, 1974a; Kappel & Lambert, 1972; McCord, McCord, & Thurber, 1963; Propper, 1972; Romer & Cherry, 1978). These strains in father–son relationships may help account for the fact that the sons (not daughters) of lower-class (not middle-class) employed mothers are more poorly adjusted than any other group (Douvan, 1963; McCord et al., 1963). Perhaps, maternal employment has worse effects on boys from lower-class families because members of this class tend to have more traditionally sex-stereotyped expectations, and are thus likely to regard maternal employment as evidence of the fathers' failure to provide for their families. These perceptions would make the fathers seem poor models with whom to identify. If this is the process of influence involved, it provides a good example of the need to consider maternal employment in the context of family relationships and cultural values when attempting to understand its effects. Not all the effects of maternal employment, in other words, are mediated directly by changes in the mothers' role and behavior. Rather their employment may affect the behavior, roles, and perceived competence of other family members, and these changes may in turn affect the attitudes and behavior of the children. It is unfortunately all too common for social scientists to focus exclusively on direct effects, while ignoring the potential importance of indirect effects.

Finally, let us consider evidence concerning the effects of maternal employment on the security of infant–mother attachment. Research of this topic is of special importance because of evidence concerning the long-term implications of security of attachment and because of the widespread assumption that maternal employment is certain to have more deleterious effects on infants than on children of any other age.

Although Hock (1980) reported no significant effects of maternal employment on the security of infant–mother attachment in the Strange Situation (Ainsworth et al., 1978), three recent studies suggest that the likelihood of insecure (especially avoidant) attachment relationships increases when the mothers of young infants are employed (Owen, Chase-Lansdale, & Lamb, 1982; Thompson, Lamb, & Estes, 1982; Vaughn et al., 1980). However, the results of these studies also highlight a number of factors that need to be taken into account when assessing the effects of maternal employment.

First, maternal employment does not inevitably and necessarily have an adverse impact on the security of attachment. Owen et al. (1982) explored the mothers' attitudes thoroughly in their longitudinal study. They found that infants who were securely attached had mothers who valued parenthood highly, whereas those who were insecurely attached tended to value work highly and parenthood less. When mothers valued parenthood highly, they tended to have securely attached infants—regardless of whether or not they were employed. These findings suggested that maternal employment per se was a less important determinant of the security of attachment than were the mothers' attitudes and values. These findings are important, because they underscore the inappropriateness of the assumption that employed mothers constitute a homogeneous group. Clearly, we will only understand the effects of maternal employment when we take into account the attitudes, values, motivations, and circumstances of both employed and unemployed mothers, and stop viewing them as homogeneous groups.

Second, Thompson et al. (1982) showed that whereas maternal employment was associated with attachment insecurity, there was a more profound relationship between maternal employment and *changes* in the security of attachment. In other words, the mothers' return to work appeared to affect the interaction between mothers and infants, but these effects could be both positive and negative. In some cases, maternal employment seemed to make insecure relationships into secure ones; in other families, the reverse occurred. Again, therefore, we need to consider not only *whether* mothers work, but why they work. Presumably, if mothers dislike being home and feel more fulfilled when employed, then the return to employment may have positive rather than negative effects.

Summary. The evidence suggests, therefore, that maternal employment has a fairly clear-cut effect on the sex role attitudes of boys and girls. Effects on the quality of parent–child relationships, and thus on the children's psychosocial adjustment, are less consistent. Their presence and nature depends on a number of factors—including the values and attitudes of the mothers, their spouses, and the members of their social networks. Presumably, effects also differ depending on the types of nonmaternal care to which children are exposed, but unfortunately this issue has not been explored empirically. The evidence available thus far demonstrates that—contrary to popular belief—maternal employment does not necessarily have harmful effects on child development. In fact, many of the effects may be beneficial.

Increased Paternal Participation

Discussions of paternal participation usually identify two factors associated with extensive paternal involvement—maternal employment, and unusually high or low involvement by the fathers' own fathers. Much more attention has been devoted to the relationship between maternal employment and paternal involvement. It is widely suggested in both the popular and professional literature that maternal employment affects family life by leading to a redistribution of the family workload (e.g., Hoffman, 1977). When mothers/wives are employed, the argument goes, their husbands start to play a greater role in child care and housework. The empirical evidence, however, suggests that men do not do much more housework and child care when their wives are employed than when their wives are full-time homemakers and mothers. The results of the most recent national time-use survey revealed no evidence that maternal employment had *any* reliable effect on the amount of time that men devoted to child care (Pleck & Rustad, 1980). However, their relative involvement certainly increases simply because their wives spend much less time in child care.

The fact that absolute levels of paternal involvement increase so little when mothers are employed is rather surprising, given the widespread claims that men today *want* to be more involved in child care than their own fathers were (e.g., Sheehy, 1979). Perhaps these men are only espousing these values because they are now socially approved, or perhaps our social and economic system is still too rigid to permit men to assume a greater role in child care without risking great personal and professional costs. At first glance, this seems unlikely, since (at least in Sweden) the provision of paid paternal leave with a guarantee of reemployment at or above the pre-leave level has induced remarkably few eligible fathers to request even small amounts of paternal leave (Lamb & Levine, 1983). On the other hand, the attitudes of peers and employers may still inhibit fathers from seeking parental leave, as may the attitudes they have internalized during years of living in a sex-stereotyped society. In addition, it is possible that men are biologically designed to be less interested and competent in child care than women are. My colleagues and I are currently engaged in a nationwide effort to identify the circumstances which limit or facilitate paternal involvement (Levine, Pleck, & Lamb, 1983). We expect our efforts to advance our understanding of paternal involvement while also identifying ways in which society could facilitate involvement by those fathers who wish to be more involved.

Other than maternal employment and institutional practices, discussions of paternal participation often identify the earlier involvement of the father's father as a key determinant of the level of involvement. Some have hypothesized that highly involved fathers are attempting to compensate for the limited involvement of their own fathers (Gersick, 1975; Mendes, 1976), whereas others have argued that highly involved fathers themselves had unusually involved fathers, whom the younger fathers are thus attempting to emulate (Manion, 1977). One recent study of Israeli fathers by Sagi (1982; Radin & Sagi, 1982) provided clear support for the identification hypothesis: highly involved fathers reported that their own fathers had been unusually involved in child care. There is little empirical support for the compensation hypothesis.

Regardless of the reasons for increased paternal participation, one wonders about the effects of paternal involvement on children's development. As noted earlier, the mother–child relationship appears to have a greater impact on most aspects of socioemotional development, presumably because mothers typically serve as primary caretakers and socialization agents. If this were true, then we would expect the relative importance of the father–child relationship to increase as the extent of paternal involvement increased. To my surprise, our recent research in Sweden failed to show this increase, at least with respect to infants: We found no relationship between degree of paternal involvement and the predictive validity of the security of infant–mother and infant–father attachments (Lamb, Hwang, Frodi, & Frodi, 1982).

Studies of older children have yielded different results, however. Russell's (1982, 1983) highly involved fathers reported that they felt much closer to their children as a result of their role-sharing or role-reversal, but unfortunately no effects on the children were assessed. Radin (1982; Radin & Sagi, 1982) reported that increased paternal involvement had positive effects on the locus of control and academic achievement of pre-schoolers. Children with highly involved fathers, like those with employed mothers, had less stereotyped attitudes regarding male and female roles. In a later study of Israeli fathers in which Sagi employed Radin's measures, results similar to but stronger than those obtained in the United States were reported (Sagi, 1982; Radin & Sagi, 1982). Presumably, the effects on sex-role attitudes occurred because the role-sharing parents provided less stereotyped models with which their children could identify and also encouraged their children to have egalitarian attitudes. The effects on intellectual performance may reflect fathers' traditional association with achievement and occupational advancement, or it could reflect the benefits of having extensive stimulation from two highly involved and relatively competent parents.

Summary. Obviously, considerably more research is needed before we will fully understand the effects of increased paternal involvement. Based on the available evidence, however, we can discount popular fears that the personal adjustment and gender identity of children will be seriously disturbed if their fathers assume an extensive role in childcare. True, many of the families in Russell's study returned to more traditional life styles when they had the opportunity to do so, but none of the children in this or any of the other studies reported here appeared to suffer adverse consequences. Several researchers are currently engaged in studies designed to explore the effects of these nontraditional childrearing styles on children, so we should be much better informed a few years from now than we are today.

Divorce and Single Parenthood

Of the deviant family forms considered in this chapter, single parenthood is the one about which there is most reason for concern. Of further concern is the fact that the number of single-parent families has risen dramatically over the last few decades. National statistics now suggest that about one third of the children in the United States will spend some portion of their childhood in a single-parent family (Glick & Norton, 1979). For 90% of them, the single parents will be their mothers.

To the extent that they do not have a spouse to supplement their parenting efforts, single mothers and fathers are in a similar predicament, with lack of supervision and control over children being possible consequences. Further, in all single-parent families one major sex role model is absent. In addition many single mothers lack the training and experience to obtain satisfying and financially rewarding jobs, and they are subject to pervasive discrimination in the work place so they are likely to be in worse economic circumstances than single fathers. Especially when the children involved are young, community attitudes are often less supportive of single mothers working than of single fathers. Social isolation is commonly experienced by both divorced parties, but may be especially serious for mothers whose social network was largely defined by their ex-husbands' work associates. For these reasons, single mothers may often be in worse straits than single fathers.

As long as these social and economic stresses remain, single parents are likely to be less effective, consistent and sensitive as parents, and this is likely to distort relationships with their children and have adverse effects on their psychological adjustment. Unfortunately, we cannot say what proportion of the adverse effects of father absence would be eliminated if single mothers could count on less financially stressful circumstances and were less isolated from social networks. We do know, however, that increasing numbers of women combine working and mothering, and these women thus retain independent sources of income and access to social networks. Divorce is substantially less stressful and disruptive for these women (Hetherington, 1979) than for previously unemployed single mothers. Marital dissolution is inherently stressful for almost all people, however, making at least temporary disturbances of psychological functioning almost inevitable (Hetherington, Cox, & Cox, 1978).

There have been numerous studies of children raised by single mothers and substantially fewer studies of single fathers (see Lamb, 1976a, 1981c, and Biller, 1976, 1981, for reviews). Although researchers now question whether the absence of a male model satisfactorily accounts for the effects observed, it is fairly clear that children (especially boys) raised by single mothers are "at risk." Boys raised by single mothers are more likely than those from two-parent families to be less "masculine" (which may or may not be disadvantageous, depending on the circumstances), more psychologically maladjusted, delinquent, hyper- or hypoaggressive, and to perform more poorly at school (Biller, 1981; Lamb, 1981c; Radin, 1981; Shinn, 1978, provide reviews of the literature). Girls may reveal deficits in their ability to interact with males, although these effects may not be evident prior to adolescence even when the fathers' absence occurred much earlier (Hetherington, 1972). The availability of alternative male models (e.g., stepfathers, older brothers, uncles, grandfathers) can reduce the adverse effects on sex-role development (Biller, 1974) although few substitute relationships match the intensity of close father–child relationships.

Interestingly, the only comparative study of single fathers of which I am aware (Santrock & Warshak, 1979; Santrock, Warshak, & Elliott, 1982) indicated that girls adapted more poorly than boys did in the care of single fathers. This finding is consistent with evidence suggesting that fathers are embarrassed when called upon to purchase clothing for—and to discuss menstruation and sexuality with—their pubescent daughters, and this is likely to be especially problematic for single fathers (Fox, 1978; Hipgrave, 1982). Together with the results of studies concerned with the children of single mothers, these findings suggested that single parents are more successful raising children of the same than of the opposite sex, but we obviously need further documentation of this fact.

Nevertheless, although most social scientists seem to consider single fathers to be in an especially invidious position because they typically have to assume sole parental responsibility without adequate warning or preparation, I suspect that, *on average,* today's single fathers are more likely than single mothers to succeed in meeting the extensive demands placed on them. They comprise a highly selected and self-motivated group, simply because popular and judicial skepticism regarding their motivation and ability ensures that they have to fight to obtain custody, whereas mothers often gain custody by default. In addition, society either tolerates or expects single fathers to work full time and to employ others to assist in child and home care, whereas both of these behaviors would be viewed as indices of incompetence on the part of single mothers.

Despite the above, the potential for deviant outcomes among the children of single mothers and fathers is considerably greater than with any of the other nontraditional family forms discussed here. As Eleanor Maccoby (1977) has said: "Childrearing is something that many people cannot do adequately as single adults functioning in isolation. Single parents need time off from parenting, they need the company of other adults, they need to have other voices joined with theirs in transmitting values and maturity demands to their children" (p. 17). The socialization process *need* not fail, of course. Its success depends on the availability of emotional, practical, and social supports for single parents and their children.

Three other issues must also be mentioned. First, marital disharmony appears to have more deleterious effects, especially on boys, than does divorce and father absence (Block, Block, & Morrison, 1981; Lamb, 1977d; Rutter, 1979). It is conceivable, therefore, that some of the "effects of single parenthood" may be consequences of the marital hostility that preceded divorce rather than of the divorce and subsequent period of single parenthood. Thus, if our goal is to minimize the psychological damage to developing children, single parenthood may be the most desirable of the realistic alternatives. Second, psychological father absence (which occurs when fathers are seldom available to their children) and physical father absence have qualitatively similar effects on sex-role development (Blanchard & Biller, 1971). Likewise, distant or hostile fathers and absent fathers have qualitatively similar (though quantitatively different) effects on moral development (Hoffman, 1970). These findings again imply that single parenthood may not have less desirable consequences than the alternative arrangement. Finally, it is important not to exaggerate the ill-effects of divorce or single-parenthood. Even though many studies have demonstrated statistically significant group differences between children in single- and two-parent families, many of the individuals in the groups do not deviate from the norm. In other words, we must not let the evidence of development problems in *some* children of divorce lead us to unfounded statements about the *inevitable* effects of divorce.

CONCLUSION

There is substantial evidence that experiences within the family have a major impact on social, personality, and intellectual development. Of course, socializing agents outside the family—television, peers, teachers, for example—also affect development, and later experiences can either reverse or accentuate the effects of earlier experiences; there are no magic periods during which specific experiences have irreversible effects on subsequent development. Nevertheless, it is reasonable to conclude that children who have good and rewarding early relationships within the family are probably at an advantage relative to those whose initial experiences are less satisfactory.

It is also clear that the socializing experience differs when children are raised in families that deviate from the two-parent, traditional norm, and that the differences indeed affect children's development. At this point, we still need much more work designed both to identify the effects more precisely and to define the processes by which these effects are mediated. However, we know enough to underscore some of the points made earlier. First, there is no justification for assuming that any family forms that deviate from the traditional form necessarily have harmful consequences. In fact, as I have suggested, some of these deviant styles—for example, those involving maternal employment—have what may be seen as positive effects on children. Second, we must be careful to distinguish between the objective description of findings or effects and the subjective evaluation of those findings. It is one thing to say that girls whose mothers are employed are less stereotypically feminine; a value judgment is involved if we then describe this effect as either desirable or undesirable. Finally, we need to remember that families do not exist in isolation: they are embedded in and influenced by a wider social context. Consequently, the attitudes and values of others affect both the behavior of parents, and thus indirectly affect their children, and may also have direct effects on the latter. Because societal attitudes change over time, the same "deviant" family form may have different effects in different historical epochs or in different social contexts. For example, maternal employment was formerly viewed very negatively; three decades later, maternal employment is the normative practice. Changing perceptions of maternal employment surely change the likely pattern of effects on children.

REFERENCES

Ainsworth, M.D.S. The development of mother–infant attachment. In B.M. Caldwell & H.N. Ricciuti (Eds.), *Review of child development research* (Vol. 3). Chicago, IL: University of Chicago Press, 1973.

Ainsworth, M.D.S., Bell, S.M., & Stayton, D.J. Individual differences in the development of some attachment behaviors. *Merrill-Palmer Quarterly*, 1972, *18,* 123–143.

Ainsworth, M.D.S., Bell, S.M., & Stayton, D.J. Infant–mother attachment and social development: "Socialisation" as a product of reciprocal responsiveness to signals. In M.P.M. Richards (Ed.), *The integration of a child into a social world*. Cambridge, England: Cambridge University Press, 1974.

Ainsworth, M.D.S., Blehar, M., Waters, E., & Wall, S. *Patterns of attachment*. Hillsdale, N.J.: Erlbaum, 1978.

Ainsworth, M.D.S., & Wittig, B.A. Attachment and exploratory behavior of one-year-olds in a strange situation. In B.M.Foss (Ed.), *Determinants of infant behavior IV*. London: Methuen, 1969.

Almquist, E.M., & Angrist, S.S. Career salience and atypicality of occupational choice among college women. *Journal of Marriage and the Family*, 1970, *32* 242–249.

Arend, R., Gove, F.L., & Sroufe, L.A. Continuity of individual adaptation from infancy to kindergarten: A predictive study of ego-resiliency and curiosity in preschoolers. *Child Development*, 1979, *50*, 950–959.

Bandura, A. *Social learning theory*. Englewood Cliffs, NJ: Prentice-Hall, 1977.

Baruch, G.K. Maternal influences upon college women's attitudes toward women and work. *Developmental Psychology*, 1972, *6*, 32–37.

Baruch, G.K., & Barnett, R. *The competent woman*. New York: Irvington, 1978.

Baumrind, D. Current patterns of parental authority. *Developmental Psychology Monographs*, 1971, *1*, whole number 2.

Baumrind, D. *Early socialization and the discipline controversy*. Morristown, NJ: General Learning Press, 1975.

Belsky, J. Mother–father–infant interaction: A naturalistic observational study. *Developmental Psychology*, 1979, *15*, 601–607.

Belsky, J. Early human experience: A family perspective. *Developmental Psychology*, 1981, *17*, 3–23.

Biller, H.B. *Paternal deprivation: Family, school, sexuality and society*. Lexington, MA: Health, 1974.

Biller, H.B. The father and personality development: Paternal deprivation and sex-role development. In M.E. Lamb (Ed.), *The role of the father in child development*. New York: Wiley, 1976.

Biller, H.B. Father absence, divorce, and personality development. In M.E. Lamb (Ed.), *The role of the father in child development* (rev. ed.). New York: Wiley, 1981.

Blanchard, R.W., & Biller, H.B. Father availability and academic performance among third grade boys. *Developmental Psychology*, 1971, *4*, 301–305.

Block, J.H., Block, J., & Morrison, A. Parental agreement–disagreement on child-rearing orientations and gender-related personality correlates in children. *Child Development*, 1981, *52*, 965–974.

Bowlby, J. *Attachment and loss*. Vol. 1. *Attachment*. New York: Basic Books, 1969.

Bronfenbrenner, U. The changing American child. *Journal of Social Issues*, 1961, *17*, 6–18.

Clarke-Stewart, K.A. And daddy makes three: The father's impact on mother and young child. *Child Development*, 1978, *49*, 466–478.

Connell, D.B. Individual differences in attachment behavior. Unpublished doctoral dissertation, Syracuse University, NY, 1976.

Douvan, E. Employment and the adolescent. In F.I. Nye & L.W. Hoffman (Eds.), *The employed mother in America*. Chicago, IL: Rand McNally, 1963.

Duvall, E.B. Conceptions of mother roles by five and six-year-old children of working and non-working mothers. Unpublished doctoral dissertation, Florida State University, FL, 1955.

Dweck, C.S. Achievement. In M.E. Lamb (Ed.) *Social and personality development*. New York: Holt, Rinehart & Winston, 1978.

Estes, D., Lamb, M.E., Thompson, R.A., & Dickstein, S. Maternal affective quality and security of attachment at 12 and 19 months. Paper presented to the Society for Research in Child Development, Boston, MA, April 1981.

Fagot, B.I. Consequences of moderate cross-gender behavior in preschool children. *Child Development*, 1977, *48*, 902–907.

Fagot, B.I., & Patterson, G.R. An in vivo analysis of reinforcing contingencies for sex-role behavior in the preschool child. *Developmental Psychology*, 1969, *1*, 563–568.

Finkelman, J.J. Maternal employment, family relationships, and parental role perception. Unpublished doctoral dissertation, Yeshiva University, NY, 1966.

Fox, G.L. The family's role in adolescent sexual behavior. Paper presented to the Family Impact Seminar, Washington, DC, October 1978.

Fox, N. Attachment of kibbutz infants to mother and metapelet. *Child Development*, 1977, *48*, 1228–1239.

Frieze, I., Parsons, J., & Ruble, D. Some determinants of career aspirations in college women. Unpublished manuscript, University of California at Los Angeles, May 1972.

Gersick, K. Fathers by choice: Characteristics of men who do and do not seek custody of their children following divorce. Unpublished doctoral dissertation, Harvard University, MA, 1975.

Glick, P.C. Future American families. *COFU Memo*, 1979, *2* (3), 2–5.

Glick, P.C., & Norton, A.J. Marrying, divorcing, and living together in the U.S. today. *Population Bulletin*, 1979, *32*, whole number 5.

Gold, D., & Andres, D. Comparisons of adolescent children with employed and unemployed mothers. *Merrill-Palmer Quarterly*, 1978, *24*, 243–254. (a)

Gold, D., & Andres, D. Developmental comparisons between ten-year-old children with employed and unemployed mothers. *Child Development*, 1978, *49*, 78–84. (b)

Gold, D., & Andres, D. Relations between maternal employment and development of nursery school children. *Canadian Journal of Behavioral Science*, 1978, *10*, 116–129. (c)

Goodenough, F.W. Interest in persons as an aspect of sex difference in the early years. *Genetic Psychology Monographs*, 1957, *55*, 287–323.

Grossmann, K.E., & Grossmann, K. The development of relationship patterns during the first two years of life. Paper presented to the International Congress of Psychology, Leipzig, DDR, July 1980.

Grossmann, K.E., Grossmann, K., Huber, F., & Wartner, U. German children's behavior towards their mothers at 12 months and their fathers at 18 months in Ainsworth's Strange Situation. *International Journal of Behavioural Development*, 1980, *4*, 157–181.

Hartley, R.E. Children's concepts of male and female roles. *Merrill-Palmer Quarterly*, 1960, *6*, 83–91.

Heilbrun, A.B. An empirical test of the modeling theory of sex-role learning. *Child Development*, 1965, *36*, 789–799.

Hetherington, E.M. Effects of father-absence on personality development in adolescent daughters. *Developmental Psychology*, 1972, *7*, 313–326.

Hetherington, E.M. Divorce: A child's perspective. *American Psychologist*, 1979, *34*, 851–858.

Hetherington, E.M., Cox, M., & Cox, R. The aftermath of divorce. In J.P. Stevens & M. Matthews (Eds.), *Mother/child, father/child relationships*. Washington, DC: NAEYC, 1978.

Hipgrave, T. Childrearing by lone fathers. In R. Chester, P. Diggory & M. Sutherland (Eds.), *Changing patterns of child bearing and child rearing*. London: Academic Press, 1982.

Hock, E. Working and nonworking mothers with infants: Perceptions of their careers, their infant's needs, and satisfaction with mothering. *Developmental Psychology*, 1978, *14*, 37–43.

Hock, E. Working and nonworking mothers and their infants: A comparative study of maternal caregiving characteristics and infant social behavior. *Merrill-Palmer Quarterly*, 1980, *26*, 79–101.

Hoffman, L.W. Mother's enjoyment of work and effects on the child. In F.I. Nye & L.W. Hoffman (Eds.), *The employed mother in America*. Chicago, IL: Rand McNally, 1963.

Hoffman, L.W. Effects of maternal employment on the child: A review of the research. *Developmental Psychology*, 1974, *10*, 204–228.

Hoffman, L.W. Changes in family roles, socialization, and sex differences. *American Psychologist*, 1977, *32*, 644–657.

Hoffman, L.W. Maternal employment: 1979. *American Psychologist,* 1979, *34,* 859–865.

Hoffman, L.W., & Nye, F.I. *Working mothers.* San Francisco, CA: Jossey-Bass, 1974.

Hoffman, M.L. Moral development. In P.H. Mussen (Ed.), *Carmichael's manual of child psychology* (Vol. 2). New York: Wiley, 1970.

Hoffman, M.L. The role of the father in moral internalization. In M.E. Lamb (Ed.), *The role of the father in child development* (rev. ed.). New York: Wiley, 1981.

Johnson, M.M. Sex role learning in the nuclear family. *Child Development,* 1963, *34,* 315–333.

Kappel, B.E., & Lambert, R.D. Self worth among children of working mothers. Unpublished manuscript, University of Waterloo, 1982.

King, K., McIntyre, J., & Axelson, L.J. Adolescents' views of maternal employment as a threat to the marital relationship. *Journal of Marriage and the Family,* 1968, *30,* 633–637.

Kohlberg, L. Stage and sequence: The cognitive-developmental approach to socialization. In D.A. Goslin (Ed.), *Handbook of socialization theory and research.* Chicago, IL: Rand McNally, 1969.

Lamb, M.E. Effects of stress and cohort on mother– and father–infant interaction. *Developmental Psychology,* 1976, *12,* 435–443. (a)

Lamb, M.E. Interactions between eight-month-old children and their fathers and mothers. In M.E. Lamb (Ed.), *The role of the father in child development.* New York: Wiley, 1976. (b)

Lamb, M.E. Interactions between two-year-olds and their mothers and fathers. *Psychological Reports,* 1976, *38,* 447–450. (c)

Lamb, M.E. The role of the father: An overview. In M.E. Lamb (Ed.), *The role of the father in child development.* New York: Wiley, 1976. (d).

Lamb, M.E. (Ed.) *The role of the father in child development.* New York: Wiley, 1976, (e)

Lamb, M.E. Twelve-month-olds and their parents: Interaction in a laboratory playroom. *Developmental Psychology,* 1976, *12,* 237–244. (f)

Lamb, M.E. The development of mother–infant and father–infant attachments in the second year of life. *Developmental Psychology,* 1977, *13,* 637–648. (a)

Lamb, M.E. The development of parental preferences in the first two years of life. *Sex Roles,* 1977, *3,* 495–497. (b)

Lamb, M.E. Father–infant and mother–infant interaction in the first year of life. *Child Development,* 1977, *48,* 167–181. (c)

Lamb, M.E. The effects of divorce on children's personality development. *Journal of Divorce,* 1977, *1,* 163–174. (d)

Lamb, M.E. Social interaction in infancy and the development of personality. In M.E. Lamb (Ed.), *Social and personality development.* New York: Holt, Rinehart & Winston, 1978. (a)

Lamb, M.E. Qualitative aspects of mother– and father–infant attachments. *Infant Behavior and Development,* 1978, *1,* 265–275. (b)

Lamb, M.E. The development of parent-infant attachments in the first two years of life. In F.A. Pedersen (Ed.), *The father–infant relationship: Observational studies in a family setting.* New York: Praeger Special Studies, 1980.

Lamb, M.E. Developing trust and perceived effectance in infancy. In L.P. Lipsitt (Ed.), *Advances in infancy research* (Vol. 1). Norwood, NJ: Ablex, 1981. (a)

Lamb, M.E. The development of social expectations in the first year of life. In M.E.Lamb & L.R. Sherrod (Eds.), *Infant social cognition: Empirical and theoretical considerations.* Hillsdale, NJ: Erlbaum, 1981. (b)

Lamb, M.E. Paternal influences on child development: An overview. In M.E. Lamb (Ed.), *The role of the father in child development* (rev. ed.). New York: Wiley, 1981. (c)

Lamb, M.E. Maternal employment and child development: A review. In M.E. Lamb (Ed.), *Nontraditional families: Parenting and child development*. Hillsdale, NJ: Erlbaum, 1982.

Lamb, M.E., Thompson, R.A., Gardner, W., Charnov, E.L., & Estes, D. Security of infantile attachment as assessed in the "Strange Situation": Its study and biological interpretation. *Behavioral and Brain Sciences*, 1984, *7*, 127–171.

Lamb, M.E., & Easterbrooks, M.A. Individual differences in parental sensitivity: Origins, components, and consequences. In M.E. Lamb & L.R. Sherrod (Eds.), *Infant social cognition: Empirical and theoretical considerations*. Hillsdale, NJ: Erlbaum, 1981.

Lamb, M.E., Easterbrooks, M.A., & Holden, G.W. Reinforcement and punishment among preschoolers: Characteristics, effects, and correlates. *Child Development*, 1980, *51*, 1230–1236.

Lamb, M.E., Hwang, C.-P., Frodi, A.M., & Frodi, M. Security of mother– and father–infant attachment and its relation to sociability with strangers in traditional and non-traditional Swedish families. *Infant Behavior and Development*, 1982, *5*, 355–367.

Lamb, M.E., & Lamb, J.E. The nature and importance of the father–infant relationship. *The Family Coordinator*, 1976, *25*, 379–385.

Lamb, M.E., & Levine, J.A. The Swedish parental insurance policy: An experiment in social engineering. In M.E. Lamb & A. Sagi (Eds.), *Fatherhood and family policy*. Hillsdale, NJ: Erlbaum, 1983.

Lamb, M.E., & Roopnarine, J.L. Peer influences on sex-role development in preschoolers. *Child Development*, 1979, *50*, 1219–1222.

Lamb, M.E., & Stevenson, M.B. Father–infant relationships: Their nature and importance. *Youth & Society*, 1978, *9*, 277–298.

Langlois, J.H., & Downs, A.C. Mothers, fathers, and peers as socialization agents of sex-typed play behaviors in young children. *Child Development*, 1980, *51*, 1237–1247.

Lewis, M., & Feiring, C. Direct and indirect interactions in social relationships. In L.P. Lipsitt (Ed.), *Advances in infancy research* (Vol. 1). Norwood, NJ: Ablex, 1981.

Levine, J.A., Pleck, J.H., & Lamb, M.E. The Fatherhood Project. In M.E. Lamb & A. Sagi (Eds.), *Fatherhood and family policy*. Hillsdale, NJ: Erlbaum, 1983.

Lynn, D.B., & Cross, A.R. Parent preferences of preschool children. *Journal of Marriage and the Family*, 1974, *36*, 555–559.

Maccoby, E.E. Current changes in the family and their impact upon the socialization of children. Paper presented to the American Sociological Association, Chicago, IL, September, 1977.

Main, M.B. Exploration, play, and cognitive functioning as related to child–mother attachment. Unpublished doctoral dissertation, Johns Hopkins University, MD, 1973.

Main, M.B., Tomasini, L., & Tolan, W. Differences among mothers of infants judged to differ in security. *Developmental Psychology*, 1979, *15*, 472–473.

Main, M.B., & Weston, D.R. Security of attachment to mother and father: Related to conflict behavior and the readiness to establish new relationships. *Child Development*, 1981, *52*, 932–940.

Manion, J. A study of fathers and infant caretaking. *Birth and the Family Journal*, 1977, *4*, 174–179.

Matas, L., Arend, R.A., & Sroufe, L.A. Continuity of adaptation in the second year: The relationship between quality of attachment and later competence. *Child Development*, 1978, *49*, 547–556.

McCord, J., McCord, W., & Thurber, E. Effects of maternal employment on lower-class boys. *Journal of Abnormal and Social Psychology*, 1963, *67*, 177–182.

Meir, J.C. Mother-centeredness and college youth's attitudes toward social equality for women: Some empirical findings. *Journal of Marriage and the Family*, 1972, *34*, 115–121.

Mendes, H. Single fatherhood. *Social Work,* 1976, *21,* 308–312.

Miller, S.M. Effects of maternal employment on sex-role perception, interests and self-esteem in kindergarten girls. *Developmental Psychology,* 1975, *11,* 405–406.

Money, J., & Ehrhardt, A.A. *Man and woman: Boy and girl.* Baltimore, MD: Johns Hopkins Press, 1972.

Mussen, P.H. Early socialization: Learning and identification. In T.M. Newcomb (Ed.), *New directions in psychology III.* New York: Holt, Rinehart, & Winston, 1967.

Mussen, P.H., & Rutherford, E. Parent–child relations and parental personality in relation to young children's sex-role preferences. *Child Development,* 1963, *34,* 589–607.

Nash, S.C., & Feldman, S.S. Sex role and sex-related attributions: Constancy or change across the family life cycle? In M.E. Lamb & A.L. Brown (Eds.), *Advances in developmental psychology* (Vol. 1). Hillsdale, NJ: Erlbaum, 1981.

Owen, M.T., Chase-Lansdale, P.L., & Lamb, M.E. Mothers' and fathers' attitudes, maternal employment, and the security of infant–parent attachment. Unpublished manuscript, 1982.

Parke, R.D., Power, T.G., & Gottman, J. Conceptualizing and quantifying influence patterns in the family triad. In M.E. Lamb, S.J. Suomi, & G.R. Stephenson (Eds.), *Social interaction analysis.* Madison, WI: University of Wisconsin Press, 1979.

Parke, R.D., & Sawin, D.B. The family in early infancy: Social interactional and attitudinal analysis. In F.A. Pedersen (Ed.), *The father–infant relationship: Observational studies in the family setting.* New York: Praeger Special Studies, 1980.

Pastor, D.L. The quality of mother–infant attachment and its relationship to toddlers' initial sociability with peers. *Developmental Psychology,* 1981, *17,* 326–335.

Payne, D.E., & Mussen, P.H. Parent-child relations and father identification among adolescent boys. *Journal of Abnormal and Social Psychology,* 1956, *52,* 358–362.

Peterson, E.T. The impact of maternal employment on the mother–daughter relationship and on the daughter's role orientation. Unpublished doctoral dissertation, University of Michigan, MI, 1958.

Pleck, J.H., & Rustad, M. Husbands' and wives' time in family work and paid work in the 1975–76 study of time use. Unpublished manuscript, Wellesley College, 1980.

Propper, A.M. The relationship of maternal employment to adolescent roles, activities, and parental relationships. *Journal of Marriage and the Family,* 1972, *34,* 417–421.

Radin, N. The role of the father in cognitive, academic and intellectual development. In M.E. Lamb (Ed.), *The role of the father in child development.* New York: Wiley, 1976.

Radin, N. *Childrearing fathers in intact families with preschoolers.* Paper presented to the American Psychological Association, Toronto, September 1978.

Radin, N. The role of the father in cognitive, academic, and intellectual development. In M.E. Lamb (Ed.), *The role of the father in child development* (revised edition). New York: Wiley, 1981.

Radin, N. Primary caregiving and role-sharing fathers. In M.E. Lamb (Ed.), *Nontraditional families: Parenting and child development.* Hillsdale, NJ: Erlbaum, 1982.

Radin, N., & Sagi, A. Childrearing fathers in intact families in Israel and the U.S.A. *Merrill-Palmer Quarterly,* 1982, *28,* 111–136.

Rajecki, D.W., Lamb, M.E., & Obmascher, P. Toward a general theory of infantile attachment: A comparative review of aspects of the social bond. *Behavioral and Brain Sciences,* 1978, *1,* 417–463.

Romer, N., & Cherry, D. Developmental effects of preschool and school age maternal employment on children's sex role concepts. Unpublished manuscript, Brooklyn College, 1978.

Rosen, B.C., & D'Andrade, R. The psychosocial origins of achievement motivation. *Sociometry,* 1959, *22,* 185–218.

Russell, G. Shared-caregiving families: An Australian study. In M.E. Lamb (Ed.), *Nontraditional families: Parenting and child development*. Hillsdale, NJ: Erlbaum, 1982.

Russell, G. *The changing role of fathers?* St. Lucia, Queensland: University of Queensland Press, 1983.

Rutter, M. Why are London children so disturbed? *Proceedings of the Royal Society of Medicine*, 1973, *66*, 1221–1225.

Rutter, M. Maternal deprivation, 1972–1978: New findings, new concepts, new approaches. *Child Development*, 1979, *50*, 283–305.

Sagi, A. Antecedents and consequences of various degrees of paternal involvement in child rearing: The Israeli project. In M.E. Lamb (Ed.), *Nontraditional families: Parenting and child development*. Hillsdale, NJ: Erlbaum, 1982.

Santrock, J.W., & Warshak, R.A. Father custody and social development in boys and girls, *Journal of Social Issues*, 1979, *35*, 112–125.

Santrock, J.W., Warshak, R.A., & Elliott, G.L. Social development and parent-child interaction in father-custody and stepmother families. In M.E. Lamb (Ed.), *Nontraditional families: Parenting and child development*. Hillsdale, NJ: Erlbaum, 1982.

Schaffer, H.R., & Emerson, P.E. The development of social attachments in infancy. *Monographs of the Society for Research in Child Development*, 1964, *29*, serial number 94.

Sears, R.R., Maccoby, E.E., & Levin, H. *Patterns of child rearing*. Evanston, IL: Row Peterson, 1957.

Sears, R.R., Rau, L., & Alpert, R. *Identification and child rearing*. Stanford, CA: Stanford University Press, 1965.

Serbin, L.A., Tonick, L.J., & Sternglanz, S.H. Shaping cooperative cross-sex play. *Child Development*, 1977, *48*, 924–929.

Sheehy, G. Introducing the postponing generation. *Esquire*, 1979, *92* (4), 25–33.

Shinn, M. Father absence and children's cognitive development. *Psychological Bulletin*, 1978, *85*, 295–324.

Smith, H.C. An investigation of the attitudes of adolescent girls toward combining marriage, motherhood and a career. Unpublished doctoral dissertation, Columbia University, 1969.

Sroufe, L.A. Attachment and the roots of competence. *Human Nature*, 1978, *1* (10), 50–57.

Sroufe, L.A. The problem of continuity in development. Presentation to the Society for Research in Child Development, San Francisco, CA, March 1979.

Sroufe, L.A. Infant–caregiver attachment and patterns of adaptation in preschool: The roots of maladaptation and competence. In M.J. Perlmutter (Ed.), *Minnesota symposia on child psychology*, Vol. 16. Hillsdale, NJ: Erlbaum, in press.

Stayton, D.J., Ainsworth, M.D.S., & Main, M. The development of separation behavior in the first year of life: Protest, following and greeting. *Developmental Psychology*, 1973, *9*, 213–225.

Stevenson, M.B., & Lamb, M.E. The effects of social experience and social style on cognitive competence and performance. In M.E. Lamb & L.R. Sherrod (Eds.), *Infant social cognition: Empirical and theoretical considerations*. Hillsdale, NJ: Erlbaum 1981.

Tasch, R.J. Interpersonal perceptions of fathers and mothers. *Journal of Genetic Psychology*, 1955, *87*, 59–65.

Thompson, R.A., & Lamb, M.E. Infants, mothers, families, and strangers. In M. Lewis & L.A. Rosenblum (Eds.), *Beyond the dyad*. New York: Plenum, 1983.

Thompson, R.A., Lamb, M.E., & Estes, D. Stability of infant–mother attachment and its relationship to changing life circumstances in an unselected middle-class sample. *Child Development*, 1982, *53*, 144–148.

Vaughn, B.E., Egeland, B., Sroufe, L.A., & Waters, E. Individual differences in infant–mother attachment at twelve and eighteen months: Stability and change in families under stress. *Child Development*, 1979, *50*, 971–975.

Vaughn, B.E., Gove, F.L., & Egeland, B. The relationship between out-of-home care and the quality of infant–mother attachment in an economically disadvantaged population. *Child Development*, 1980, *51*, 1203–1214.

Vogel, S.R., Broverman, I.K., Broverman, D.M., Clarkson, F.E., & Rosenkrantz, P.S. Maternal employment and perception of sex roles among college students. *Developmental Psychology*, 1970, *3*, 384–391.

Waters, E. The reliability and stability of individual differences in infant–mother attachment. *Child Development*, 1978, *49*, 483–494.

Waters, E., Wippman, J., & Sroufe, L.A. Attachment, positive affect, and competence in the peer group: Two studies in construct validation. *Child Development*, 1979, *50*, 821–829.

Weiner, B. *Achievement motivation and attribution theory.* Morristown, NJ: General Learning Press, 1974.

Winterbottom, M. The relation of need for achievement in learning experiences in independence and mastery. In J. Atkinson (Ed.), *Motives in fantasy, action, and society.* Princeton, NJ: Van Nostrand, 1958.

Chapter 3
Child Care Options and Decisions:
Facts and Figurings for Families*

Alice Sterling Honig

College for Human Development
Syracuse University

The problem of the care of children of working parents arose in the United States only within the past century, as industrialization increased. The first day nursery was opened in New York City in 1854. Well into the twentieth century nurseries served mainly working mothers who, because of death, divorce, or desertion, were without husbands. In the first decades of this century, analysis of mortality statistics showed that the likelihood of death during the first year of life was higher if mothers worked outside the home. Social workers used these data in order to press for such social reforms as increased wages, mother's pensions, and improved housing conditions.

By the 1930s, the prevailing societal attitude was that no mother should work outside the home unless she had to because of economic need; even then, welfare workers should do all they could to help her meet her needs without outside work. During the Depression in the thirties, studies appeared which attempted to assess the impact of working mothers on their children (Matthews, 1934). The nation's need for women's labor during World War II caused a surge in nurseries for children of working women, a surge that ebbed after the war. In contrast, the marked increase in employment for mothers in the last decades of the 20th century seems to presage a more permanent change in the life of the nation, rather than an emergency adjustment to temporary needs for working women.

---

* This paper was presented at the Conference on "Families in Transition: Children, Work, and Housework," in Cincinnati, OH, May, 1981.

This shift toward permanent participation by a majority of mothers in working places outside the home has aroused passionate concern among social scientists interested in its effects on the quality of family life. For example, Urie Bronfenbrenner (1981), speaking at the biennial meetings of the Society for Research in Child Development, charged that the progressive fragmentation and isolation of the family since World War II posed grave risks for children. He spoke of his concern for the kinds of supports that Americans might offer to bolster childrearing efforts. He speculated as to whether citizens yet have the know-how, the means, and the intentions to implement alternative child-care arrangements outside of the family that would represent positive, enabling childrearing environments.

Research facts and figures can illuminate current needs of working parents and their children for societal supports. Such a knowledge base can also provide guidelines for more equitable and optimal resolutions of the problems faced by women who work outside the home and who must find quality child care. The following discussion will examine these several questions:

- What do we know about the demographic and sociological situations in which children are growing up today?
- What, if any, are the effects of working parents on child development? Are there specific aspects of the relationship between the child and working parents that researchers have identified as supportive of or inimical to the child-nourishing function of families?
- What are the currently available child care facilities and techniques available for coping with the needs of working parents for alternative child care? How successful have day care facilities been as environments for rearing children?
- What child-care trends for working parents can be predicted for the future? What innovative coordinations, joint efforts, and liaisons among persons and organizations offer potentially more adequate choices for working parents?

Facts are crucial for both personal decisions and more broadly based, societal solutions to child care issues and problems. I refer to public policies that can avoid or cushion distressful and stressful situations for children and families.

DEMOGRAPHICS

Women in the Work Force

A majority of women work because of an economic need. Thus, current employment conditions for women reflect both market demands, as suggested by Glazer in this volume, and individual needs. Nearly two thirds of women in the labor force in 1979 were single, widowed, divorced, separated, or had husbands whose earnings were less than $10,000 in 1978. In 1974, 5.3 million working women were married to men earning less than $7,000 annually and 4.5 million more families with incomes over $10,000 depended on the wife's wages to keep their income above the poverty line (League of Women Voters Educational Fund, 1978). The facts reported below are extrapolated from a U.S. Department of Labor (1980) publication.

- The number of working mothers has increased more than tenfold since the period just before World War II. Fifty-five percent of all mothers with children under 18 years (16.6 million) were working in 1979; 45% of mothers of preschoolers were working.
- The 6.0 million working mothers with preschoolers in 1979 had 7.2 million children under six years of age.
- Women constituted one fifth of the labor force in 1900. In 1979, 43 million women constituted *more* than two fifths of all workers. These proportions are expected to continue to increase over the next decades.
- The average woman worker is as well educated as the average man worker; both have completed a median of 12.6 years of schooling.
- The more education a woman has, the greater the probability that she will seek paid employment. Among women with four-year college degrees, almost 2 out of 3 were working in 1979.
- The average woman worker earns only about three fifths of what a man does, even when both work full time, year round.
- Full-time, year-round women workers who are high school graduates with no college had less income than men who had not completed elementary school ($9,769 vs. $10,474, respectively) in 1978. Women with four years of college also had less income than men with only an 8th grade education ($12,347 vs. $12,965 respectively).
- One out of seven families was maintained by a woman in 1979 compared to about 1 in 10 in 1969.

A 1981 Labor Department study shows that women were paid considerably less than men in the same occupations. Men averaged $366 a week in sales work, women only $190. Men janitors and cleaners earned $238 per week, women only $170. Thus, women are more likely than men to be poor. For example, 69% of food stamps are issued to households headed by women, and 80% of households receiving money from the Aid to Families with Dependent Children Program (AFDC) are headed by women.

Poverty and its attendant aggravations therefore can be expected to weigh heavily on many families that are female-headed. How prevalent is this pattern? Family composition and the presence or absence of supportive relatives will have important implications for children in need of care.

Family Configurations

Once upon a time, the ideal American family configuration consisted of an at-home wife, a working husband, two children, a puppy dog, and a house with a white picket fence. So the cultural myth goes. This family configuration now comprises 13% of families. In another 16%, children are present and both parents work. There is no breadwinner in 1% of families, a widowed, divorced, or separated head of family in 21%, and a single parent as head in 16% of families. Extended families (6%), experimental or cohabiting families (4%) and currently child-free families (23%) represent the remainder of family configurations (Honig, 1979a). Nine tenths of single parent families are headed by women, and 2.3 million children under six years live with mother alone as head of family. In some central core, low-income areas, this figure rises to above 80% (Bronfenbrenner, 1981).

Since the single breadwinner family may have particularly urgent needs for child care, let us examine the statistical dimensions of this situation. The Census Bureau in 1980 reported that female-headed households increased by 51% during the 1970s from 5.6 to 8.5 million households. By the end of the eighties, it is predicted that one in every three children born in the decade will spend all or part of growing-up time in a single parent family (Levine, 1981). Currently, one out of six children lives in a single parent family. "The average length of time spent by children in a single-parent home as a result of marital disruption is about six years" (Hetherington, 1979). One third of black children and one fifth of Hispanic children currently live in female-headed households. Six million children live with stepparents.

The proportion of children living in father-headed, single parent families has tripled since 1960, but of these 1½ million children, more school-age children than preschoolers are likely to live with the father only (Glick & Norton, 1978). In father-headed single-parent families, the mean income, according to the 1980 Census figures, was $9,200—about three times the figure for female-headed households with a mother under 21 years.

The economic news in single parent families is not good for children. Single parenting by a mother drastically reduces the monetary wherewithal to provide for children. In these families, the median income is $6,195 for working mothers, $3,678 for unemployed mothers, and $3,758 for non-working single mothers (Glickman & Springer, 1978). These incomes are, of course, well below poverty level.

Birth and Fertility Patterns

Birth and fertility patterns are changing in the United States. In 1957, there were 3.8 children per family; in 1980 there were 1.8 children per family. There are fewer children for companionship and for learning interpersonal skills within each household. The gross expenditures involved in giving birth to, and rearing, children have discouraged many families from having many children. Also, since more women prefer to spend as little time as possible out of the work force, spacing between children is getting smaller. There are fewer older children in a family to care for younger siblings.

Of women who marry more than once, 25% give birth during a period of marital disruption, 11% give birth between separation and divorce, and 14% between divorce and remarriage (Hetherington, 1979). Thus, many children are being born into families where stress far beyond that occasioned by pregnancy alone can be considered part of the birth legacy of the child.

Such facts are especially alarming, since a secure and intimate marital relationship has been found to predict fewer pregnancy risks (Grossman, Eichler & Winickoff, 1980). Several researchers have found, in general, that "couples with good marital relationships before the birth of the child had little postpartum difficulty and those couples with poor marital adjustment were more likely to experience postpartum depressions and more frequent complications during pregnancy" (Valentine, 1982, p. 20). Sherefsky & Yarrow (1973) found that the overall marital adjustment of a couple affected the quality of later parenting as well as individual adjustment to pregnancy and childbirth.

Teen Parenting. The numbers of births to teenagers have more than doubled from 1960 (92,000) to 1974 (221,400) (Baldwin & Cain, 1980). Every year, more than one million 15- to 19-year-olds (10% of this age group) become pregnant. About 1 out of 5 of the three million babies born annually are born to adolescent mothers. The prognosis for these children is somber in terms of medical and educational risk (Phipps–Yonas, 1980). Teenagers run a four-to-five-times higher risk of pregnancy complications and possible developmental risks for children. Yet 9 out of 10 mothers are keeping their babies, and births to the youngest teens are increasing fastest.

If adolescent parents marry, somewhat more than half of these marriages end in divorce. Also, the leading cause of school dropouts among young women is pregnancy. In either of the above two critical situations, there will be particularly urgent needs for high quality chid care so that adolescent mothers can get continued education, job training, and jobs. There are also particularly urgent needs for high quality child care in order

to prevent possible developmental deficits (Honig, 1978b). The social situation into which the baby was born may increase chances that the infant
will be at risk for developmental delays (Honig, 1980).

Child Neglect and Abuse

Many children lead troubled lives today, despite the increase in material
amenities of life and despite advances in health care which have improved
the physical quality of family life. For example, one out of four fathers
died in the 19th century during the family-building years, whereas only
one in seven fathers die nowadays during this phase of family life. But at
the same time, child suicide rates have increased markedly in some affluent
suburbs.

Despite the widespread existence of health care services, ten million
children receive no medical care and eighteen million children receive no
dental care. A conservatively estimated 2,000 children die from physical
child abuse each year, and about one million children are sublethally
abused. Emotional abuse figures are hard to come by, but these add to
the toll. Incest figures are rising alarmingly in communities across the
nation. Two million children are left alone during the day to care for themselves while mothers work. Of these, 100,000 are less than six years of
age.

Malnutrition is an important factor in increased sickness, irritability,
apathy, and developmental delay among young children. Almost 20% of
American children suffer from iron depletion. Honig and Oski (1978) report
that when intramuscular iron was administered to infants with iron defi-
ciency anemia, they were found to gain significantly in IQ points and have
more normal responsivity (rather than over- or underreactivity during assessment) on a posttest one week later, compared to randomly selected
controls who received placebo initially and then iron therapy immediately
after the posttest.

Divorce and Remarriage

What are the current figures on divorce and remarriage? How do these
figures affect the national need of working parents for child care? In the
Eighties, 30–40% of marriages are likely to end in divorce (Levine, 1981).
Forty-five percent of fathers remarry. Only one third of mothers remarry.
The remarriage rate is four times higher if the divorced father is raising
a child than if the divorced mother is raising a child. Fewer than one third
of ex-husbands contribute to support of families, and the provision of
support drops off rapidly after the first year.

Longitudinal research of the past decade has produced troubling data about the effects of divorce and single parenting on family functioning and child adjustment. The divorce experience represents a transition from a family situation existant prior to divorce, the disorder and stress associated with separation and divorce, the postdivorce disequilibrium, and finally, the struggle to cope in order to reach new equilibrium in the reorganization into a single-parent family (Hetherington, 1979).

Divorce can be incredibly disruptive in the lives of children of all ages. In a five-year postdivorce longitudinal study, Wallerstein and Kelly (1980) found disturbance in almost all children during the first two years following divorce as families readjusted. But beyond that period, about one third of the children adjusted quite well, and somewhat more than a third had remnants of serious anger, depression, guilt, resentment and sorrow; about one third of the children were muddling through. They had come to terms with the disruption, but occasionally had difficulties in some aspect of their lives.

What childhood age seems most vulnerable to the effects of divorce? Summary of the research of Goren (1982) on impact of divorce reports that boys and girls from three to six seem to need both parents more than at any other stage of development. She found that 6- to 9-year-old children often assume blame for their parents' break-up. Kurdek (1981) reviewed the research literature on effects of divorce. He reported that some researchers find that adolescents are better able to cope with divorce because of their increased conceptual ability, while other researchers find that even adolescents are vulnerable because of their own emerging struggles with adult sexuality and responsibilities. Kurdek stresses the importance of family support systems. Goren (1982) found that the adolescents in her research developed feelings of fear or abandonment, so that new relationships were approached "apprehensively, with the expectation of being rejected or losing love" (p. 3).

Research has shown that a child living with the same sex parent after divorce has a better chance of adjustment. Both boys and girls show an increase after divorce in dependent help-seeking and in affection-seeking overtures. Boys, particularly, exhibit more aggressive behaviors and act more noncompliantly with mothers (Hetherington, Cox, & Cox, 1978).

Maintenance of postseparation parenting predicts better child adjustment. That is, children with frequent, regular, positive contact with both parents seem to have fewer problems. Thus, the interesting fact emerges that preseparation parent–child relationships do *not* predict postseparation relationships. Loving, consistent parent interactions with children postdivorce can ameliorate distress. Also, if bitterness and denial of home access to the child exists between parents, then child care arrangements that permit a noncustodial parent regular access to the child can make an important difference in consistency of contact. For example, a father denied frequent visitation by an angry ex-wife can visit his pre-schooler every lunch hour in the on-site child care center at his work place.

Women who are working prior to divorce have an easier time adjusting after divorce. If a postdivorce mother newly enters into a job, then disruption and sense of loss increases for children (Hetherington, 1979). Since 1970, divorced women have the highest participation rate of working of any group of women classified by marital status (American Orthopsychiatric Assn., 1982). These figures point up the acute need for societal supports for quality child care for working parents, particularly where children of divorce are involved. Unfortunately, this has yet to become a national priority.

WORKING PARENTS AND CHILD ADJUSTMENT

In 1980, 65.4% of women 25–34 years of age worked (American Orthopsychiatric Assn., 1982). Thus, the most significant growth rate for those entering the work force is in just that age group of women most likely to be mothers of young children. How does maternal employment affect children? The effects of maternal employment on children depend on a complex of factors which include:

- Child age, sex, needs, and adaptation to stress
- Maternal attitudes toward work and toward the importance of childrearing
- Stresses and strengths within the family
- Maternal behaviors when with the child
- How the child perceives maternal work
- Availability cost, proximity, and quality of child care
- Number of hours child is in alternate care situation
- How stable or unstable the substitute care situation is

Recent research suggests that working women are more satisfied with their lives than nonworking mothers, and role satisfaction of the mother increases her effectiveness as a parent (Gold & Andres, 1978a). The frequency of positive interactions between mother and child has been related negatively to the importance of housework for the mother. The more the parent valued housework, the more likely she was to restrict her child's behavior (Olson, 1981). Thirty years ago, Nye (1952) reported that adolescent children of part-time working mothers had better relationships with their parents than did children of full-time working mothers or of mothers who did not work outside the home. More recently, Burr (1973), in reviewing the literature in this area, concluded that no relationship exists between the amount of time the wife–mother works and the personality maladjustment of her children.

Reactive depression has been found higher for women who had more than two children under the age of 14 compared to mothers with fewer than two children. But when mothers worked outside the home, this incidence of depression was reduced by 50% among single mothers without a supportive relationship with a male companion (Brown & Harris, 1978).

Working Mothers and Sex of Child.

Differential effects of working mothers on sons and daughters have been reported. In a Canadian study of 223 10-year-olds, maternal employment did not affect daughters (Gold & Andres, 1978b). But within working-class families, sons of employed mothers were described more negatively by their fathers, were more shy and nervous, disliked school more, and had lower grades. Within middle-class families, the sons of working mothers had lower math and language achievement scores. However, if the father was actively involved with his children and if the mother was satisfied with her roles, the children in all cases tended to have fewer problems. Indeed, in order to predict satisfactory child adjustment, the satisfaction of mothers seems to be a more critical variable per se than whether or not mother works outside the home (Etaugh, 1974).

Hoffman (1974, 1979) reviewed research related to the effects of maternal employment on children and found that daughters of working mothers had less traditional sex-role concepts, a higher level of female competence, and achievement and independence comparable to daughters of mothers not working outside the home. As for maternal emotional state and its effects, mothers did quite well when they (a) were satisfied with their work, (b) had adequate arrangements so that their dual role did not involve too much stress, and (c) did not feel so guilty toward children that overcompensation resulted.

Yarrow, Scott, Leeuw, and Heenig (1978) have summarized their data on the relationship between mothers' satisfaction with outside work or nonwork status and with childrearing:

> Mothers' employment status (work versus nonwork) is not related to child-rearing characteristics [but] mothers' fulfillments or frustrations in non-mother roles are related to child rearing. When mothers' motivations regarding working are taken into account, the non-working mothers who are dissatisfied with not working (who want to work but, out of a feeling of "duty" do not work) show the greatest problem in child rearing. . . . Working mothers who prefer to work and those who do not wish to work

show few group differences in child-rearing practices, probably because the working mothers (of this sample) who prefer not to work are nonetheless achieving certain valued family goals. (p. 128)

Working Mothers and Lack of Supervision

Less adequate supervision among children of lower socioeconomic families may result in more delinquency (Hoffman, 1974). There was also some evidence for a higher delinquency rate among children of middle-class working mothers, although not for reasons of inadequate supervision. Pilling & Pringle (1978) found that mothers were less happy and children more likely to show signs of stress when the child was unsupervised while the mother was away at work. Moore (1972), in a longitudinal British study, found that working mothers with unstable child care arrangements had children who, in middle childhood, were more attention seeking and had more fears, sleep problems, and toileting accidents, compared to children whose working mothers had had consistent child care support available.

Working Mothers and Television Viewing

In a cross-national study of television viewing habits of school-aged children and the development of aggression, Eron (1982) has recently reported some differences among children of working and nonworking mothers: "The children of working mothers obtain significantly higher aggression scores than children of nonworking mothers" (p. 204). This relationship was found to hold for Finland, Australia, Poland, and the United States. Interpretation is difficult. Perhaps lack of supervision permits children of employed mothers to watch more violent programs. Such data need to be considered carefully in advocating for increased support for after-school quality care situations for school-aged children of working parents.

Working Mothers and Infants

Concern for the vulnerability of infants whose mothers work is, of course, highest. The importance of development of basic trust and secure attachment to primary caregiving figure(s) in the first year of life has been well documented (see Sroufe, 1979, and his chapter in this volume).

Cohen (1978) studied mother–child interaction observed at 21 months for a group of children all born preterm. Half of the mothers were either employed two or more days per week or attended school full time. Mothers were instructed to play with and talk to their children as they normally did. Four presented tasks were videotaped: a four-minute dramatic play situation with miniature doll and family items; a two-minute dressing task where mother had to show her child how to put on mittens and get the child to do so, a four-minute book task, where both were to look at books together; and a four-minute block building task, where mother was asked to show the child how to build a simple construction according to a picture and attempt to get the child to do so. Cohen found that mothers who were not employed gave more positive attentiveness to their children. These toddlers, in turn, vocalized more to their mothers. Mean Bayley Mental Scale scores at 25 months for the children of nonemployed mothers in contrast to employed mothers were 116.5 and 94.6, respectively. These differences were highly significant. It must be remembered that the premature children in this study can be considered a group at risk for developmental problems. Cohen (1978) remarks that "it is possible that the effects of maternal employment may be heightened in such vulnerable groups. On the other hand, it may be that the second year of life is a sensitive period in which the effects of employment on the child may be particularly pronounced" (p. 197).

Thus, research suggests that working families seeking quality alternate care situations for children should be particularly sensitive to *potential problems for infants, for male children and for all children if unstable substitute care arrangements prevail.*

Quality of Time Spent with Children.

When mothers were asked to record all their activities and the time spent on each for a given recent day, differences emerged between working and nonworking mothers. Full-time employed mothers gave less time to their five-year-old children on weekdays than did housewives, but gave more attention on days off from work (Goldberg, 1981). Goldberg combined time use methodology with a lengthy standard day interview checklist. One third of the mothers were nonemployed, one third worked part time and one third worked full time. On the average, mothers spent a little over one hour per week reading to their children. They spent less than two hours teaching their children and in activities helpful to preparing the child for kindergarten. Mothers watched TV with their children for about three hours per week, more time than they spent in teaching and reading combined. The most unexpected result of the study was that mothers who worked full time reported the same amount of direct, one-to-one contact time with children in their diaries as did mothers who did not work at all. Goldberg (1981) concluded that "mothers who stay home with their children are not necessarily giving their children any more one-to-one contact time than mothers who are separated from their children all day because they are employed" (p. 12).

If the quality of time preschoolers spend with adults is important for future success at school tasks, then the next area of concern should be an inquiry into the quality of children's lives while in alternate child care arrangements such as day care.

CHILD CARE ARRANGEMENTS

In choosing child care, most parents opt for family members, such as grandparents or other relatives. Some children are left to care for themselves. Some are left in the care of older siblings. The majority of children of working parents are cared for by babysitters or in family day care homes, most of which are unlicensed. In 1975, the ratio was 777,000 children in licensed homes, compared to 6,755,000 in unlicensed homes. About 12% (850,000) of children needing care were in group day care centers in 1975 (America's Children, 1976).

Group Care in Other Cultures

Children have been successfully reared in other cultures in group care. But often, special circumstances exist. For example, infant-toddler day care centers in China visited by the author (Honig, 1978a), whether attached to factory or to commune, allowed for an hour of maternal nursing during the morning and during the afternoon. Since the centers were attached to work places nursing could continue uninterrupted, although the mother returned to agricultural work in the commune or machine work in the factory. In Israeli kibbutzim, too, the circumstances of parents' work life permits them to visit on "breaks" during the day, since day care houses are not far from the location of work. Also, when the agricultural day ends in the afternoons, parents and children can spend a couple of uninterrupted hours of playtime together before dinner. The metapelet (child care worker) is often superbly trained (see Dr. Joseph Stone's film "Day Care for a Kibbutz Toddler") and is seen by the children as a friend and partner of the parents. Thus, some societies have programs and provisions for child care at or near parents' workplaces.

Research on the Effects of Day Care

Since group day care is being chosen by more and more parents, and especially for younger children, it is important to examine some of the findings on the effects of group day care on children in order that working parents can make informed choices about the type of care they prefer for their child.

Research in the United States has shown that how much a child benefits from group care depends both on the quality of home nurturance *and* on the quality of center care. Day care centers range from custodial centers (that provide meals and exercise) to developmental centers that also provide opportunities for exploring and creating, for positive social interactions, and for language learning.

Children from poverty environments who are enrolled in high quality day care centers, with loving responsive adults, much verbal interaction and rich provision of toys usually learn more than they would at home, and they often show IQ gains (Caldwell, Wright, Honig, & Tannenbaum, 1970; Doyle, 1975; Keister, 1977).

Lally & Honig (1977) found that for infants of low education, low-income teenage mothers in (mostly) fatherless families, quality day care increased the children's IQ scores significantly above matched controls after three years in program. Eriksonian and Piagetian theory were combined to implement program goals of loving social interactions and enriched experiences for young children. Sensitive attention to individual infant needs as well as provision of sensorimotor games and experiences enhanced the cognitive competence of the children. Language interactions were embedded in daily routines such as diapering and feeding in order to promote language learning. Elaborate curricular materials and guidelines were created for training quality caregivers (Honig, 1979b; Honig & Lally 1981).

One of the most remarkable demonstrations, albeit also among the most expensive, of the positive effects of high quality, infant–toddler care for low-income infants was carried out in Milwaukee (Heber, Garber, Harrington, & Hoffman, 1972). Children were initially selected at birth, because they were born into poverty families living in high density housing areas. Their mothers had IQs under 70. These infants were particularly at risk for later sociocultural mental retardation. At first, each infant in the center had one tutor. By 18 months one caregiver was responsible for three infants. A highly enriched program from 3–60 months eventuated in mean IQ scores of 126 for these at-risk children by age 5, whereas control children scored at 95.7. Thus, at-risk infants and preschoolers are likely to do *better* than home-reared comparison children when in enriched group care (Honig, 1983).

On the other hand, poor quality day care can be inimical to the cognitive development of children from disadvantaged homes. Peaslee (1976) found that when the adult–child ratio was 1 to 16 for two-year-olds, then those toddlers scored lower on language skills and on the Bayley developmental scales than did toddlers from similar home environments who were home-reared.

For working- and middle-class children, high quality day care has

been found to be without any disadvantageous developmental consequences when preschoolers are compared with home-reared children (Kagan, Kearsley, & Zelazo, 1978). Caldwell et al. (1970) reported than when
middle and low socioeconomic infants attended a high quality day care
center together for two years, the middle class infants gained 17 IQ points
and the low-income infants gained 9 IQ points. Thus, the question as to
whether optimally nurturing and educational group care with a high ratio
of adults to children (1 to 3 or 4) can facilitate development of very young
children has been answered affirmatively in several major studies across
social class groups.

   Day Care and Attachment. Another question that has concerned spe-
cialists is whether or not group care would attenuate the attachment of
mothers and children who are separated for hours during each day. The
high quality day care centers that have provided research results have,
however, not been ten-hour-a-day centers. Thus, findings to date must
be carefully qualified by the proviso that we do not know whether or not
the long day care day would have differential effects on parent-child attachment. Caldwell et al. did, however, interview mothers carefully and
systematically in order to discover whether there was any dilution of the
attachment relationship between mothers and their infants and toddlers
who had attended the Syracuse University Children's Center for two years.
The infants attended a half-day program until 15 months and a full-day
program after that. A matched control group of mothers of home-reared
infants was also interviewed. Day care was definitely not associated with
the quality of mother–child attachment. However, the home environment
was significantly related to attachment ratings. That is, in homes where
developmental stimulation was low, where there was a lack of positive
emotional and verbal responsivity, as measured by Caldwell's Home
Stimulation Inventory (STIM), then attachment was indeed weaker. But
this outcome was found whether or not the children had attended day
care. Ramey (1981) has recently used a situational test to demonstrate
that low-income infants who attended high quality day care were still well-
attached to mothers and went to them in preference to caregivers.

Ordinary Day Care

Most children do not attend high quality university-based group day care
centers. They attend day care centers in the metropolitan or rural areas
where they live. And, as Belsky and Steinberg (1978) have so rightly noted:
"We know shockingly little about the impact of day care on children, on
their parents, and on the society in which these children and parents live"
(p. 929). Increasingly, mothers of very young children are going to work

and seeking alternative care for their infants and toddlers. How aware are caregivers in ordinary day care centers of the needs for responsive, loving interactions, and communication games that allow infants to control the amount of stimulation they receive (Honig, 1982a)? We need more studies of caregivers in ordinary day care, but there is some research that can help families make better decisions in choosing child care.

Family Day Care vs. Group Day Care. The New York City day care study (Golden et al., 1978) attempted to analyze differential benefits of family day care and of center-based care in a large metropolitan area. None of the care settings were associated with university-based research projects. There was more social interaction and positive socioemotional stimulation provided by caregivers to children during the lunch meal in family day care. But on cognitive findings and health care findings, the results favored metropolitan center day care. More of these children also had had a medical checkup and required shots.

> By three years of age, the children enrolled in group care obtained significantly higher scores on the Stanford Binet than their matched controls enrolled in family day care (IQs of 99 versus 92). Moreover, whereas the children in center care had maintained the same level of intellectual performance between eighteen and thirty-six months of age, their counterparts in family day care had shown a significant decline from ninety-eight to ninety-two. (Bronfenbrenner, 1979, p. 195)

Group Size and Adult–Child Ratios. What are favorable ratios of adults to children in ordinary day care? The Abt (1979) national day care study discovered that small group size and higher adult–child ratios were strongly related to measure of programmatic quality for infants and toddlers.

The Abt findings are important because the study's staff observed and tested 1,800 children in 57 centers located in Atlanta, Detroit, and Seattle. They observed and interviewed caregivers in 129 day care classrooms. For infant care, the more infants there were per staff member, the more the caregiver engaged in management and control behavior, rather than teaching or playing or cuddling. For preschool-aged children, *small groups* of 15 or fewer children were found to be associated with higher gains on the Caldwell Preschool Inventory and the Peabody Picture Vocabulary Test. Also, in smaller groups, more desirable child and teacher behaviors were observed.

Center size as well as group size can affect the quality of child care. Prescott (1973) had reported a decade earlier that large centers serving over 100 children tended to be more authoritarian than smaller sized centers.

Teacher Responsiveness. Honig and Wittmer (1982b) studied teacher–child–peer interactions for 100 two- and three-year-old boys and girls attending seven ordinary metropolitan day care centers that served families whose fees were paid by Title XX funds.[1] Microanalysis of the chains of responses between caregivers and children revealed that almost 75% of toddler communications with teachers in day care were in order to seek adult help or attention. On almost two thirds of the occasions that toddlers approached caregivers needing assistance, they received a positive adult response. Yet, the researchers noted that receiving a negative response or no response to one third of their attempts to get adult help may be quite discouraging to toddlers. Two-year-olds are still dependent on adults for reassurance and for assistance in many tasks. If caregivers ignore a toddler's bid for help, that toddler may give up on a task or try negative behaviors to gain the help needed.

In general, Honig and Wittmer found that in ordinary day care almost 22% of toddlers bids of all kinds were ignored. In contrast, data from high quality university-run day care suggests that well-trained toddler teachers very rarely (less than 1%) ignore toddler overtures (Honig & Lally, 1975).

Particularly disturbing were Honig and Wittmer's findings that when toddlers approached teachers in a distressed or (more rarely) negative way, they were ignored or responded to in a negative or unsympathetic manner on nearly one half of such occasions. Male toddlers also received significantly *more* attention for their noncompliance than did female toddlers, although both sexes had equal rates of compliance with caregivers. In ordinary group care, young boys may possibly be treated more stereotypically as "causing more trouble than girls" for teachers (Honig & Wittmer, 1982a).

Although toddlers only sought information in about 5% of their bids to caregivers, almost two thirds of the adult responses to such bids involved teaching or questioning or giving positive emotional comments. Thus, in ordinary day care, teachers seemed mostly to respond quite appropriately to toddlers' intellective bids. Yet even here, 25% of such bids were ignored. Some parents might be concerned that so low a level of child information-seeking was present in ordinary day care classrooms.

If working parents place their children in ordinary day care, they may need to inquire closely about the philosophy of the center in terms of the quality and frequency of responses given when children seek help or comfort from teachers. Parents may also need actively to seek out centers providing more intellectual stimulation.

---

[1] In Title XX programs, federal funds are provided to match state expenditures for a wide range of social services such as day care for low-income families.

INNOVATIONS IN CHILD CARE ARRANGEMENTS

What are the child care trends for the future? Societal and economic barriers may make some of the ideas to be discussed in this section less likely to be tried. Yet it is important to think imaginatively in assessing options that communities and parents *can* provide for quality child care. If they recognize the importance of such provisions, then determined voters can indeed allocate resources to make quality care options possible.

Some of the future trends can be predicted from innovative experiments and undertakings currently being tried or planned. First, there may be a shift in the fundamental societal attitude toward day care. Day care may come to be seen not as a necessary but disapproved social service for poor children—the current view of some media and policymakers (Caldwell, 1982)—but as a potentially facilitative environment in which young children can be safely and lovingly nurtured and intellectually encouraged in their development. Parents need to become much more energetic and well-advised consumers of quality day care.

More alliances between public schools, parents, and day care providers should occur in the future. Many communities have public school classrooms that are empty. As more and more children need after-school care, linkages between social service agencies, families and public schools should increase the provision of quality *after-school day care* in school facilities, as well as the use of empty classrooms for preschool care.

Diversity in day care offerings will increase. Already, there are on-site day care centers for hospital personnel in many medical facilities. Hospitals are the fastest growing sites for the provision of day care today. More and more industry or service agency-based day care facilities may arise as employees actively seek to promote quality child care on the premises where they work. Indeed, employee unions in some communities are providing seed money for starting up quality day care centers at work places. An example is the Nurturing World infant/toddler day care program recently begun with seed money from the New York State Employee's local union at the Hutching's Psychiatric Center in Syracuse, NY.

These developments will reverse a pattern that existed from 1960 to 1974, when 82% of industrial on-site day care closed, because it was not profitable and had low utilization (Levine, 1981).

More partnerships between private sector and public sector should occur. For example, working parents need child care in the summer as well as during the usual school year. Day camps may team up with day care operators who provide service ten months of the year in order to provide continuity of child care throughout the year.

Industry may choose more flexible options to attract workers by offering their employees *vouchers* for slots in family day care or in child care centers. Companies that offer such vouchers for reserved spaces in child care facilities should reap benefits of decreased employee absenteeism resulting from child care problems.

Flextime in jobs may permit more families to become co-caregivers. If one parent works as an employee in the morning, and another in the afternoon, they may be able to trade child–care services with and for each other.

More private day care homes may coordinate with each other under the auspices of civic organizations in order to upgrade the quality of care provided. In Syracuse, the Children's Consortium, a private philanthropic agency, supports the activities of a Magic Bus that carries materials and training personnel around the community to family day care home providers.

Levine (1981) reports that the Ford Foundation lent money recently for an experiment in networking by family day-care providers. Providers used the money to rent space in a building at low and stable rent. Then, instead of providing family day care in their separate homes, the providers each used separate space in the same building to set up a small family day-care operation. By combining resources, they are able to buy equipment and share resources at lower cost to each.

Although eligibility requirements have recently become far more restrictive, federal support for child care (some $2 billion in 1977) occurs mainly in three ways:

- Day care tax credits by the government allow families with two working parents, single parents, and some students to subtract 20% of day care costs (up to $400 for one child and $800 for two or more) from federal tax owed.
- For AFDC recipients, there is an "income disregard." That is, for welfare recipients who work, all day care expenses are disregarded when benefit reductions resulting from earnings are calculated.
- Headstart provides year-round care to 349,000 preschool-age children, mostly from low-income families. (League of Women Voters Education Fund, 1978)

Parents spent a total of $7 billion on child care in 1977. Although the costs of child care in day care centers ranges from $105 per month to the same amount per week (for infant care for upper-class families in a large metropolis), there is much uncertainty currently over government child care support for families. Funds for CETA workers who could serve as trained aides in day care centers have been withdrawn. Food supports have been cut. Strenuous public efforts to persuade legislators to restore budgetary supports for quality child care are necessary. Legislators have often viewed out-of-home child care as destructive of home and family values. Yet governmental support for a variety of quality child care options can increase family stability, tranquility, and ability to care well for children.

More community facilities that have heretofore served other needs may move into provision of child care. Community libraries, churches, health centers, etc., may find ways to set up small service components within their buildings, where child care could be provided at less cost, since major rent and service fees may already be covered within the location concerned.

More innovative private networks for occasional child care will be formed. In a suburban Virginia community outside Washington, DC, about 25 parents have set up a system of plastic chips. When a newcomer moves into their community, the family is given 25 chips, each good for one hour of child care. The family cannot leave the child care network without eventually returning this loan. Each month, one family serves as secretary for coordinating families, desired dates, and child care providers. No family in the network need ever pay for child care in money. They meet each others needs for service whenever their time permits. Barter in child care arrangements should grow as working parents seek less expensive ways to meet their child care needs. Such a system may work better for part-time rather than full-time working parents.

Agencies that currently have more conventional nursery-school or day-care programs may increase the flexibility of their provision by adding drop-in centers, so that family needs for emergency or occasional child care can be met.

High School Sites

Quality child care as a practicum site actively in use for the community, for teachers, and for any pregnant teenagers may become important aspects of high schools. Such quality care centers would serve as living laboratories for young people to study how young children grow and flourish, given the skilled and tender care that well-trained teachers can provide. Since parenting skills are often in short supply, such centers could serve as the focus for courses to increase the ability of young people eventually to meet the needs of their own children more ably (Honig, 1982b). The kind of communicative dance whereby parent and infant tune into each other's signals, and keep long interactions going as they learn the positive aspects of an intimate caring relationship is difficult to learn in a society geared so heavily toward consumerism and industry. Such in-school centers could go far toward reducing the national incidence of child abuse and inappropriate parental behaviors.

CONCLUSIONS

Working parents will continue to need more and better alternative child care facilities. Corporate cooperation with such needs may eventuate in more quality facilities for children on the premises of company plants. Special privileges for nursing mothers could be arranged particularly well for on-site child care. More networking by families and more networking by family day care workers will help to keep child care costs down, add to community spirit, and increase options for parents. Community coalitions of organizations, such as Child Care Councils, can connect citizens with babysitters, centers, and other providers. Such councils may well become more common in urban areas, as the need for coordinating a variety of child care facilities and arrangements becomes more urgent.

Despite the increase in innovative ideas for child care, the most serious obstacle currently is the lack of governmental commitment to fiscal support for working families needing out-of-home child care. Current federal priorities do not put child development ahead of more missiles, more marching band uniforms, or more tobacco subsidies. Only a concerned and articulate citizenry that perceives supports for families and children as a positive national benefit will be able to effect changes in political priorities. Legislation that offers tax incentives for quality child care use by citizens would be a wise public policy commitment to the future citizens that small children will grow up to be.

Whatever the innovations of the next decades, quality child care will still need to demonstrate such time and research-honored characteristics as provision of safe, healthy environments, where needs for bodily and spiritual nourishment are met; where children can find responsive nurturing adults whose patience, delight, and genuine interest in children further the development of curiosity and love of learning in little ones. If, as a society, we long for well-organized, persistent, curious and self-energized learners who know how to relate lovingly with peers and to treat adults as trusted helpers, friends and teachers, then we need a societal commitment to provide more adequate child care supports for working families with children.

REFERENCES

Abt Associates, Inc. *Children at the center: Final report of the National Day Care Study, Executive Summary*. Cambridge, MA., 1979 (ERIC Document Reproduction Service No. ED 168 706).

American Orthopsychiatric Association. *Newsletter*. Winter, 1982, p. 12.

America's Children, 1976. Washington, DC: The National Council of Organizations for Children and Youth, 1976.

Arend, R.A., Gove, F.L., & Sroufe, L.A. Continuity of early adaptation: From attachment in infancy to ego-resiliency and curiosity at age 5. *Child Development,* 1979, *50,* 950–959.

Baldwin, W., & Cain, V.S. The children of teenage parents. *Family Planning Perspectives,* 1980, *12,* 34–43.

Belsky, J., & Steinberg, L. The effects of day care: A critical review. *Child Development,* 1978, *49,* 929–950.

Bronfenbrenner, U. *The ecology of human development.* Cambridge, MA: Harvard University Press, 1979.

Bronfenbrenner, U. The evolution of context in developmental research: Retrospect and prospect. Invited Address presented at the biennial meetings of the Society for Research in Child Development, Boston, MA, April 1981.

Brown, G.W., & Harris, T.M. *Social origins of depression: A study of psychiatric disorder in women.* New York: Free Press, 1978.

Burr W.R. Theory construction and the sociology of the family. New York: Wiley Interscience, 1973.

Caldwell, B.M. How can we educate the American public about the child care profession? Presidential address delivered at the annual meetings of the National Association for the Education of Young Children, Washington, DC, November 1982.

Caldwell, B.M., Wright, C., Honig, A.S., & Tannenbaum, J. Infant daycare and attachment. *American Journal of Orthopsychiatry,* 1970, *40,* 397–412.

Cohen, S.E. Maternal employment and mother–child interaction. *Merill–Palmer Quarterly,* 1978, *24,* 189–197.

Doyle, A.B. Infant development in day care. *Developmental Psychology,* 1975, *11,* 655–656.

Eron, L.D. Parent–child interaction, television violence, and aggression of children. *American Psychologist,* 1982, *37,* 197–211.

Etaugh, C. Effects of maternal employment on children: A review of recent research. *Merill–Palmer Quarterly,* 1974, *20,* 71–98.

Glick, P.G., & Norton, A.J. Marrying, divorcing, and living together in the U.S. Today. *Population Bulletin,* 1978, *32,* 3–38.

Glickman, B.M., & Springer, N.B. *Who cares for the baby?: Choices in child care.* New York: Schocken Books, 1978.

Gold, D., & Andres, D. Developmental comparisons between 10-year-old children with employed and non-employed mothers. *Child Development,* 1978, *49,* 75–84. (a)

Gold, D. & Andres, D. Relations between maternal employment and development of nursery school children. *Canadian Journal of Behavioral Science,* 1978, *10,* 116–129. (b)

Goldberg, R. Adapting time budget methodology for child development research: Effects of family variables on allocation of time to child rearing activities and developmental outcomes. Paper presented at the annual meetings of the Society for Research in Child Development, Boston, MA, April 1981.

Golden, M., Rosenbluth, L., Grossi, M., Policare, H., Freeman, H., and Brownlee, E. *The New York City infant day care study.* New York: Medical and Health Research Association of New York City, 1978.

Goren, B.H. Synopsis of research findings on impact of divorce. *Behavior Today,* 1982, September 13, 2–3.

Grossman, F.K., Eichler, L.S. & Winickoff, S.A. *Pregnancy, birth, and parenthood.* San Francisco, CA: Jossey-Bass, 1980.

Heber, R., Garber, H., Harrington, S., & Hoffman, C. *Rehabilitation of families at risk for mental retardation: A progress report.* Madison, WI: University of Wisconsin, December 1972.

Hetherington, E.M. Divorce: A child's perspective. *American Psychologist,* 1979, *34,* 851–858.

Hetherington, E.M., Cox, M., & Cox, R. The aftermath of divorce. In J.H. Stevens, Jr. & M. Matthews (Eds.) *Mother–child, father–child relations*. Washington, DC: National Association for the Education of Young Children, 1978.

Hoffman, L.W. Effects on child. In L.W. Hoffman & F.I. Nye (Eds.), *Working mothers*. San Francisco, CA: Jossey-Bass, 1974.

Hoffman, L.W. Maternal employment: *American Psychologist*, 1979, *34*, 859–865.

Honig, A.S. Comparison of child-rearing practices in Japan and in the People's Republic of China: A personal view. *International Journal of Group Tensions*, 1978, *8*, 6–32. (a)

Honig, A.S. What we need to know to help the teenage parent. *The Family Coordinator*, 1978, *27*, 113–120. (b)

Honig, A.S. Child care alternatives and options for parents. *Viewpoints on Teaching and Learning*, 1979, *55*, 57–65. (a)

Honig, A.S. What you need to know to select and train your day care staff. *Child Care Quarterly*, 1979, *8*, 19–35. (b)

Honig, A.S. Developmental effects on children of pregnant adolescents. Paper presented at the meetings of the American Medical Association subgroup on Adolescent Childbearing. Chicago, IL, September 1980.

Honig, A.S. Infant–mother communication. *Young Children*, 1982, *37*, 52–62. (a)

Honig, A.S. Intervention strategies to optimize infant development. In E. Aronwitz (Ed.), *Prevention strategies for mental health*. New York: Neale Watson Academic Publications, 1982. (b)

Honig, A.S. Evaluation of infant/toddler intervention programs. In B. Spodek (Ed.), *Studies in education evaluation*. London: Pergamon Press, 1983, pp. 305–316.

Honig, A.S., & Lally, J.R. How good is your infant-toddler program? Use an observation method to find out. *Child Care Quarterly*, 1975, *1*, 194–207.

Honig, A.S., & Lally, J.R. *Infant caregiving: A design for training*, 2nd edition. Syracuse, NY: Syracuse University Press, 1981.

Honig, A.S., & Oski, F.A. Developmental scores of iron deficient infants and effects of treatment. *Infant Behavior and Development*, 1978, *1*, 168–176.

Honig, A.S. & Wittmer, D.S. Early signs of sex role stereotyping. Paper presented at the biennial meetings of the Southeastern Conference on Human Development, Baltimore, MD, April 1982. (a)

Honig, A.S., & Wittmer, D.S. Teachers and low-income toddlers in metropolitan day care. *Early Child Development and Care*, 1982, *10*, 95–112. (b)

Kagan, J., Kearsley, R.B., & Zelazo, P.R. *Infancy: Its place in human development*, Cambridge, MA: Harvard University Press, 1978.

Keister, M. *The good life for infants and toddlers: Group care of infants*, 2nd edition. Washington, DC: National Association for the Education of Young Children, 1977.

Kurdek, L.A. An integrative perspective on children's divorce adjustment. *American Psychologist*, 1981, *36*, 856–866.

Lally, J.R., & Honig, A.S. The Family Development Research Program. In M.C. Day & R.K. Parker (Eds.), *The preschool in action*. Boston, MA: Allyn & Bacon, 1977.

League of Women Voters Educational Fund. *Women & work: The day care dilemma*. Washington, DC: League of Women Voters, 1978.

Levine, J. Day care challenges and opportunities in a new decade. Paper presented at the Fourth Annual National Symposium *Building Family Strengths*, Lincoln, NE, May 1981.

Matthews, S.M. The development of children's attitudes concerning mothers' out-of-home employment. *Journal of Educational Sociology*, 1934, *6*, 259–271.

Moore, T. The later outcomes of early care by the mother and substitute daily regimes. In F. J. Monks, W.W. Hartup, & J. DeWitt (Eds.), *Determinants of behavioral development*. New York: Academic Press, 1972.

Nye, F.I. Adolescent–parent adjustment: Age, sex, sibling number, broken homes, and employed mothers as variables. *Marriage and Family Living,* 1952, *14,* 327–332.

Olson, J.T. The impact of housework on child care in the home. *Family Relations,* 1981, *31,* 75–81.

Peaslee, M. The development of competency in 2-year old infants in daycare and home-reared environments. *Ph.D.* Dissertation, Florida State University, 1976.

Phipps-Yonas, S. Teenage pregnancy and motherhood: A review of the literature. *American Journal of Orthopsychiatry,* 1980, *50,* 403–431.

Pilling, D., & Pringle, M.K. *Controversial issues in child development.* New York: Schocken Books, 1978.

Prescott, E.T. A comparison of three types of day care and nursery-school-home care. Paper presented at the biennial meetings of the Society for Research in Child Development, Philadelphia, PA, April 1973.

Ramey, C. Consequences of infant day care. In B. Weissbourd & J. Musick (Eds.), *Infants: Their social environments.* Washington, DC: National Association for the Education of Young Children, 1981.

Sherefsky, P.M. & Yarrow, L.J. *Psychological aspects of a first pregnancy and early postnatal adaptation.* New York: Raven Press, 1973.

Sroufe, L. The coherence of individual development: Early care, attachment, and subsequent developmental issues. *American Psychologist,* 1979, *34,* 834–841.

U.S. Department of Labor. *Facts on women workers.* Washington, DC: by Women's Bureau, Office of the Secretary, 1980.

Valentine, D. Adaptation to pregnancy: Some implications for individual and family mental health. *Children Today,* 1982, *11,* 17–20, 36.

Wallerstein, J.S., & Kelly, J.B. *Surviving the break-up: How children actually cope with divorce.* New York: Basic Books, 1980.

Yarrow, M.R. Scott, P., de Leeuw, L., & Heinig, C. Child-rearing families of working and non-working mothers. In H. Bee (Ed.), *Social issues in developmental psychology,* 2nd ed. New York: Harper & Row, 1978.

Chapter 4
Gender Inequities in Childhood Social Life and Adult Work Life*

Kathryn M. Borman
Judith Frankel
University of Cincinnati

INTRODUCTION

The discussion in this chapter centers upon the social demands of organizational life. Of particular interest are gender inequities associated with the performance of managerial roles in organizations. Although we can argue only by analogy, we take the position that performance demands in highly complex games played in childhood are similar to demands to be a good team player, coach, or captain in the organizational setting. Their exclusion from complex games in childhood deprives most girls of experiences in an important early managerial training ground. We refer particularly to experiences in negotiating power, rules, and roles. Children demonstrate at least an elementary mastery of these applied social skills in their routine organization of complex game structures. It is boys and not girls who regularly participate in complex game negotiations. We argue that there are similar interpersonal dynamics in organizational settings although they have not been systematically studied. These dynamics can be summarized as the political life of organizational members.

* This material is based upon work supported by the National Institute of Education under the grant NIE-G-79-0123 made to the first author. Any opinions, findings, etc., expressed in this paper are those of the authors and do not necessarily reflect the view of the Institute or the Department of Education.

   Thanks are gratefully extended to Sarah Gideonse, Maita Levine, Jeylan Mortimer, Patricia O'Reilly, and Shirley Piazza for their helpful comments on the original draft of this chapter.

The chapter is divided in two major sections, the first concerned with adult managerial work and the second with the world of children's play. The purpose of the first section is to provide a context for understanding the significance of socialization in children's games for future organizational careers. In this section we turn initially to a brief analysis of constraints inhibiting women's managerial success. Then we consider a study (England, Chassie & McCormack, 1982) demonstrating occupational inequities associated with gender. In moving next to an analysis of children's games, our specific concern is in understanding the interactional milieu of complex games, particularly the nature of social skills demanded by play in soccer, football, and the like. We conclude by analyzing the parallel strategies exhibited by competent females in complex games and complex organizational structures.

Three common themes characterize the separate worlds of children's games and adult managerial work: (a) access, (b) male dominance, and (c) complexity.

Access

Like life in organizations, life in children's games is governed by access to an ongoing group. Rates of participation are highly regulated by gatekeepers who screen participants for evidence of attributes deemed necessary for comembership. These attributes, however, may be only marginally related to the actual skills (including social skills) demanded by the game (or organizational) structure. Although access is determined by demonstration or assessment of some minimal level of competence (especially in games) or related training and education (especially in organizations), it is clear that personnel decisions in the world of work show bias in favor of men and against women at all stages: entry, evaluation, and promotion (Nieva & Gutek, 1980).

Male Dominance

Children's games, especially team sports, are dominated by boys (Lever, 1978); managerial roles are typically held by men. In 1980, managerial jobs requiring complex social skills (persuading, diverting, supervising, negotiating, mentoring) were held by a small proportion of women who occupied less than 25% of the available positions. In 1981, the median salary for white women managers and administrators was $14,664 as compared to $24,492 for white men in similar positions. There is clearly a persistent male bias in both adult occupational and children's play activities. Obstructions to female participation in both cases are inherent in organizational structures, general stereotypes and in the attitudes of girls' peers and women's colleagues and supervisors (Nieva & Gutek, 1980).

Complexity

It is important at the outset to clarify the several meanings of the term "complexity" as it is used here. Organizational complexity refers to the patterned relationships among structural features such as roles, group goals, and rules.

To negotiate complex organizations, the individual presumably must wield relatively complex social skills. Social skills are presumed to reside in one individual as a set of personality traits or characteristics. Congruent with this assumption, previous studies of children's social development and their social cognitive skills have been measured by standard tasks constructed by developmental psychologists. Research in this tradition has judged the child's capacity to take the perspective of another on the basis of performance in a laboratory setting (see, for example, Ford, 1979). In our discussion, by contrast, we emphasize "applied" social intelligence, the demonstration in real life of a capacity to organize, manage, and negotiate complex social interactions. This capacity is transparent in children's spontaneously organized games.

Games and managerial occupations both require participants to engage in complex interactions with others. In games, particularly in team activities such as soccer and football, children must undertake relatively complex verbal exchanges to settle issues of power, rules, roles, and strategies (Borman, Barrett, & Sheoran, 1982). Managerial roles demand skill in supervising, negotiating, and mentoring (U.S. Dept. of Labor, 1977).

Complexity in games was observed by Lever (1978) who judged complexity along six dimensions: division of labor based on specialization of roles; interdependence between individual members; size of the membership; explicitness of the group goals; number and specificity of impersonal rules; and action of members as a unified collective. It should be noted that Lever's system of classification draws from the literature on complex organizations. Thus, the unit of analysis is the social group and not the individual.

Although individuals participate in organizational structures which are more or less complex, *it does not necessarily follow that such participation requires more complex social skills.* For example, according to Lever's typology, baseball is more complex than chess, and tennis is more complex than golf. Moreover, structural barriers, particularly norms associated with stereotypic expectations for girls' (as opposed to boys') behavior may inhibit girls from entering games traditionally played by boys.

In summary, complex childhood games and adult work organizations, particularly the structures of organizational management, are characterized by (a) biased (promale) rules of access requiring attributes considered critical for comembership, (b) predominantly male memberships, and (c) complex patterns of social interactions.

ADULT MANAGERIAL WORK

Barriers in the Workplace

Barriers to successful performance in the social settings of games and work considered here do not reside in female attitudes or "traits" such as fear of success. Rather, as we have previously noted, the dificulties faced by girls and women are inherent in external factors. Inequities are manifest in all aspects of organizational careers of women and are perpetuated by the nature of organizational life. We believe the central issue is power. Power is the capacity to determine the allocation of benefits and privileges in any social setting. In the world of work, wages, promotions, and less tangible rewards such as comfort, job clarity, and autonomy are disproportionately awarded to men and perhaps surprisingly, to low status women (Nieva & Gutek, 1981; Miller, Labovitz, & Fry, 1975). Throughout the remainder of the chapter we will examine the social forces and processes which serve to enhance the power of men and boys and limit the power of women and girls.

Barriers in the workplace can be located in all aspects of women's job related experiences. In finding a job, women are more likely than men to make direct application to employers or to rely upon college placement services. In contrast, college-educated men are more likely than similarly trained women to rely upon friends or relatives in finding a job. These differences in job search behaviors suggest that men are more likely than women to gain access to jobs through an "old boys' network" that facilitates their organizational entrée (Young, 1974).

As an example of work inequities, wage differentials between men and women are often explained as a direct result of discontinuous work force participation by women whose childbearing and family responsibilities intrude upon their work lives. Indeed, women *do* suffer lower total years of job experience and less seniority than men, whose careers typically encounter no similar interruptions. In a study reviewed by Nieva and Gutek (1981), comparisons were made of men and women with similar job experience. In this research Suter and Miller (1973) found that, given continuous work histories, large salary differentials still persisted between men and women across occupational categories. "Among professionals, women earned 66 percent of the male average; among clerical workers, 79 percent; and among operatives and service workers, 50 percent. (Furthermore) . . . the payoff for each additional year of work experience was higher for white men than for other groups" (Nieva & Gutek, 1981, p. 108). In explaining persistent inequities in work life, Nieva and Gutek, (1981) argue that findings across the board support a "vested interest" interpretation, by which they mean that the "organizational structure functions to protect men's vested interests by allowing interpersonal barriers to exist that are not explainable by a rational view of organizational influence,'' i.e., the legitimate authority conveyed to organizational decision makers by virtue of their greater experience, lengthier training, etc. (p. 12).

Moreover, women who occupy managerial positions are more likely to experience greater job strain than most women who occupy more traditional feminine roles in the same organization. We have already seen that executive women earn a smaller percentage of comparable male salaries than female clerical workers as a percentage of their male counterparts' wages. The notion of "sex role incongruence" explains much of these effects. Women whose career lives have required them to attain some graduate training and job authority are frequently perceived by coworkers to be "out of role." Not only do coworkers evaluate such women harshly, but women themselves view their positions more negatively than most women occupying lower status jobs in the same work setting. Specifically, higher status women experience more difficulties with job clarity, autonomy issues, and job tension than lower-ranking females. Thus, in terms of distributive justice, high achieving women accurately perceive the unfair treatment accorded them and react appropriately (Suter & Miller, 1973).

The promale bias pervasive in organizational settings that we have just examined has historical antecedents. Organizational structures were plotted around the dispositions of white, Protestant men from elite schools, who were the earliest architects of current work organization formulations (Kanter, 1975). The formulation of a managerial ideology to define appropriate values and behaviors in organizations resulted in a "masculine ethic" which persists into the 20th century. According to Kanter (1975):

> A "masculine ethic" of rationality and reason can be identified in the early image of managers. This "masculine ethic" elevates the traits assumed to belong to men with educational advantages to necessities for effective organizations: a tough minded approach to problems; analytic abilities to abstract and plan; a capacity to set aside personal, emotional considerations in the interests of task accomplishment; and a cognitive superiority in problem-solving and decision making. (p. 43)

As much a part of this ideology as a belief in rationality is a view of organizational structures as hierarchically organized and constructed of easily manipulated parts. Departmental offices and other structures are controlled by managers to make organizations run smoothly and efficiently in accord with rational planning. There is little room for social interaction in this model and no room at all for emotions and politics, which presumably are deposited at the company door. Women, whose sex roles cast them as emotional, irrational, and ineffective in abstract reasoning are, by their "nature" excluded from consideration in this model.

Although later models of organizational life are more accommodative to social interaction (informal ties, friendship networks), nonetheless these models also characterize differences in work settings as attributable to leadership styles. The most effective settings are associated with a leadership style emphasizing authority and rationality. The human relations model underscores the "importance for productivity of primary informal relations among workers" and is illustrated in the Hawthorne studies conducted by Elton Mayo and others in the 1930s (Kanter, 1975, p. 46). The human relations model characterizes good managers as tough, even heroic, in their effective control of office workers who, in turn, are seen as governed by "sentiment, emotion, and social instincts" (Kanter, 1975, p. 47). Organizational life is seen as analogous to family life with a cool, patriarchal manager in charge of his self-indulgent, emotional, undirected charges. In the human relations model, "life at the top" is free from selfish self-interest, while relationships among office staff members are alive with petty alliances which are potentially destructive to organizational goals. This model is perhaps even more denigrating to women than the rational model of organizational life, since office workers in clerical positions are typically female and managers male.

An adequate model of organizational life must incorporate an understanding of organizations as complex and differentiated by the positions and responsibilities held by organizational members. This portrayal acknowledges the central importance to careers in organizations of power and politics and the applied social skills these require for negotiation. By virtue of holding membership in work units carrying out different tasks, individuals belong to competing reference groups. These groups command differential patterns of allegiance from members in the same organization. Alliances form across task groups according to positions held within each division. Thus, interest groups of clerical workers and middle managers, for example, form across task structures in the same organization.

In Kanter's structuralist model, rather than seeing relationships forming on the basis of social interests and activities as in the human relations model, relationships are considered to stem from political considerations. Thus, within large organizations, membership in several groups is quite likely, and membership is keyed to the perceived political power and advantage inherent in allegiance to the group. Also, individuals, much like community residents, may be governed by "local" interests as opposed to a "national" orientation. In other words, membership in professional groups outside the organization or identification with a career line extending beyond the immediate work setting may temper a worker's organizational affiliation.

The structuralist view of organizational life is a useful model for understanding patterns of interactions that inhibit or encourage the acquisition of organizational power by allied individuals. This perspective allows examination of variable complexity in patterns of social interaction within and between status groups. A far more accurate picture than is currently available regarding day-to-day experience in work settings would flow from studies of group processes. These studies, it should be emphasized, would be centrally focused upon power and related issues of informal organizational rules and roles, a far different emphasis than the characteristic view of everyday experience in work settings taken by the human relations studies. For example, there are countless organizational domains and systems of interaction that have never been given consideration. As we suggested earlier, we do not understand the dynamics of how (female) members of the typing pool negotiate power issues among group members (much less what those issues are!), or how (male) managers allocate resources such as office space or secretarial support. Examining these and other similar issues would provide a clearer understanding (and validation) of the skills assumed to reside in the performance of the clerical as opposed to the managerial role with its supposed emphasis on supervising, negotiating, and mentoring.

Social Skill Demands in Occupations

Although a chief empirical concern in this chapter is with anticipatory socialization to the managerial role in children's games, we will pause to review a recent, highly relevant study of skill demands in characteristically male and female jobs.

England, Chassie, and McCormack (1982) used regression analysis to determine how much of the sex-earnings gap is explained by the net effect of occupational sex composition (e.g., predominant numbers of job holders of a single gender) as opposed to skills requirements for 378 occupations employing 77% of the labor force in 1970. Measures of cognitive, manual, perceptual, and social skill requirements, in addition to educational and on-the-job training requirements, were taken from the *Dictionary of Occupational Titles (DOT)* descriptors. We will only consider variation in the social skill and training requirements here. Social skills were dimensionalized, in accordance with the *DOT* descriptors, as (a) no significant relationship to people; (b) serving, speaking, or signaling; (c) persuading, diverting, or supervising; (d) instructing; (e) negotiation; and (f) mentoring.

In an initial, descriptive analysis, England et al. determined that men disproportionately held jobs at both extremes of the social skills continuum, corresponding to their greater participation in blue collar jobs on the one hand and managerial jobs on the other. Women were disproportionately located in occupations demanding social skills of the middle range (serving, speaking, or signaling; instructing). The one exception to this general trend was the higher involvement of men in jobs demanding skill in persuading, diverting, or supervising, skills falling between the female-dominated skill categories. In summarizing the relationship, England et al. (1982) note:

> The sporadic nonlinearity of the relationship between social skills and occupational sex composition suggests that social skills comprise two separate dimensions, power wielding and nurturing, each of which varies in complexity. Women's jobs often entail serving, teaching, or counseling; these tasks vary in complexity but have in common a nurturant stance. Male jobs which entail social skills often involve supervising, persuading (as in commission sales or law) or managing; these tasks also vary in complexity but have in common the wielding of power. (p. 158)

Thus, women cluster in occupations with relatively high social skill demands in nurturance, but low demands in power. In contrast, men's jobs are considerably variable in social skill requirements; however, male occupations with social skills requirements are uniformly high in power.

In the subsequent regressions, analyses were run separately by sex to assess the net effect of occupational sex composition and skill requirements on earnings. The skill measures and sex composition of the 378 occupations were independent variables in each analysis with the 378 occupations serving as cases. Each occupation in the equation was weighted separately for men and women by dividing the number of members in a particular occupation for each sex in all occupations. Also, analyses were carried out for median annual earnings of full-time workers to avoid attributing the greater tendency of women to be employed part time to the occupation's general sex composition effects.

The impact of occupational sex composition on earnings was judged as apparent only if both men and women had lower earnings when employed in predominantly female occupations (England et al., 1982, p. 159). Social skill was dimensionalized as power wielding and nurturance. To avoid a perfect linear dependency among all dimensions of social skill, a series of dummy variables comprising the social skill domain were entered into the equations with the lowest category (no relationship to people) suppressed.

Women pay a heavy price for holding positions in predominantly female occupational categories. The earnings gap overall between the salaries of men and women was $4,089 in 1980. Indications are that this disparity was widened (*U.S. Bureau of the Census*, 1981, p. 687). In 1980, the median weekly earnings for men was $332, for women $204. Based on these figures, the median yearly earnings for men was $6,136 more than the median yearly earnings for women in 1980. The most striking finding of the analyses performed by England et al. is that occupational sex composition explains four times as much of the variation in salaries as either of the other sets of job-related factors (discussed below) contributing to the sex earnings gap. This central finding cannot be overlooked in our discussion of this study, since it underscores the general male bias in the occupational reward structure—in this case earnings—that has been described throughout this chapter. It is critical for our purposes to note that of all the skill groups, including manual, perceptual, cognitive, and social variables in addition to education and training factors, only two variables demonstrated an effect on the earnings gap. The first is the set of training skills learned following formal education: differences in on-the-job training account for $291 of the annual sex-earnings gap. Favorable on-the-job training opportunities for men have long been noted and in this study account for approximately 7% of the observed differences in wages. The second set of factors comprises differences in social skills demanded by characteristically male and female jobs. Here, skills in negotiating, persuading, mentoring, etc., associated with male jobs are more lucrative than female skills in nurturance. In fact, the skills explain almost 8% of the variation in pay.

The researchers conclude their discussion of findings in this study by noting that there is no consistent, linear relationship between occupational skill demands and occupational sex composition. Rather, "women's occupations offer less remuneration because of their sex composition" (England et al, 1982, p. 164). Since on-the-job training experience and social skills are the only job-related factors that explain any of the variance in wages, the question of "*how sex role socialization affects what kinds of skills are thought appropriate for males and females to practice*" becomes the central issue (England et al, 1982, p. 164, emphasis added). In other words, we need to learn the ways in which men are encouraged to develop skills that win them power, while women are encouraged to pursue experiences that develop social skills in nurturance. These related issues are important because of the clear relationships between social skills, occupational sex composition, and salary.

WORLD OF CHILDREN'S PLAY

Learning Power, Rules, and Roles in Games

As we suggested earlier, children's spontaneously organized play activities and, particularly, competitive play in complex games, allows the rehearsal of complex social skills related to future performance in managerial roles. With few exceptions, girls are systematically excluded from these games and, by extension, from important experiences in manipulating power, rules, and roles.

Before we begin a discussion of social interactions and negotiations in children's playground games, we wish to offer an important caveat. We are by no means suggesting that developing skills in power negotiating is somehow "better" than learning skills in nurturance. In fact, we are in fundamental agreement with Gilligan (1982) and others, who argue that women's moral development typically takes a substantively different course than men's. In contemporary Western societies, women's moral development emphasizes the significance in ethical problem-solving of conflicting responsibilities as opposed to the emphasis in men's moral development on competing individual rights. The argument instead is that a male bias persists in U.S. society such that power, competitiveness, and rational planning are rewarded, and nurturance, cooperation, and intimacy are devalued throughout the life cycle. This pattern of societal "reinforcement" of one set of values and behaviors over another severely penalizes women, as we have seen.

Further, we are arguing that social learning in childhood, particularly in games, much like on-the-job training in adulthood, has important outcomes in allowing access to privileged occupational positions. Here, it is important to recognize that experience gained in informal learning modifies and structures the individual's world view. Cross-cultural studies suggest that regular, recurrent experience in abstract problem-solving tasks systematically organizes cognitive structures which mediate subsequent approaches to problem solving in similar contexts (Cole & Means, 1981). We argue that the same principle applies to social problem-solving contexts and that complex games are social problem solving milieus *par excellence*.

There are several factors that common sense suggests as likely to contribute to the more frequent involvement by boys in complex, competitive games. First, traditional patterns of sex-role socialization exert pressure to compete (as opposed to nurture). As toddlers, boys are provided with toys and play equipment that emphasize active engagement and manipulation of things (Fagot, 1974).

Other external factors contribute to different roles of involvement in complex games. The physical resources of the playground (e.g., the condition of available equipment) were found in a pertinent study to be related to the socioeconomic background of students attending the school (Borman et al., 1981). Thus, we might expect that affluent students attending well-provisioned schools would be more likely to have the space and equipment to organize a soccer or baseball game than less advantaged students attending other schools.

Still other factors might contribute to differential rates of participation in complex games. Social intelligence has been linked to performance in jobs, as we have seen. Social intelligence as a construct has generally been considered to consist of two component parts: "The ability to understand and manage men and women, boys and girls—to act wisely in human relations'' (E.L. Thorndike, 1920, as quoted in Walker & Foley, 1973, p. 840). The recent emphasis in defining job-related social skills has clearly been on the applications of social intelligence in *both* nurturing *and* managing others. This emphasis is clear in the *DOT* descriptors mentioned earlier. However, in its application to the world of work, the earliest emphasis was upon social intelligence as it defined the managerial role. As Walker and Foley point out, the use of the term "social intelligence" by the Bureau of Public Personnel Administration in 1930, though explicitly referencing Thorndike, "narrows social intelligence to managerial leadership", as is clear in the following:

> The essential thing is that the person having a high degree of social intelligence is able to get others consistently and voluntarily to do the things he [sic] wants them to do and even like doing so, while the person without considerable social intelligence cannot consistently bring about such results. (Bureau of Public Personnel Administration, 1930, quoted in Walker & Foley, 1973, p. 846)

As is clear in the above passage, the component of *social understanding* present in Thorndike's conceptualization is lost in a pragmatic and male-biased view of social intelligence as equated with social power-in-action.

It is beyond the scope of this discussion to examine the several factors of the social intelligence construct that have more recently become of interest to social psychologists and developmentalists (see Walker & Foley, 1973, for a review). However, it is important to note that several domains comprise the general construct of social intelligence: (a) what the other sees (visual/spatial or perceptual); (b) what the other feels (affective); and (c) what the other thinks (cognitive/communicative or conceptual) (Ford, 1979). It should also be emphasized that social intelligence mediates social behaviors observed in the adult, job-related skills of nurturance, mentoring and so forth, as well as in children's game-related behaviors—particularly their verbal negotiations of power, rules, and roles in highly complex games (Lever, 1978; Mathews, 1977; Rubin & Pepler, 1976). Thus, individuals with higher levels of social intelligence could be expected to participate more frequently in activities demanding these skills. In children, the expectation is that individuals with greater social intelligence will participate in more highly complex games.

Borman and her coworkers undertook a two-year study of informal interaction on school playgrounds among elementary school children in three diverse settings in the Cincinnati metropolitan area. The major purpose of the study was to investigate differences in reported and observed rates of participation in highly complex games during lunch time recess at the three schools. All children attending the three schools in the second and fifth grades during the first year of study were included in the initial playground log phase of the research. During this period, children kept a daily account of their major playground activity during recess. Logs were kept during a three-week period at the beginning of each year of research. A major purpose for collecting diary data in this fashion was to identify children who varied in rates of participation in playground activities, including highly complex games. A subgroup of children, representative of the two grades, three schools, and of both sexes, was subsequently selected for further, more detailed study, including participation in a series of individually administered tasks designed to measure social intelligence (specifically the social cognitive dimension, i.e., the ability to determine what another thinks in an ethically charged social dilemma).

Three aspects of the study concern us here. First are overall differences in participation in highly complex games; second is the pattern of association between sex and social interaction in playground games; and third is the effect of sex on the capacity to understand what another thinks in an ethically charged dilemma for the subgroup of children.

The overall finding of greater participation in highly complex games by boys is in keeping with the findings in other related research, notably Lever's earlier and methodologically similar work. Using cluster analysis, Borman and Sheoran (1981) initially analyzed all games and activities reported by children in their daily logs along the six dimensions of complexity identified by Lever and mentioned near the outset of this chapter. Games and activities fell along a continuum of three game clusters and a single activities cluster. Not surprisingly, the least complex pastimes according to Lever's typology are pursuits such as walking, talking, observing others, helping in the lunch room, and so on, which depend upon social skills in nurturance as opposed to skills in power brokering. The three game clusters correspond to games of low, middle, and high complexity. Games of low complexity include hopscotch, jumprope, tag, and tetherball; games of middle complexity include racquetball, kickball, and foursquare; finally, games of high complexity are softball, baseball, football, soccer, and basketball. Clearly, according to this typology which incorporates dimensions of organizational complexity, predominantly girls' games of hopscotch, tetherball, etc., offer less opportunity for rehearsal of power, rules, and roles than games typically played by boys. By the same token, boys have reduced opportunity for rehearsal of skills in nurturance than girls.

To determine the nature of the actual linkages between sex, school, age, and participation in more or less complex games and activities, a series of Chi Square analyses were composed. These results are reported in Tables 1, 2, and 3. These tables report results for all children (N = 370) included in the study during the second year's playground log phase.

As is evident in Table 1, girls are more likely than boys to participate with frequency in activities such as walking, talking, or lunch-room duty (the Nongame Category) and in games of low- and middle-complexity. A disproportionately large number of boys participate in games of high complexity in comparison to girls. Although both boys and girls report occasional involvement in uncharacteristic pasttimes, i.e., nongames and low-complexity games for boys and both low-complexity and high-complexity games for girls, they *most* often engage in stereotyped activities as reported in Table 1. Girls' play revolves around skills of nurturance and intimate interaction which characterize dyadic play in hopscotch, tetherball, and in conversational interaction (i.e., walking, talking, kibbitzing while others play). Boys' highly complex games require skills in negotiating, power brokering, and managing others in the context of team games which are highly competitive in nature.

Not only are boys more likely than girls to engage in highly complex games, but, as is clear in Table 2, the social context of the school exerts an influence upon activity selection for both boys and girls. As reported in Table 2, disproportionate numbers of children at School 2 participate in nongame activities. School 2 is characterized by a divided student body

Table 1
Percentages of Boys and Girls Participating in Nongames, Low-, Middle-, and High-Complexity Games

Complexity Categories	Boys	Girls
Nongames	9	28
Low-complexity games	4	7
Middle-complexity games	24	42
High-complexity games	63	23

*($X^2 = 63.21, p < .001$).

Table 2
Percentage of Children in Schools 1, 2, 3. Participating in Nongames, Low-, Middle-, and High-Complexity Games

Complexity Categories	School 1	School 2	School 3
Nongames	12	28	11
Low-complexity games	6	1	10
Middle-complexity games	22	26	46
High-complexity games	60	45	33

*($X^2 = 45., p < .001$).

since Black students, approximating 30% of the total school enrollment, are bused in from outside the local neighborhood. Poor Black students constitute an alienated minority in School 2 which is located in a white, lower-middle-class neighborhood in Cincinnati. In contrast, a disproportionate number of children at School 1 participate in games of high complexity, although School 1 is also a desegregated setting. However, School 1 is located in an integrated lower-middle-class suburban community recognized by the NAACP for its well managed program of districtwide school desegregation. Finally, a larger proportion of students than expected at School 3 participate in games, such as kickball, of middle complexity. Resources, or the lack of them, is at issue in School 3, attended by a large number (90%) of urban Appalachian students from low-income households. Unlike either Schools 1 or 2, School 3 does not have extensive playground facilities. Grounds are limited to a small, asphalt yard adjacent to the school building. Thus, to summarize results reported in Tables 1 and 2, there is a strong and predictable relationship between sex and complexity of play and between school and play complexity.

However, no such relationship is present for age as shown in Table 3. Although common sense might suggest that 6th grade children, by virtue of maturation and experience, participate in more complex games than 3rd grade children, results reported in Table 3 suggest that activities are fixed by age 9 in children's recreational repertoires. These results are consistent with research in recreation and sport that show little variation in the physical activities of children between ages 9 and 12 (Cratty, 1979).

Given the pattern of involvement in games just described, it is important to examine the consequences of participation in more or less complex game structures by girls and boys. A series of audiotaped transcripts were made of children's verbal interactions throughout the period of observed play during lunch-time recess. Children were randomly selected from among the subgroup of 3rd and 6th graders at the three schools. A

Table 3
Percentages of Grade 3 and Grade 6 Children Participating
in Nongames, Low-, Middle-, and High-Complexity Games

Complexity Categories	Grade 3 Children	Grade 6 Children
Nongames	20	17
Low-complexity games	5	6
Middle-complexity games	37	28
Low-complexity games	38	49

$^*X^2 = 5.3, p = $ ns

single child on a particular occasion of lunch-time recess was thus selected for observation. A repeated measures analysis was used to determine variation in time spent preceding, negotiating, and playing the observed and recorded games. Analyses were made separately for observed cases ($N = 8$) of kickball, a boys' game, and hopscotch ($N = 3$), a girls' game. It is interesting to note that *all* boys whose game play was observed and recorded during this phase of the research spontaneously joined kickball games. This included both younger and older boys at each of the three schools. By the same token, three girls played hopscotch while other recorded activities for observed girls included jumprope, tag, racquetball, four square, softball, and tetherball. In other words, while all observed boys played games of high complexity, i.e., kickball, observed girls elected to play a wide variety of games on the complexity continuum.

On data for kickball players, the repeated measures analysis for the three different time periods yielded a statistically significant main effect for time and a significant two-way interaction for time × players as reported in Table 4. Children at School 3 took less time to negotiate play in kickball than children at either School 1 or School 2, while children at School 2 were generally less quick to enter either negotiations or game play. Children at School 1 spent less time finding a game and spent more time both negotiating and playing kickball than their counterparts at the two other schools. The general trend at all three schools was for kickball players to spend more time in the game itself than in activity preceding or organizing the game.

For hopscotch play, as reported in Table 5, a repeated measures analysis similar to the analysis reported for kickball in Table 4 yielded no significant main effects or two-way interaction for time × players. Figure 1 clarifies the two sets of findings for kickball and hopscotch just reported. The marked contrast is in time spent in game play itself. Kickball players spend four times the amount of time involved in their play than hopscotch players, all of them girls. Moreover, organizing play and negotiating rules, positions and so forth is also a lengthier process in kickball game preli-

Table 4
Repeated Measures Analysis for Kickball Players' Time Spent Preceding Game, Negotiating Game and Playing Game

Source of Variation	SS	MS	df	F	P
Players	655991.97		7		
Time	2102829.1	1051515.6	2	13.76	<.01
2-Way Interaction					
Time x players	1069488.2	76392.014	2.14	13.76	<.01

Table 5
**Repeated Measures Analysis for Hopscotch Player's Time Spent Preceding Game,
Negotiating Game and Playing Game**

Source of Variation	SS	MS	F		P
Main Effects					
Players	13662.82				
Time	53280.223	26640.112	2	4.778	n.s.
2-Way Interaction					
Time x Players	22301.777	5575.44	2.4	4.778	n.s.

minaries. Kickball players take ten times as long as girls in hopscotch to sort through these matters before play begins.

Kickball typically involves a large number of players possessing varying levels of athletic skill and thus requires a lengthier process to set things in order than in organizing hopscotch. Since two players are the usual number in hopscotch, there is really very little to organize in the game, except to establish the order of turntaking. This process was often done nonverbally, as in the case of a 3rd grade girl at School 2 who walks toward the hopscotch grid with a friend with whom she had been eating lunch three minutes earlier. Her companion says, "Let's play hopscotch," and the focal child replies, "Okay." They pause briefly to pick up flat stones to use as markers in the game. As they approach the grid, the girl who had suggested the game takes her position and initiates play by throwing her marker. Consensus on turntaking is accomplished without a word of negotiation! A tacit understanding appears to exist between the players, such that the individual who suggests the game is allowed the first turn.

In contrast, boys' negotiations reflect a profound interest in power relationships and the establishment in the social order of the game of a relatively equal balance of power based upon athletic ability. Entry into the game is predicated upon the capacity to perform. Approaching a 6th-grade boy at School 1 who is choosing team members, a boy asks, "Can I play?" The response is "Can you run?" Later, a boy urges, "Get Emerson! Get Emerson! He can kick far." When an "unfair" distribution of skill is perceived by a player, and particularly when the balance of power favors the opposition, the player is likely to threaten to quit, as did Eddie, a focal player at School 1.

When the game is about to begin, the division of roles is negotiated: Unknown boy: "Curt, play third. Mark, you got first? I got short stop." The lengthiest negotiations centered upon the kicking order. Moreover,

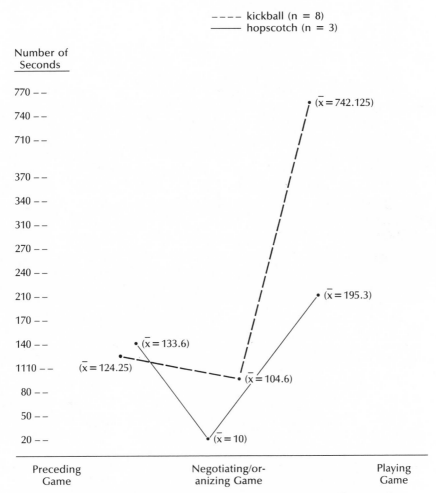

Figure 1. Profile of mean number of seconds for kickball and hopscotch players' time spent preceding game, negotiating game and playing game.

an order established at the outset of the game would likely be revamped
later by players jostling each other in line:

(   ):   I'm after Kerry.
Mike: Ah, I'm after ((   )).
Unknown boy: You're third and he's fourth.
Unknown boy: Mike . . . then Mike 'n' then me.
Unknown boy: No. You're after Mike, 'n' Stay's after Deacon 'n' . . .

(Transcript made at School 1, April, 1980.)

Even though roles and power relationships are explicitly discussed
in the manner illustrated, rules are only obliquely stated and generally
with reference to a specific player action. For example, a member of the
defense warns a runner, "No leadin' off at all. Not a inch! Not even a
centimeter!" During pregame negotiations, children typically did not either
review among themselves an established code of rules or argue about
playing according to one or another set. Instead, once player roles had
been established, game play is initiated without mention of rules governing
play. Rules may be consensually established by kickball players who, by
spring, are seasoned colleagues. Rules become problematic and are discussed only when the continuity of the game is threatened. The analyses
just reported suggest that interaction varies for boys and girls engaged in
establishing game structures. Kickball players not only spend more time
in negotiating positions and game organization beforehand than hopscotch
players but also in playing the game. While girls rely upon a consensual,
often nonverbally expressed agreement, boys appear to relish the give
and take of a lengthy process of negotiation for rights and privileges.

To determine whether the more complex game structures characteristic of boys' games entailed an expression of greater social cognitive ability
compared to girls, an analysis of variance (ANOVA) was calculated for
scores obtained in a series of individually administered moral dilemmas.
Girls' mean scores were slightly higher than boys' on this measure (girls'
$X = 25.22$; boys' $X = 24.71$). There was no effect for sex on scores ($F
= 0.06$; $df = 1$, n.s.) This finding suggests that factors other than social
intelligence underlie the greater tendency of boys to negotiate power, rules,
and roles in complex games.

We argue instead that the characteristics of game structures exert
differential demands for "applied" social intelligence. Boys' games emphasize social power-in-action closely identified with the managerial role,
while girls' games emphasize intimacy and solidarity congruent with the
nurturant role. Furthermore, since there are no significant gender effects

upon social cognitive abilities, it cannot be presumed that boys take up more complex games because they possess more measured social intelligence than girls. Thus, as they are currently played on most school playgrounds, games provide differential access to learning power, rules and roles, the hallmarks of managerial practice. And it is quite clear that boys are the ones exercising these skills.

The question might then be asked: Why don't girls exercise these skills? It is clear in the case of girls who play boys' games—they do, once allowed to participate! Some girls are allowed in the game with the male gatekeeper's permission, as seen by the behavior of Michelle, a 3rd-grader in School 3, who walks right into a boys' kickball game without any resistance from the male players. The transcript records her entry:

Michelle: (while walking toward the diamond)
            "Hey," ((Curtis)). 2 seconds.
Michelle: #"Can I play?" (2 seconds) "Can I play?"
Curtis: "OK, you're after us."
            #She ((   )) him.
Michelle: (to a player) "Be after you . . ."

Girls like Michelle, who "pass inspection" and are permitted access to the game are particularly aggressive, charismatic, and frequently display comic skills. They also possess two constitutional factors, competency and high energy levels. These attributes are similar to the applied social skills and credentialing characteristics identified by Kanter as consistent with successful performance by women in managerial roles (Kanter & Stein, 1979).

Figure 2 provides examples of strategies successful players use on the playground (Borman et al., 1982) and in the workplace (Kanter & Stein, 1979). While the examples in Fig. 2 show that some girls and some women can gain entry into the playfield and into the workplace, not all, even those with notable skills, can force their way into male-dominated games and jobs. Powerful norms and stereotypes function as a barrier to their easy access.

CONCLUSION

In summarizing the parallel course of occupational and playground experiences for females, we wish to conclude by highlighting the structural constraints we have addressed in this chapter that restrict the full participation by women in games and in work. First, gatekeeping in both contexts keeps most, but not all, the women out. In order for a woman to get into

Figure 2. Examples of parallel strategies used by successful players on the playground and in the workplace.

Strategy

Examples from the playground	Examples from the workplace
(a) Aggressiveness	
L: (black female) Want to play French? (jump rope)	"I learned when I'm demanding, I get equal time". p. 150
Little black boy: I go with you. (said in a taunting voice)	"I always did what I wanted, despite my parents' restrictions." p. 136
SF: (black female) Uh, uh. (assertively)	
L: Want to play French?	
SF: Yeah, you want to play French?	
(b) Self-Confidence	
Alesia: (a successful girl player in boys' games) I'm only wonderful, I didn't say how far.	"I'm a goddam good lawyer," he says.
	"I'm a very capable guy—this company is lucky to have me." p. 169
(c) Charisma	
SF: (an attractive girl whose classmates seek her attention) Kids are always following me. All the time. Every time I turn around, that kid is following me, messin' with me.	And there is ample evidence, (Stein 1976; Silverman & Jones 1971) that decisions about who will move in or move up are often made on the basis of social characteristics and personal acceptance rather than any direct measure of competence in the position or the job. pp. 86–87
(d) Humor	
MW: He's OUT! HE'S OUT YAAY . . .	"Guts and sense of humor" are the capacities one woman stresses—"I develop my ability to see the funny side of situations, and I wait for men to get over their problems." p. 136
(( )): (Objecting to out call)	
MW: HE'S OUT!	
(( )): (No, he's not.)	
MW: HE'S . . . OUT.	
(Scott Abernathy runs out to argue)	
(White girl): You wanna fight about it?	
Scott: Yeah.	
(White girl): Go join the Army!	

(e) Energy

(Angie guards the perimeters of a jump rope game by chasing marauding boys away)

Angie: Uh, uh!! (Angie continues to run and run, stops and watches—10 seconds elapse)

Girl: (jumping rope and chanting) 1, 2, 3, 4, 5, 6, 7, 8, 9, 10, 11, 12, 13, 14, 15, 16, 17, 18, 19, 20, 21, 22, 23, 24, 25, 26, 27, 28, 29, 30, 31.

(Boy runs into game and yells Pow! Wow!)

(Game is disrupted for a second or 2).

Girl: (continues to count) 32, 33, 34, 35, 36.

(2 boys near the jump rope interrupt game again.)

Angie: Let go of the rope, I said.

N: Okay

(Angie runs after the boys who hassle for 12 seconds)

N: One more

(More running by Angie)

Despite their own successes and ability to cope, a few of the women stressed the extra energy that it took to deal with many of the situations they faced because they were women. "It's not that I can't make it okay", one said. "It's just that there are so many more things I have to deal with than a man does." p. 137

(f) General Competence

JM: Hey wait a minute, Michelle.

(she kicks it anyway, but waits, momentarily).

((   )) Run! (she does, winds up on 1st).

MK: (chuckles to self) (to the kicker at the plate) READY THOMAS?

(12 seconds pass while MK waits on 1st. There is talk back at homeplate but none of it picked up by MK who is well out of earshot. MK takes off on Thomas's good kick, pauses 2 seconds at second base, runs home and is welcomed.)

Competence, and particularly knowledge of the company and the procedure, is by far the most important factor in the effectiveness of women as well as men. There is no substitute for competence. p. 136

Key to figure:

(   ) = information obtained from field notes

((   )) = speaker unidentified

Capitals = shouted words

the field, play or work, she must be a very special person—charismatic, aggressive, self-assured, witty, energetic, and extremely competent. Men, on the other hand, often enter the ranks as players without displaying these extraordinary skills and characteristics.

Second, women are not socialized to value and to learn the rules one needs to know to play complex male games on the play or work field. In fact, quite the opposite. They are discouraged from integrating this information into their personalities, subtly and not so subtly by sex-role stereotyping and outright rejection and negative reinforcement. Their drive to achieve has been so balanced or overshadowed by their highly developed need to nurture that this development has lessened their chances for successfully competing with men who are driven by finely honed achievement motives matched by strategies for meeting their singleminded needs.

The third and strongest point in support of our thesis is that the structure of children's games and the structure of the workplace are themselves designed to mediate against women. Even where men and women perform equally in some objective sense, we have shown that the playfield and the workplace are so constructed that male and female performances are perceived differently to the detriment of women.

We believe that the first step toward rectifying the disparity between male and female success on the playground or workplace is to recognize once and for all, without hedging and excuses, that the source of the problem lies not with the structure of the women themselves but with the structure of games and work.

REFERENCES

Borman, K.M., Barrett, D., & Sheoran, P. Negotiating Playground Games. Paper presented at American Sociological Association Annual Meeting, San Francisco, CA, September 1982.

Borman, K. & Sheoran, P. Analyzing children's games using cluster analysis. Paper presented at American Educational Research Association Annual Meeting, Los Angeles, CA, April 1981.

Cole, M., & Means, B. *Comparative studies of how people think*. Cambridge, MA: Harvard University Press, 1981.

Cratty, B.J. *Perceptual and motor development in infants and children,* 2nd edition. Englewood Cliffs, NJ: Prentice-Hall, 1979.

England, P., Chassie, M., & McCormack, L. Skill demands and earnings in female and male occupations. *Sociology on Social Research,* 1982, *66,* No. 2, 147–167.

Fagot, B.I. Sex-related stereotyping of toddlers' behavior and parental reaction. *Developmental Psychology,* 1974, *10,* 554–558.

Ford, M. The construct validity of egocentrism. *Psychological Bulletin,* 1979, *86,* No. 1, 1169–1188.

Gilligan, C. *In a different voice*. Cambridge, MA.: Harvard University Press, 1982.

Kanter, R.M. Women and the structure of organizations: explorations in theory and behavior. In R.M. Kanter & M. Millman, (Eds.), *Another voice*. New York: Anchor Press, 1975.

Kanter, R.M., & Stein, B.A. *Life in organizations*. New York: Basic Books, 1979.

Lever, J. Sex differences in the complexity of childrens' play. *American Sociological Review*. 1978, *43*, 471–483.

Mathews, W.S. Sex role perception, portrayal and preference in Biennial Conference of the Society for Research in Child Development. New Orleans, LA, March 1977.

Miller, J., Labovitz, S., & Fry, L. Inequities in the organizational experiences of women and men. *Social Forces, 1975, 54*, 365–381.

Nieva, V.F., & Gutek, B.A. *Women and work*. New York: Praeger, 1981.

Nieva, V.F., & Gutek, B.A.   Six effects in evaluation. *Academy of Management Review, 1980, 5*, 267–276.

Rubin, K.H. & Pepler, D.J. The relationships of social play preference to role taking skills in pre-school children. *Psychological Reports*. 1976, *39*, 823–826.

Suter, L.E. & Miller, H.P. Income differences between men and career women. *American Journal of Sociology*. 1973, *78*, 962–974.

U.S. Bureau of the Census. *Statistical Abstracts of the United States: 1981* (102nd edition). Washington, DC, 1981.

U.S. Department of Labor. *Dictionary of Occupational Titles* Fourth Edition. Washington, DC, 1977.

Walker, R.E. & Foley, J.M. Social itelligence: Its history and measurement. *Psychological Reports*. 1973, *33*, 839–864.

Young, A.M. Labor market experience of recent college graduates. *Monthly Labor Review, 1974, 97*, No. 10, 33–40.

II
WORK AND HOUSEWORK

Chapter 5
Men, Women, Work, and Family

Jeylan T. Mortimer

Department of Sociology
University of Minnesota

Glorian Sorensen

School of Public Health
University of Minnesota

During the past several decades, there have been major structural changes in the family. Declining fertility, rising divorce rates, and the increasing prevalence of the single-parent family have accompanied the rapid influx of married women into the labor force. These concurrent changes have focused public attention on the interrelations of work and the family. The increasing concern with these linkages is manifest in the growing number of corporate task forces and surveys, conferences, and articles in the popular media. The growth of scholarly literature has clearly demolished the "myth of separate worlds" (Kanter 1977a). It is now well recognized that work and the family are linked together and dependent upon one another in numerous ways, despite their institutional separation. Moreover, there is substantial evidence that their relationship is highly reciprocal; work not only influences family life, but the family also influences behavior in the work place. While some of these effects are contemporaneous, for example, events in the workplace often have more or less immediate impacts on the family; others, like the effects of vocational socialization in the family, may be lagged over long periods of time.

Recently, scholars have become increasingly critical of the manner in which work and family ties have been investigated (Spade, 1981). Bronfenbrenner and Crouter (1981), in their recent review of work and family research, have described the disparate assumptions underlying early work on the subject. Attention was focused on the deleterious consequences of unemployment for men's families and the detrimental implications of employment for women's families. Thus, for men, work was considered normal; a disruption in work likewise was expected to disrupt the family. But at a time when women were generally outside the labor force, investigators searched for evidence of negative consequences of employment, especially for children (Nye & Hoffman, 1963).

Such divergent assumptions, consistent with traditional sex role norms, persist in more recent work. Feldberg and Glenn (1979) speak of the "work model" for men and the "gender model" for women. When men are studied, attention is focused on the variations in their occupational experiences and the manner in which these experiences influence their lives off the job. But when women are studied, the mere fact of working assumes major importance. Moreover, family characteristics, not work attributes, often assume the status of independent variables, and their ramifications for women's occupational attainment, role conflict, etc., are examined. But now that a majority of married women, like men, are employed, there is considerable justification for a more balanced approach.

In this review, we attempt to apply the same conceptual framework to an examination of the linkages of work and family for men as well as for women. Whether the special circumstances of men or of women are the subject of attention, the impacts of work on family life can be divided into three general categories: work provides socioeconomic resources for the family; it sets time and spatial constraints on family members' activities, particularly the time in which they can be together; and finally, it influences the family through its effects on the attitudes, values, and personality of the working member. The impacts of the family on work can be subsumed in two categories: occupational socialization—the family prepares each new generation of workers; and implications for attainment—it can support or obstruct the occupational achievement of its members. In this chapter, we will first briefly review the nature of these mutual influences. We will then consider some of the literature on work and family, reviewing the findings of research on men and women. We will see that these studies, though differing in their particular concerns and frames of reference, converge in several respects and point to similar policy recommendations.

THE MUTUAL INTERRELATIONS OF WORK AND THE FAMILY

Of foremost importance, work provides social status for the family in the community and economic resources for consumption, thereby setting upper limits on its standard of living. Work also can give substantial opportunity for social mobility, as when the occupation is structured as a career. Alternatively, it may represent threats to economic security, as in many blue collar and service jobs when layoffs are frequent. Perceived opportunities and threats to economic well-being strongly influence family decision-making regarding the employment of its members (Ghez & Becker, 1975). When families perceive new occupational opportunities or when they are confronted with a disruption in ongoing resources, they must alter their activities and sometimes change their entire organization. The family might move to another geographical region where employment prospects are better; attempt to find additional jobs for the wage earner or earners—overtime work or moonlighting; or send additional earners into the labor force, most frequently wives, but sometimes also, adolescent children.

Second, work sets external constraints on family organization and activities. These constraints include the amount of time spent working and the scheduling of work. Working parents often complain that the demands of their work do not allow sufficient time with their children. The particular patterning of work time may also unduly interfere with, and disrupt, family functioning. In a recent nationwide survey, the issues surrounding work time and scheduling emerged as highly problematic for working parents (Quinn & Staines, 1979). Further constraints on the family are set by requirements for travel and geographic mobility. Though there is evidence that families are balking at some of these demands, such as frequent geographic moves, they often have little choice. They must either meet the requirements of the employer or seek a position elsewhere.

Third, work experiences influence the family by affecting the attitudes, values, and personality of the working member(s). There may be experiences in the workplace that cause dissatisfaction and stress for the worker, which the family must cope with when the worker returns home. In other cases, the work may be so demanding and involving that the worker has little energy left to become involved with other family members. There has been considerable scholarly debate over whether the responses of workers to their jobs are characterized by processes of segmentation and compensation, on the one hand, or generalization and spillover, on the other (Piotrkowski, 1978). According to the first hypothesis, workers segment their lives, blocking out thoughts of work when at home, or attempt to compensate for the dissatisfactions of work by seeking out stimulation and gratification in leisure or family activities. According to the second, the job's effects on the worker carry over to nonwork spheres. There appears to be far more evidence for the "generalization hypothesis" than for the segmentation or compensation model.

Let us now consider the effects of the family on work. In most past studies, the family has been viewed as accommodative to work, for only recently has change in the family begun to stimulate changes in work roles and organizational requirements. But the family makes vital contributions to the work place. It socializes each new generation of workers, instilling the most basic attitudes and values concerning the meaning of work (Mortimer, 1975, 1976), which influence vocational preferences and eventual occupational destinations (Mortimer & Kumka, 1982; Spenner, 1981). A large body of research has investigated the status attainment process, demonstrating the manner in which the family of origin influences the occupational destinations of its offspring (Featherman, 1980).

The family of procreation likewise influences the occupational attainments of its members. Family economic needs provide a major motivation for both men and women to seek employment and to be successful in the occupational career (Harris et al., 1981; Piotrkowski, 1978; Rubin, 1976; Sennett & Cobb, 1972). Researchers have directed considerable attention to the limitations to women's occupational attainment associated with marriage and fertility (Card, Steel, & Abeles, 1980; Havens, 1973; Sewell, Hauser, & Wolf, 1980). At the same time, there is consistent evidence that married men have higher socioeconomic attainment than unmarried men (Abeles, Steel, & Wise, 1980; Duncan, Featherman, & Duncan, 1972; Mortimer, Lorence, & Kumka, 1982). Thus, there is evidence that families generally impede women's careers, but support the careers of men.

Findings from a recent panel study, conducted by Mortimer and her colleagues, are used in this chapter to illustrate the linkages of work and family for professional and managerial men. They followed up, ten years after graduation, men who had previously participated in an extensive University of Michigan study of the influences of college life. Eighty-eight percent of the seniors in the original study were successfully located, and 84% of these were persuaded to return a mailed questionnaire, yielding a panel of 512 men. The questionnaire assessed their education and work histories, current work experiences, the psychological attributes that had been measured earlier, and information about their family lives. This study will henceforth be referred to as the "Michigan Panel Study." (For further information about the design and findings of this research, see Mortimer and Lorence, 1979a, 1979b; Mortimer, 1980; Mortimer and Kumka, 1982.)

Since this study refers to a rather socioeconomically advantaged stratum of the population, we also will consider a broad range of literature. It must be recognized that the particular character of the linkages of work and family vary tremendously.[1] Important structural dimensions of both work and family provide quite different contexts for their interrelationships. First, the special demands of professional and managerial occupations, in contrast to those of lower white-collar and blue-collar work,

---

[1] The variation in the linkages of work and the family is fully explored in Mortimer and London (1984). The present chapter draws heavily on this earlier work.

pose very different external constraints on the family, and generate different dynamics of work–family interface. Second, one must consider the features of the family. Is there only one, or are there two working members? Is there only one, or are there two parents? Because these work and family characteristics set different work opportunities and demands, as well as different family needs and resources (Moen, 1982), they are of major importance in considering work–family linkages for men and women.

EFFECTS OF WORK ON THE FAMILY

The Provision of Socioeconomic Resources

Much of the research focused on the work and family linkages of men has been developed in the context of the traditional, single-provider family. Though single-provider families are a diminishing minority, constituting approximately one third of husband–wife families (Aldous, 1981), it is important to understand the linkages of work and family in this context. Because in previous generations single-provider families were the majority, work often continues to be structured as if this traditional family type were the most prevalent. Requirements of work, particularly at high socioeconomic levels, seem most compatible with the single provider structure. The study of single-provider families illuminates the stresses of the homemaker role, and shows that the husband's occupational role can structure the wife's family role as well.

According to the exchange model of family dynamics (Scanzoni, 1970; 1972), the husband in the traditional single-provider family provides economic support to the wife in exchange for her household duties, child care, companionship, and support. In general, as the husband's occupational prestige and income increase, marital satisfaction and stability likewise increase, as does the husband's power and legitimacy as the family head (Scanzoni, 1970). But at the highest status levels, demands on the family may to a large extent offset high occupational rewards (Aldous, Osmond, & Hicks, 1979; Dizard, 1968; Young & Willmott, 1973). Professional and managerial families often face the unique pressures of the career, a vertically structured sequence of positions through which individuals expect to move (Wilensky, 1960). The Michigan Panel Study supports Aldous's "success constraint theory" (see Aldous et al., 1979) that the husband's occupational attainment may have costs as well as benefits for the family. The more successful of the married men reported greater strains in their families caused by work, strains caused by long working hours, fatigue, preoccupation with problems at the office, extensive travel, and residential moves (Mortimer, 1980).

At the other end of the socioeconomic spectrum, in blue-collar jobs, rarely is there a vertical career line. Young blue-collar men have rather unstable work histories. They move from job to job in search of higher wages and better working conditions (Rubin, 1976). But by midlife, most blue-collar men become "locked in" to their jobs, unable to improve their working conditions and rewards by changing employers. Such mobility may threaten seniority, retirement, and other benefits, constituting a substantial risk to the family. As a result, blue-collar men (and their families) are often stuck in dead-end jobs. Unlike men of professional or managerial status, their incomes do not grow at a pace commensurate with increasing family economic needs. Their "life cycle squeeze" (Oppenheimer, 1974) at midlife is a factor which may propel their wives into the labor force.

Moreover, blue-collar men and their families often live with a fear of cutbacks in their hours, reduction of overtime pay, and layoffs. Many of these men have little security in their jobs due to the fluctuations in the economy. Numerous studies have documented the deleterious consequences of marginal employment and unemployment for the family (Elder, 1974; Rubin, 1976; Schorr & Moen, 1979; Sennett & Cobb, 1972; Steinmetz & Straus, 1974).

The growing prevalence of women's employment outside the home has increased family resources and reduced the costs for families when unemployment strikes the male breadwinner. Indeed, the dual-work family is becoming the dominant pattern of family life. In 1900, only 18% of all women over 14 years of age were employed, most of whom were unmarried (Smith, 1979). By 1980, the labor force included 51% of married women with husbands present (U.S. Dept. of Labor, 1980a). In March of that year, 57% of mothers of children under 18 were in the labor force, and almost half of mothers of children under 6.

However, despite this influx of women into the work force, the jobs women occupy and the salaries they earn have not radically changed. Overall, the income of women is about 59% that of men, a situation which has persisted over the past several decades. Over the course of their work careers, men more often move to positions of higher prestige, whereas women tend to remain at the same prestige level or decline (Rosenfeld, 1979; Sewell et al., 1980). Men's earnings also rise substantially more during their careers than do the earnings of women (Barrett, 1979). Moreover, in terms of their incomes, men benefit far more from their education and occupational prestige than do women (Featherman & Hauser, 1976).

In part, this occupational attainment and earnings gap reflects the sex-role socialization prevalent in our society. Young girls have envisioned their future roles as wives and mothers, deemphasizing their roles as workers. Their underestimation of their eventual labor force participation (as compared with the actual labor force experience of adult women) may limit their investments in education, training, and work experiences, placing them at a disadvantage in their adult work lives (Sexton, 1977). However, recent evidence suggests that young women increasingly are expecting to combine family and career responsibilities (Regan & Roland, 1982).

Sex-role socialization and differing human capital investments do not adequately account for the income gap between men and women, however. It has been estimated that if the educational and labor force experiences of husbands and wives were equalized, women would still earn only two-thirds of the income of men (Treiman & Terrell, 1975). On the basis of 1973 data, Featherman and Hauser (1976) estimated that 84% of the income gap between men and women was attributable to sex discrimination. The erroneous assumption that women are secondary earners, receiving superfluous income, is sometimes used to justify their income disadvantage. Such a perception overlooks the strong economic need forcing many women to work. In fact, two thirds of working women are single, divorced, widowed, or separated, or married to men with earnings less than $10,000 (National Commission on Working Women, 1982).

Clearly, the large difference in the incomes of men and women cannot be attributed to socialization and human capital investments alone. Rather, much of the income differential is linked to occupational segregation. In a segmented labor market, particular occupations are earmarked for women, generally positions offering little opportunity for advancement. Despite their high educational requirements, sex-typed female positions pay relatively little (Oppenheimer, 1975). This segmenting of the labor market that crowds women into relatively few positions has shown little change despite the influx of women into the labor force. According to Oppenheimer (1975), 14 out of 17 jobs that were 70% or more female in 1900 continued to be occupied predominantly by women in 1960. Unfortunately, the number of jobs in this female sector has not kept pace with the rising number of women seeking work (Barrett, 1979). The occupational crowding of women tends to reduce their wages and increase their unemployment.

The characteristics of "female jobs" coincide with traditional sex-typed traits (Oppenheimer, 1975). Women are viewed as supportive, nurturing and expressive, traits that mesh well with their stereotypic occupational roles. Women also are viewed as receiving their satisfaction vicariously, i.e., through the success of their male bosses, rather than directly (Kanter, 1977b). Women are seldom placed in positions of authority, unless they supervise other women. Lacking a vertical career line and geographic mobility requirements, these female occupations are consistent with demands of husbands' careers (Mortimer, Hall, & Hill, 1978). When women attempt to enter traditionally male positions, they frequently face sexual harassment and a tightly knit male buddy system (Barrett, 1979).

This segregation of the labor market is perpetuated by "statistical discrimination'': employers assess individual job applicants on the basis of their categorical membership (Stevenson, 1978). The assumption that women are unstable workers thus becomes a self-fulfilling prophecy. Due to employers' expectations, women are placed in dead-end positions offering little opportunity for training and advancement. However, both men and women workers in such low level jobs have relatively low commitment to the employing organization and manifest high rates of absenteeism and turnover (Kanter, 1977b). The concentration of women in these kinds of positions thus reinforces their image as unstable workers.

Women's relatively low earning power has important implications for their families. Employed married women do enhance their families' economic resources, contributing, on the average, about one fourth of family income, and 40%, if employed full time (Hayghe 1979). But according to the resource theory of family dynamics, power in the family increases directly with economic contributions (Scanzoni, 1972, 1979). Women's relatively low economic contributions and their consequent dependence on their husbands decreases their power, and may put them in a relatively poor bargaining position with regard to negotiations over household work, child care, family geographic moves in response to employment opportunities, working hours, and so forth. Hence, women are caught in a vicious circle. Their economic contributions to the family do not provide them with a sufficient resource base to alter their traditional responsibilities, and this very subordination to the demands of their families and their husbands' careers perpetuates their economic disadvantage. Furthermore, as long as women are restricted to low paying jobs in the segmented labor market, the restriction of their occupational careers is the most economically rational course for their families to pursue.

A major consequence of occupational segregation is the profound economic difficulties faced by many women, especially single mothers (Kamerman, 1980). About one third of female-headed families in the United States are poor, that is, below the government's poverty standard (U.S. Commission on Civil Rights, 1982: 22). Although women continue to be treated as secondary workers in the labor force, the courts have begun to consider them capable of supporting themselves and their children without the assistance of ex-husbands. Thus, in 1978, only 60% of divorced mothers were awarded child support, and only half of those received the full amount they were due (U.S. Census Bureau, 1981).

The External Constraints Which Work Poses for the Family

The demands of work certainly limit the time workers can spend with their families. In professional and managerial occupations, there are often heavy time commitments which draw the husband away from the family, placing the major burden of family responsibility upon the wife (Bailyn, 1971; Pahl & Pahl, 1971; Young & Willmott, 1973). Since careers are generally quite demanding and open-ended in their requirements, particularly in the early phases, the career aspirant may feel that work is never finished. It is not uncommon for young professionals and managers to have 60-hour-or-longer work weeks, with little time for the family even in the evenings and on weekends. In such circumstances, the wife becomes, in effect, a single parent. In the Michigan Panel Study, work time emerged as a major constraint on family life. When the men were asked, "Have any of the following requirements of your work caused disruption or strain in your family life?", 59% reported "long hours, the need to work at night or on weekends." Increasing hours at work and time pressure on the job were associated with greater perception of family strain. Kanter (1977b) and Machlowitz (1980) have also described strains in the family surrounding the long working hours of highly successful men.

A common solution to the economic problems of blue collar families is for the husband to work overtime or to take a second job, either of which results in the husband–father being less physically and emotionally available to other family members (Piotrkowski, 1978; Sennett & Cobb, 1972). Another possible solution is for the wife–mother to enter the labor market. But this increasingly prevalent mode of coping violates traditional sex-role expectations—the husband as economic provider and the wife as mother–homemaker—which are central to conceptions of the "good life" in the working class (Komarovsky, 1972; Rainwater, 1971; Rubin, 1976).

Piotrkowski (1978), in her study of the work and family interface of blue collar, mainly single-provider families, describes the difficulties families experience in bridging the spatial boundaries of work. She points out that the ease of communicating with working members on the job varies directly with their position in the hierarchy of the organization. The wives in her study often experienced difficulty in crossing the work–family boundary—even in emergencies, they were sometimes unable to contact their husbands.

Thus, husbands' long work hours generally place major responsibility for household and child care upon the wife. Because of the assymetrical sex-role norms applying to men and women (Pleck, 1977), men are permitted to disrupt their families as they pursue their occupational goals. However, women receive relatively little help from their families in accommodating to the time demands and pressures of work. When a wife becomes gainfully employed, she generally maintains the role expectations incumbent upon her as housewife, mother, and contributor to her husband's career. Moreover, it is normatively approved that the woman's family role, if necessary, will lessen or curtail her work activity. Thus, women have a dual work load, in both work and family, even when employed full time.

Pleck and Rustad's (1980) study of time use indicates that although employed women spend about 28 hours on family work each week, their husbands contribute only about 13 hours. Furthermore, the amount of time husbands spend on household tasks does not vary significantly according to the employment status of their wives. When the husband does contribute, he is more likely to care for children than to do routine household tasks (Pleck, 1977). Though employed married women spend less time on housework than do full-time homemakers, their total work time, including both employment and housework, is considerably greater than that of housewives (Pleck & Rustad, 1980).

Clearly, the combined work and home responsibilities of working women are a serious source of role overload and strain. In consequence, many married women prefer to work part time or to work intermittently. In 1978, only 44% of employed women were year-round full-time workers (U.S. Dept. of Labor, 1980b, Table 19). Moen's (1982) analysis of data from the Panel Study of Income Dynamics showed that only 23% of the female panel had continuous full-time employment from 1972 to 1976. Many women choose employment that is close to their homes, that involves little overtime, overnight travel, and geographic mobility. These constraints on employment surely limit women's socioeconomic attainment, their ability to contribute to the financial resources of their families and to support themselves in the event of marital dissolution.

For couples in which the wife pursues a professional or managerial career with high time demands, the implications for the family are quite pronounced. In these "dual career families" (see Mortimer, 1978, for a review of the literature) both spouses lack the support the wife provides for the single-provider "two-person career" family (Papanek, 1973). They may also feel extreme pressure of time, trying to meet all the demands of two careers plus household and child care duties. Consequently, both spouses may feel that their productivity and occupational achievement is constrained by home responsibilities (Holmstrom, 1972; Hunt & Hunt, 1981). Career demands, including overnight travel and the need to bring work home in the evenings and on weekends, may pose particular problems for mothers, who feel the opposing demands of their children's needs (Poloma, Pendleton, & Garland, 1981). These diverse pressures and strains have led some sociologists to question the viability of the dual career family (Benenson, 1981; Hunt & Hunt, 1981).

The Psychological Impacts of Work Experience

There is considerable evidence, mainly derived from research on men, that work experiences induce psychological change, with important implications for family life. Kohn and Schooler's (1982) ten-year longitudinal study of a nationwide representative panel of male workers demonstrates that experiences in the workplace, especially relating to self-direction, influence parental values, self-confidence and self-deprecation, intellectual flexibility, and authoritarian conservatism. Thus, work generalizes or "spills over" to nonwork areas of life.

The work of Mortimer and her colleagues provides further evidence for the generalization model, that work experience, particularly autonomy on the job, influences broad dimensions of personality. Over a ten-year period, work autonomy—involving decision-making latitude, challenge, and requirements for innovative thinking—strengthened the men's self-concepts (see Mortimer & Lorence, 1979a). Under these conditions of work, the individual's sense of personal competence or efficacy increased. Experiences of autonomy in the workplace also enhanced the level of involvement in work (Lorence & Mortimer, 1981) and both intrinsic and people-oriented occupational reward values (Mortimer & Lorence, 1979b).

Such shifts in the psychological attributes of male workers, shown by the Michigan Panel of college graduates and Kohn's more representative panel, demonstrate the pervasive changes in personality that are linked to work experiences, changes which other family members must come to terms with in their daily interactions with those who are employed. For example, at professional and managerial levels, wives often complain that their husbands are so highly involved or "absorbed" (Kanter, 1977b) in their careers, that they are psychologically unavailable—inaccessible to family members even when they are at home (Fowlkes, 1980; Machlowitz, 1980; Maccoby, 1976). In the Michigan Panel Study (Mortimer, 1980), husbands' high occupational involvement had a direct negative effect on their marital satisfaction. The evidence suggests that men's excessive involvement in work can limit their ability to derive satisfaction from their families. Furthermore, changes in attitudes and orientation toward self and others, found to be linked to work, would likely have pervasive effects on patterns of relationships with family members.

Another body of literature focuses on job stress and its popularized cousin, "burnout." Job stress refers to the subjective experience of workers when they are confronted with a situation on the job (the job stressor) with potentially serious consequences for which their usual modes of behavior are inadequate (House & Wells, 1978; Lazarus & Launier, 1978; McGrath, 1976). New modes of behavior, coping, and adaptation are necessary. Job stressors may take the form of pressures or deprivations. Pressures are produced by a discrepancy between the demands of the job and the worker's abilities. Although pressures are usually the result of excessive demands, or role overload, stress is also produced by the boredom and monotony characterizing work underload (Ferguson, 1973). Deprivations are produced when job rewards do not meet the worker's needs or expectations (French, Rodgers, & Cobb, 1974; House, 1980).

Job stress may have substantial importance for the life satisfaction and health of workers and for their behavior when they return home.

Research on blue collar men shows how their problems on the job influence family interaction (Farrell & Rosenberg, 1981). Piotrkowski (1978) reports that when workers were stressed and upset at work, due to role conflict and overload, boredom, and the underutilization of skills, they came home fatigued, irritable, and worried. They also attempted to create "personal space" between themselves and other family members, blocking out their wives and children. The wives tried to help their husbands by keeping the children "out of their hair," allowing time for rest and recuperation. The children, too, learned to distance themselves from the working parent. When they did not, the fathers became angry and irritable. Piotrkowski called this pattern of linkage between work and family life "negative carryover." A second pattern was called "energy depletion"—there was simply little energy left to become involved with wives and children, and the workers withdrew from their families. But when fathers felt satisfied and challenged by their jobs a very different pattern emerged—one of "positive carryover." The worker, upon returning home, actively initiated contact with family members. The ensuing interactions were characterized by interest, concern, closeness, and warmth.

Some workers in Piotrkowski's study claimed that they didn't care about work and denied any connections between their work and family lives. But this attempted disengagement had its own costs—an inability to gain a sense of esteem from the work role and less closeness with the spouse and children. They could not share the father's work life, if he refused to discuss it. Piotrkowski's study suggests that the traditional function of the family, as an oasis of support that replenishes the male provider who experiences stresses at work, may occur at some cost to wives and children and to the character of family life in general. If the worker is exposed to prolonged and unrelieved stress, his depletion of energy and lowered resistance to illness (Veninga & Spradley, 1981) will have major consequences for other family members.

It is widely assumed that women are less affected than men by the work they do, because of their primary involvement in the home. But research has demonstrated that women and men respond very similarly to their job environments. Although the majority of women enter the labor force in response to economic incentives, they receive more than just financial rewards from their jobs (Komarovsky, 1972; Lein, 1979; Rubin, 1979). Indeed, as in the case of men, the work role can offer women a sense of usefulness and self-esteem (Rubin, 1979; Feree, 1976; Walshok, 1979).

In a recent study of 2500 employed men and women living in the

Minneapolis-St. Paul area, Sorensen (1983) found that despite differing levels of occupational attainment and time spent on the job, women's and men's attitudes and behaviors were influenced similarly by their job experiences. Specifically, demanding work hours contributed to increases in women's and men's job absorption, distress symptoms, hard-driving behavior, and speed and impatience. In contrast, social support diminished their sense of distress and hard-driving, competitive orientation.

Similarly, Miller and her colleagues (1979) found that for both men and women in a nationwide sample, job conditions allowing self-direction are related to favorable self-evaluation, flexible and tolerant orientations toward others, and effective intellectual functioning. In contrast, job pressures and uncertainties produce negative self-conceptions, anxiety, and diminished intellectual flexibility. These relationships were not conditional on the woman's occupational commitment, sense of responsibility for contributing to family income, hours worked, or the presence of young children in the home. Moreover, there was evidence that the covariation of occupational self-direction and psychological attributes is not merely the reflection of self-selection to jobs, but demonstrates the causal effect of women's work experiences on their self-conceptions and social orientations.

But while men and women respond similarly to the same work conditions, they do not generally have comparable work experiences. In addition to the constraints on their leisure time and the possible work overload resulting from their dual responsibilities, women may face social disapproval for the breaching of traditional social norms. The prevailing attitudes toward maternal employment may lead working mothers to experience anxiety and guilt and to feel compelled to compensate in their behaviors toward their children (Hoffman, 1974). Employed wives and mothers sometimes feel frustrated over their inabilities to meet other role commitments, such as maintaining contact with friends, participating in the school and community, and spending time with extended family. The work role also can have implications for a woman's relationship with her husband. The demands on the marital relationship are especially heightened by the dual career situation (Rice, 1979), particularly when both spouses simultaneously experience peak requirements in their careers (Rapoport & Rapoport, 1971).

Work experiences, therefore, have important implications for mental and physical well-being. Most studies on the effects of employment on health have focused on men, although their findings have implications for women as well. Given that gender makes little difference in workers' psychological responses to the job environment (Miller et al., 1979; Sorensen, 1983), similar effects on health are likely to be observed in both men and women workers under conditions of work overload (Frankenhaeuser, 1977;

French & Caplan, 1973; Kahn et al., 1964), restricted advancement opportunity or threatened job security (Cherniss, 1980; Kahn, 1981; Kasl,
Gore, & Cobb, 1975; Suls & Mullen, 1981), and limited ability to control
work activities and participate in decisions affecting the job environment
(Aiken & Hage, 1966; Antonovsky, 1979; Cooper & Marshall, 1976; Levi,
1978). Moreover, women may be at greater health risk than men, due to
their disproportionate exposure to these conditions as a result of their
segregation into traditionally "female" jobs that allow little opportunity
for advancement or self-direction. Women's health risks also may be exacerbated by the work overload associated with their dual responsibilities
at home and on the job.

The few studies focused on the effects of women's employment on
health have identified the key characteristics of women's jobs which increase health risks, as well as the syngeristic impact of home and job
responsibilities (Haynes & Feinleib, 1980; Severne, 1982). Haynes and
Feinleib (1980), for example, followed a group of men, employed women,
and housewives between the ages of 45 and 64 for eight years, and observed
the development of coronary heart disease (CHD). Employment status
alone did not affect the development of coronary heart disease; indeed,
single working women who had the longest job tenures of all employed
women had the lowest incidence of CHD. However, among working
women, the risk of CHD was highest among women with the greatest
household responsibilities, as assessed by marital status and the number
of children, and was particularly high among clerical workers. (Other
studies have noted the lack of opportunity for advancement and self-direction in clerical work; see the National Commission on Working Women,
1979).

In summary, although women respond to job conditions similarly to
men, they generally do not face the same job conditions. Discrimination
and labor market segmentation confine women to low paying jobs offering
little opportunity for mobility. Furthermore, employed married women
continue to shoulder the major responsibility for household tasks and child
care. Nonetheless, despite the stresses they face in meeting these conflicting demands, women are generally satisfied with their jobs and report
that employment offers them a heightened sense of usefulness.

EFFECTS OF THE FAMILY ON WORK

Socialization of Children

A major theme in research on fathering is that men try to inculcate attitudes
and values in their children, especially in their sons, which are useful in
their own occupations. Kohn's (1969) findings relating social class and

parental values are highly consistent with this proposition. According to Kohn, when work is routine and closely supervised and lacks substantive complexity, men will place a high value on children's conformity and obedience to authority, behaviors that are necessary in their work environments. Alternatively, when their work requires independent and complex thought, they will value self-direction for their children as well as for themselves. These class differences in childrearing values have been replicated in many studies in several different national contexts (Kohn, 1977).

There is also some evidence that the father's work situation affects his parental behavior (Kohn, 1977; Rubin, 1976). In comparison to men of higher social-class position, blue collar men are more directive (rather than supportive) in their parenting styles and rely more on physical forms of punishment than appeals to reasoning or guilt (Gecas, 1979). McKinley (1964) believed that lower-class men more severely discipline and punish their children because of their frustration, due to low job satisfaction and work autonomy.

It is often reported in the literature that parental socioeconomic status is positively related to close and supportive relationships with children (Gecas, 1979). This finding was replicated in the Michigan Panel Study (Mortimer, Lorence, & Kumka, forthcoming). Paternal support also induced a range of psychological attributes in sons that enhanced their subsequent occupational attainment: a greater sense of competence or personal efficacy, higher involvement in work, and a stronger crystallization of occupation values.

Study of the status attainment process has emphasized the implications of parental socioeconomic level for parental encouragement and for children's educational and occupational aspirations. However, research has also identified other, nonvertical dimensions of the father's occupation as sources of variation in socialization (Aberle & Naegele, 1952; Benson, 1968; McKinley, 1964; Steinmetz, 1972). Fathers' occupational functions and attributes have consistently been found to be related to sons' vocational orientations (Kahn, 1968; Turner, 1970). Mortimer's research (1975, 1976) provides evidence that the particular character of the father's occupation, that is, its professional or business orientation, is an important determinant of sons' occupational values. She found that as closeness and communication with the father increased, the intrinsic and people-oriented values of professionals' sons were enhanced. In contrast, in business families, paternal support seemed to strengthen extrinsic occupational values. These differences in socialization, by the father's occupational sector, are consistent with survey data that show that businessmen do, in fact, give more extrinsically oriented responses when asked to evaluate the importance of different occupational rewards, emphasizing high income and advancement, while professionals are likely to indicate concern with the more intrinsic satisfactions of work (Gurin, Veroff, & Feld, 1960; Kilpatrick, Cummings, & Jennings, 1964; Robinson, Athanasiou, & Head, 1969; see also Parsons, 1939, and Goode, 1957). Moreover, these differences in value socialization were found to have implications for sons' later occupational destinations (Mortimer & Kumka, 1982; Mortimer & Lorence, 1979b). Intrinsic and people-oriented values furthered the acquisition of autonomous jobs and work with high social content; extrinsic values predicted high adult income levels. This research supports the conclusion that the father's position in the occupational structure and his particular work experiences have important implications for sons' vocational development and career attainment.

It is thus clear from research on men that the family plays a crucial role in the socialization of the next generation of workers. As parental work patterns and social norms change, the socialization of children is also likely to be affected. Numerous studies have examined the impact of the increasing employment of women on their children. (For reviews of the literature, which we draw upon heavily here, see Hoffman, 1974, 1980).

The implications of maternal employment certainly vary with the age of the child. Because the relationships between the child and its major adult caretakers are so important during the formative period of infancy, and because of the mother's traditional responsibility for the care of the child, considerable attention has been paid to the effects of the mother's employment on infants. However, since this is the topic of another chapter (see Sroufe and Ward, this volume), we will not address it further here. Moreover, it is necessary to look beyond the immediate periods of infancy and childhood to assess the full impacts of maternal employment and various forms of "substitute care." Bronfenbrenner (1979) has warned that some effects may be manifested only in later developmental periods. His thorough review of extant longitudinal studies suggests that children cared for in large group settings (with many children per adult) become more peer oriented than children reared in more traditional, familylike settings. This peer orientation may make the older child (especially boys) less responsive to adult supervision and result in lower achievement in school. Any such achievement deficit, if it does occur, would have implications for the subsequent attainment of the children of working mothers. Bronfenbrenner's findings suggest a need for more longitudinal research focused on the effects, in later life, of different substitute childcare settings.

From cross-sectional studies, it is apparent that the major effect of the mother's employment on adolescent girls is to enlarge their conceptions of their future roles, raising their aspirations and encouraging them to consider a wider range of vocational possibilities (Hoffman, 1974; Hartley, 1961). Daughters of employed women have been found to be more likely than those with nonemployed mothers to plan to work in adulthood, and, at the college level, to aspire to nontraditional occupational roles (Tangri, 1972). This relationship between maternal employment and daughter's occupational aspirations may be mediated by the mother's attitudes toward her work.

Working mothers, especially those who are well educated and who enjoy their jobs, may be more likely than nonworking mothers to encourage independence in their children, particularly during adolescence (Hoffman, 1974, 1980). This independence training, coupled with the role model working mothers present, would heighten the aspirations and long-term achievements of daughters (Hoffman, 1974, 1980; Miller & Garrison, 1982; Tangri, 1972).

While most attention has been focused on the impacts of maternal employment on girls' vocational attitudes and choices, there is evidence that maternal employment also strengthens the career interests of boys (Hoffman, 1974). Both sons and daughters of employed women have been found to have more flexible sex-role conceptions, perceiving male and female roles as more similar to one another, to hold less rigid conceptions of the appropriate activity spheres of men and women, to approve of female employment, to favor social equality for women, and to evaluate female competence highly. Furthermore, maternal employment appears to reduce the tendency to sex-type the personalities of each sex. That is, daughters of working mothers see women as more competent and effective. Sons of working mothers view men as warmer, perhaps due to an increased tendency on the part of their fathers to participate in childrearing (Vogel, Broverman, Broverman, & Clarkson, 1970).

Thus, the predominant weight of evidence supports the view that maternal employment has positive socialization impacts. However, Hoffman (1980) points out that there may be some negative implications for boys. For example, studies of sons of employed blue-collar women suggest a strain in the father–son relationship, possibly due to the very traditional normative definition of sex roles in this stratum. The blue collar mother's employment may appear to reflect the father's inadequacy as an economic provider.

It is certainly necessary to consider the social context in which employment occurs to understand (and predict) its long-term effects on children. Elder's (1974) panel study of adolescent girls in the Great Depression showed that the daughters of employed women were drawn into labor-intensive family work to assist their mothers and stretch the economic resources of their families. This high level of involvement in family activities led to the development of a greater commitment to the family in adulthood. This commitment was expressed in higher fertility and greater satisfaction derived from family life. These findings from Elder's monumental study, coupled with the quite different implications of maternal employment for adolescent girls today, as indicated by Hoffman's reviews of research (1974, 1980), alert us to the importance of families' interpretations of events and the character of their adaptations to the changes which accompany maternal employment. As Hoffman (1974) points out, much remains to be discovered about the processes through which the effects of maternal employment occur. It is likely that the effects on children will differ, depending on the way maternal employment influences the family's power structure, division of labor, and childrearing dynamics, and on both parents' orientations toward work and family roles.

The Effects of the Family on Occupational Attainment

As noted earlier, several studies have documented the socioeconomic advantages of married men in comparison to the unmarried. But because of the persistence of traditional sex-role norms and task assignments, the effects of marriage appear to be just the opposite for women. While married men have significant advantages over single men, women who restrict their family life have higher socioeconomic attainment than those who do not. Thus, women who never marry have higher attainment than those who marry; women with no children have higher attainment than women with children; and women with few children have higher attainment than those with many children (Card, Steel & Abeles, 1980; Havens, 1973; Sewell, Hauser, & Wolf, 1980; Sorensen, 1983). Marriage and especially the presence of children clearly have a depressing effect on the continuity of women's labor force participation (Moen, forthcoming) and occupational achievement (Poloma et al., 1981).

Pleck has observed that the boundaries between work and home are more permeable for women than for men. The family role is allowed to intrude into her work role (Pleck, 1977). The demands of marriage and of motherhood may force a woman to work part time, to interrupt her career, or to otherwise limit her occupational options. The discontinuous labor force histories and part-time employment patterns of married women account for a substantial portion of the income differential between married and never married women (Treiman & Terrell, 1975).

Ethnographic research reveals that the division of labor is quite strongly sex-typed in the blue-collar family, with wives shouldering major responsibility for housework and child care even when employed (Rubin, 1976, 1979) and for providing a comfortable refuge for their husbands after hard days at work (Piotrkowski, 1978). Though husbands may sometimes care for the children during their wives' working hours (Emlen & Perry, 1974; Kamerman, 1980; Lein, 1979), there is little evidence that wives' other responsibilities are substantially reduced when they are employed.

It is also apparent that the traditional exchange between husband and wife, in the professional and managerial single-provider family, often extends to the wife's support of the husband's career. The prospects of increasing income and economic security, through advancement in the career, provide incentives for the wife to accommodate to the excessive requirements of the husband's work (Greiff & Munter, 1980). Despite the cultural myth that individuals achieve on their own merits (Kanter, 1977b), the role of wife frequently includes the expectation that she lend active support to her husband's career. The wife's role in the "two person career" has been studied most extensively in large organizations such as corporations (Whyte, 1956; Helfrich, 1965; Handy, 1978; Kanter, 1977b; Grieff & Munter, 1980). But it has also been described in other settings, including politics (MacPherson, 1975), diplomacy (Hochschild, 1969), medicine (Fowlkes, 1980), the military (Goldman, 1973; Finlayson, 1976), academe (Hochschild, 1975; Fowlkes, 1980), and the ministry (Douglas, 1965; Scanzoni, 1965; Taylor & Hartley, 1975). The Michigan Panel study (Mortimer, 1980) documents this pattern in a wide range of professional and managerial occupations.

Women often provide necessary services to their husbands, enhancing their productivity, and benefiting the organizations that employ them. For example, wives provide services such as editing, clerical assistance, writing, and attending meetings, thus directly substituting for the work of paid employees. Their entertaining and socializing enhances the husband's position in the organization (Kanter, 1977b). Wives may participate in community and volunteer activities which enlarge their husbands' business contacts or clientele (Fowlkes, 1980), as well as the company's public image (Kanter, 1977b). Many wives provide emotional support and consultation, acting as "sounding boards" for their husbands' ideas. Given the wide range of tasks they perform in fulfilling the obligations of the "two person career," it is no wonder that wives' own careers tend to be restricted. Mortimer, Hall, & Hill (1978) have concluded on the basis of an extensive review of the literature that husbands' occupational attributes act to constrain wives' employment and occupational attainment.

It might appear that married men would be advantaged over their single counterparts, particularly in professional and managerial occupations where the two-person career pattern is most strongly institutionalized. But there has been little systematic research on the causal processes underlying the relationship between marital status and men's attainment. Specifically, it is not known to what extent the higher attainment of married men is attributable to the effects of marriage and wives' contributions to advancement, or to processes of selection to marriage, that is, on the basis of prior attributes that would promote attainment or on the basis of earlier educational and occupational achievement.

The data from the Michigan Panel Study bear directly on this issue

(Mortimer, Lorence, & Kumka, 1982). Confirming other research, the married men had greater career stability over the ten years following college, higher income, and greater work autonomy than those who never married during the decade following college graduation. Married men also made more positive evaluations of their career progress, and exhibited greater satisfaction with their work and their lives in general. This pattern of findings is consistent with earlier research, on both socioeconomic attainment and the quality of life. Married people, in comparison to the unmarried, have often been found to express more positive global evaluations of, and satisfaction with, their lives (Andrews & Withey, 1976; Campbell, Converse, & Rodgers, 1976). Moreover, the psychological advantages of the married have been found to be more pronounced for men than for women (Campbell, 1981). If marriage enhances the adjustment and satisfaction of men, it is reasonable to suppose that this advantage would influence behavior in the work setting, enhancing productivity and occupational attainment.

There was substantial evidence from the panel study that the advantages of the married men did not result solely from selection processes. Few attitudinal differences, relevant to future occupational attainment, could be discerned in the senior year of college between those who would marry and those who would remain single during the following ten years. Moreover, the vast majority of the married panel members had either married prior to embarking on their careers, or undertook these two life transitions simultaneously. Thus, for only a minority of respondents could it be argued that occupational success occurred prior to, and fostered, marriage. Finally, by estimating the antecedents and consequences of marriage within the context of a comprehensive path model, it was demonstrated that the relationships between marital status and achievements are not the result of prior variables that could influence both marriage and attainment processes (such as family socioeconomic status, prior work values and self-concept, postgraduate education, etc.). There also was evidence in this study that support from the wife was an important intervening linkage—accounting for the attainments of the more successful married men. While the "selection hypothesis" cannot be ruled out entirely, the findings support the conclusion that marriage is an important "career contingency" (Duncan, Featherman, & Duncan, 1972) for professional and managerial men.

IMPLICATIONS FOR SOCIAL POLICY

The research findings that have been discussed in this chapter point to several areas of recommendation for social policy. It is evident that most families are dependent on the workplace to provide them with a continuing flow of income, and therefore, economic security. Many studies have re-vealed the disruptive impacts of marginal and unstable employment for the family. To promote the welfare of families, surely full employment should be an overriding national goal. Second, the fact that work time impinges on family time, often excessively, is apparent throughout the literature. The number of hours spent at work and their scheduling remain problematic for all workers, men and women, particularly when they have young children. More flexible working hours and greater discretion in overtime work would help workers who are juggling the demands of jobs, maintaining households, and rearing children. Third, we have seen that work experiences have important effects on psychological functioning and also influence health status. To enhance the psychological and physical well-being of workers, efforts should be made to widen their opportunities for self-direction and work autonomy, increase the level of interest and challenge in their jobs, and reduce work pressure and overload.

Each of these directions of change could be elaborated in great detail. However, given our space limitations, we have chosen to concentrate on one very general and intractable problem: the inequality of men and women in the labor force and in the family. It is clear from our review that ine-quality in each of these spheres serves to reinforce that in the other.

The growing number of women workers may give the impression that traditional patterns of sex-role behavior have been markedly altered (Po-loma & Garland, 1971; Young & Willmott, 1973). However, examination of the types of work women perform and the range of home responsibilities they continue to fulfill demonstrates that considerable change is still nec-essary, if parity with men is to be achieved. As a result of the sex-typed division of labor, both in the home and in the workplace, women are fre-quently overloaded by excessive role demands. Changes are needed in the workplace, and ultimately in the home, if women are to fully actualize their potential.

Clearly, both traditional social norms and women's relatively low economic contributions contribute to inequality in the distribution of family work. The assymetrical pattern of spouse support enhances the husband's occupational attainment, but depresses that of the wife. It is interesting to note that these normative and resource-based forces often act counter to one another. That is, in families of higher education and social status, there is stronger ideological support for sexual equality (Farkas, 1976; Scanzoni, 1979; Tallman, 1983). But, as Benenson (1981) has observed, it is in this stratum that husbands' earnings are likely to be far greater than those of their wives. Benenson shows that it is at lower socioeconomic levels, in the lower-middle and working classes, that wives' incomes more closely approximate the earnings of their husbands. But here, as we have seen, there are strong normative supports for the traditional, sex-typed family structure.

This situation argues for a multifaceted policy approach. Traditional sex-role norms will be eroded by the elimination of sex typing in textbooks, in school curricula, and in the more subtle interactions with teachers and counselors. Girls must be socialized to plan for their futures as workers as well as mothers and wives. Boys require experiences that will reinforce their willingness and ability to be active participants in managing home and family responsibilities. For their generation, mutually strong involvement in the family and equal participation and attainment in the labor force remain a possibility. Continuing pressure from the women's movement, media attention, and legal intervention are also necessary to change norms, generating increasing acceptance of the goal of gender equality.

But equalization of the income contributions which men and women bring to their families is also necessary to enhance the resource base for women's equality in the family sphere. For women to increase their incomes, they must break out of their sex-segregated sector of the labor market, gaining access to jobs that have been defined as male positions. Strong enforcement of laws supporting equal opportunity in hiring and promotion and prohibiting discrimination and harassment in the workplace is necessary. A policy of equal pay for comparable worth will not only enhance women's positions vis-à-vis their husbands; it also will promote their economic self-sufficiency in any circumstance in which they are dependent on their own earnings—if they choose to remain single, in the event of separation, in divorce, or in widowhood.

Moreover, the present structuring of work is designed to enhance the productivity and convenience of the work organization and not to suit the needs of the family. Providing more flexible time arrangements and leave policies would allow families to meet their home obligations, with less need for the subordination of one partner to the other. Some firms are providing more opportunities for part-time work, while maintaining acceptable benefit levels, providing options to job share, or to bring work home during normal work hours (Polit, 1979). Lessening requirements for travel and geographic mobility and the provision of more liberal maternity and paternity leaves, including parental leaves for lengthy childhood illnesses, would do much to assist families. Alteration of the pressure to achieve in careers at predetermined, fixed rates would offer both men and women greater opportunity to balance their interests in, and desire for, both a career and a family.

Of great concern to mothers, fathers, and society at large, is the care of the children of employed parents while they meet their work responsibilities (Bronfenbrenner, 1979). Many families rely on diverse modes of child care and juggle a complex set of supports to assure continuous care (Kamerman, 1980). To promote the equality of women and men in the labor market, the availability of high quality day care facilities must be increased. To help parents obtain child care, some companies are providing referral information regarding day care facilities, giving child care vouchers, subsidizing community day care centers, reserving places in centers or in licensed family day care homes, or offering on-site child care. (Kamerman, 1980, documents the modes of caring for the children of working parents in European countries, which could serve as models for the United States.) There is increasing concern among employers with job dissatisfaction, turnover, and declining productivity. Changes, designed to ameliorate the conflicts of work and family, may lessen these problems in the future.

If present trends in women's employment continue, young men and women face futures in which the roles of the sexes will be less segregated than they are today. If men's rates of participation in the labor force continue to decline as they have in recent decades (Kreps & Clark, 1975, U.S. Dept. of Labor, 1980b, Table 2), and women's continue to increase, they may reach a state of parity in the future. And if attempts to break down the sex-segregated character of the labor force are successful, women's occupational attainment will increasingly become comparable to that of men. But all of this requires change in traditional family roles which subordinate women's achievement to the needs of their husbands and children. The growing literature on work and family linkages converges on the conclusion that inequality in each sphere feeds into, and perpetuates, inequality in the other. To break out of this vicious circle, substantial structural change, in both the labor market and in the family, is necessary.

REFERENCES

Abeles, R.P., Steel, L., & Wise, L.L. Patterns and implications of life-course organization: Studies from project TALENT. Pp. 307–337 in P.B. Baltes & O.G. Brim, Jr. (Eds.), *Life-span development and behavior* (Vol. 3). New York: Academic Press, 1980.

Aberle, D.F., & Naegele, K.D. Middle class fathers' occupational role and attitudes toward children. *American Journal of Orthopsychiatry,* 1952 (April), *22,* 366–378.

Aiken, M., & Hage, J. Organizational alienation: A comparative analysis. *American Sociological Review,* 1966 (August), *31,* 497–507.

Aldous, J. From dual-earner to dual-career families and back again. *Journal of Family Issues,* 1981 (June), *2,* 115–125.

Aldous, J., Osmond, M.W., & Hicks, M.W. Men's work and men's families. Pp. 227–256 in W.R. Burr, R. Hill, R.I. Nye, & I.L. Reiss, *Contemporary theories about the family* (Vol. 1). New York: The Free Press, 1979.

Andrews, F.M., & Withey, S.B. *Social indicators of well-being: Americans' perceptions of life quality.* New York: Plenum Press, 1976.

Antonovsky, A. *Health, stress, and coping.* San Francisco, CA: Jossey-Bass, 1979.

Bailyn, L. Career and family orientations of husbands and wives in relation to marital happiness. Pp. 545–567 in A. Theodore (Ed.), *The professional woman.* Cambridge, MA: Schenkman, 1971.

Barrett, N.S. Women in the job market: Occupations, earnings, and career opportunities. Pp. 31–61 in R.E. Smith (Ed.), *The subtle revolution: Women at work.* Washington, DC: Urban Institute, 1979.

Benenson, H. Family success and sexual equality: The limits of the dual-career family model. Paper presented at the American Sociological Association Meeting, August, 1981.

Benson, L. *Fatherhood: A sociological perspective.* New York: Random House, 1968.

Bronfenbrenner, U. *The ecology of human development.* Cambridge, MA: Harvard University Press, 1979.

Bronfenbrenner, U., & Crouter, A.C. Work and family through time and space. Pp. 39–83 in S.B. Kamerman and Cheryl D. Hayes (Eds.) *Families that work: Children in a changing world.* Washington, DC: National Academy Press, 1982.

Campbell, A. *The sense of well-being in America: Recent patterns and trends.* New York: McGraw-Hill, 1981.

Campbell, A., Converse, P.E., & Rodgers, W.J. *The quality of American life.* New York: Russell Sage, 1976.

Card, J.J., Steel, L., & Abeles, R.P. Sex differences in realization of individual potential for achievement. *Journal of Vocational Behavior,* 1980 (August), *17,* 1–21.

Cherniss, C. *Staff burnout: Job stress in the human services.* Beverly Hills, CA: Sage Publications, 1980.

Cooper, C., & Marshall, J. Occupational sources of stress. A review of the literature relating to coronary heart disease and mental ill health. *Journal of Occupational Psychology,* 1976 (March), *49,* 11–28.

Dizard, J. *Social change in the family.* Chicago, IL: University of Chicago, Community and Family Study Center, 1968.

Douglas, W. *Ministers' wives.* New York: Harper & Row, 1965.

Duncan, O.D., Featherman, D.L., & Duncan, B. *Socio-economic background and achievement.* New York: Seminar Press, 1972.

Elder, G.H., Jr. *Children of the great depression: Social change in life experience.* Chicago, IL: University of Chicago Press, 1974.

Emlen, A.C., & Perry, J.B. Child care arrangements. Pp. 101–125 in L.W. Hoffman & F.I. Nye (Eds.), *Working mothers: An evaluative review of the consequences for wife, husband, and child.* San Francisco, CA: Jossey-Bass, 1974.

Farkas, G. Education, wage rates, and the division of labor between husband and wife. *Journal of Marriage and the Family,* 1976 (August), *38,* 473–483.

Farrell, M.P., & Rosenberg, S. *Men at midlife.* Boston, MA: Auburn House, 1981.

Featherman, D.L. Schooling and occupational careers: Constancy and change in worldly success. Pp. 675–738 in O.G. Brim, Jr., & J. Kagan (Eds.), *Constancy and change in human development.* Cambridge, MA: Harvard University Press, 1980.

Featherman, D.L., & Hauser, R.M. *Sexual inequalities and socioeconomic achievement in the U.S., 1962–1973. American Sociological Review,* 1976 (June), *41,* 462–483.

Feldberg, R., & Glenn, E. Male and female: Job vs. gender models in the sociology of work. *Social Problems,* 1979 (June), *26,* 524–538.

Feree, M.M. Working-class jobs. *Social Problems,* 1976 (April), *23,* 431–441.

Ferguson, D. A study of occupational stress and health. *Ergonomics,* 1973, *16*(5), 649–663.

Finlayson, E.M. A study of the wife of the army officer: Her academic and career preparations, her current employment and volunteer services. In H.I. McCubbin, B.B. Dahl, & E.J. Hunter, (Eds.), *Families in the military system.* Beverly Hills, CA: Sage, 1976.

Fowlkes, M.R. *Behind every successful man: Wives of medicine and academe.* New York: Columbia University Press, 1980.

Frankenhaeuser, M. Job demands, health, and well-being. *Journal of Psychosomatic Research,* 1977, *21*(4), 313–321.

French, J.R.P., & Caplan, R.D. Organizational stress and individual strain. Pp. 30–66 in A.J. Marrow (Ed.), *The failure of success*. New York: AMACOM, 1973.

French, J.R.P., Rodgers, W., & Cobb, S. Adjustment as person-environment fit. Pp. 316–333 in G.V. Coelho, D.A. Hamburg, & J.E. Adams (Eds.), *Coping and adaptation*. New York: Basic Books, 1974.

Gecas, V. The influence of social class on socialization. Pp. 365–404 in W.R. Burr, R. Hill, F.I. Nye, & I.L. Reiss, *Contemporary theories about the family*. New York: Free Press, 1979.

Ghez, G.R., & Becker, G.S. *The allocation of time and goods over the life cycle*. New York: National Bureau of Economic Research, 1975.

Goldman, N. Women in the Armed Forces. *American Journal of Sociology*, 1973 (January), *78*, 892–911.

Goode, W. Community within a community: The professions. *American Sociological Review*, 1957 (April), *22*, 194–200.

Greiff, B.S., & Munter, P.K. *Tradeoffs: Executive, family, and organizational life*. New York: Mentor, 1980.

Gurin, G., Veroff, J., & Feld, S. *Americans view their mental health*. New York: Basic Books, 1960.

Handy, C. The family: Help or hindrance? Pp. 107–123 in C.L. Cooper & R. Payne (Eds.), *Stress at work*. New York: Wiley, 1978.

Harris, L., & Associates, Inc. *Families at work: Strengths and strains*. The General Mills American Family Report, 1980–81. Minneapolis, MN: General Mills, 1981.

Hartley, R.E. What aspects of child behavior should be studied in relation to maternal employment? In A.E. Siegel (Ed.), *Research issues related to the effects of maternal employment on children*. University Park, PA: Social Science Research Center, 1961.

Havens, E.M. Women, work, and wedlock: A note on female marital patterns in the United States. *American Journal of Sociology*, 1973 (January), *78*, 975–981.

Hayghe, H. Working wives' contributions to family income in 1977. *Monthly Labor Review*, U.S. Dept. of Labor, 1979 (October), *102*, 62–64.

Haynes, S., & Feinleib, M. Women, work and coronary heart disease: Prospective findings from the Framingham Heart Study. *American Journal of Public Health*, 1980, *70*(2), 133–141.

Helfrich, M.L. *The social role of the executive's wife*. Columbus, OH: Ohio State University, Bureau of Business Research, 1965.

Hochschild, A.R. The role of the ambassador's wife: An exploratory study. *Journal of Marriage and the Family*, 1969 (February), *31*, 73–87.

Hochschild, A.R. Inside the clockwork of the male career. Pp. 47–80 in F. Howe (Ed.), *Women and the power to change*. New York: McGraw-Hill, 1975.

Hoffman, L.W. Effects on child. Pp. 126–166 in L.W. Hoffman and F.I. Nye (Eds.), *Working mothers*. San Francisco, CA: Jossey-Bass, 1974.

Hoffman, L.W. Effects of maternal employment on children. Pp. 47–54 in C.D. Hayes (Ed.), *Work, family, and community: Summary proceedings of an ad hoc meeting*. Washington, DC: National Academy of Sciences, 1980.

Holmstrom, L.L. *The two-career family*. Boston, MA: Schenkman Publishing, 1972.

House, J. *Occupational stress and the mental and physical health of factory workers*. Research Report Series, Institute for Social Research, University of Michigan, 1980.

House, J., & Wells, J. Occupational stress, social support, and health. Pp. 8–29 in A. McLean (Ed.), *Reducing occupational stress*. Washington, DC: U.S. Dept. of Health, Education and Welfare, Public Health Service, 1978.

Hunt, J.G., & Hunt, L.L. Dual career families: Vanguard of the future or residue of the past? Paper presented at the 1981 meeting of the American Sociological Association, 1981.

Kahn, E.M. Sociometric variables, parental identification, and sons' interests. Ph.D. dissertation, Columbia University, 1968.

Kahn, R.L. *Work and health.* New York: Wiley, 1981.

Kahn, R.L., Wolfe, D., Quinn, R., Snoek, J., & Rosenthal, R. *Organizational stress: Studies in role conflict and ambiguity.* New York: Wiley, 1964.

Kamerman, S.B. *Parenting in an unresponsive society.* New York: Free Press, 1980.

Kanter, R.M. *Work and family in the United States: A critical review and agenda for research and policy.* New York: Russell Sage Foundation, 1977. (a)

Kanter, R.M. *Men and women of the corporation.* New York: Basic Books, 1977. (b)

Kasl, S., Gore, S., & Cobb, S. The experience of losing a job: Reported changes in health, symptoms, and illness behavior. *Psychosomatic Medicine,* 1975 (March/April), *37,* 106–121.

Kilpatrick, F.P., Cummings, M.C., & Jennings, M.K. *The image of the federal service.* Washington, DC: Brookings, 1964.

Kohn, M.L. *Class and conformity: A study in values.* Homewood, IL: Dorsey, 1969.

Kohn, M.L. *Class and conformity: A study in values,* second edition. Chicago, IL: University of Chicago Press, 1977.

Kohn, M.L., & Schooler, C. Job conditions and personality: A longitudinal assessment of their reciprocal effects. *American Journal of Sociology,* 1982 (May), *87,* 1257–1286.

Komarovsky, M. *Blue-collar marriage.* New York: Random House, 1972.

Kreps, J., & Clark, R. *Sex, age, and work: The changing composition of the labor force.* Studies in Employment and Welfare, Number 23, Johns Hopkins University Press, Baltimore, MD, 1975.

Lazarus, R.S., & Launier, R. *Stress-related transactions between person and environment.* In L.A. Pervin & M. Lewis (Eds.), *Perspectives in interactional psychology.* New York: Plenum Press, 1978.

Lein, L. Working couples as parents. Pp. 299–321 in E. Corfman (Ed.), *Families today,* Volume 1. Rockville, MD: National Institute of Mental Health, 1979.

Lorence, J., & Mortimer, J.T. Work experience and work involvement. *Sociology of Work and Occupations,* 1981 (August), *8,* 297–326.

Levi, L. Psychosocial stress at work: Problems and prevention. Pp. 216–222 in A. McLean (Ed.), *Reducing occupational stress.* Washington, DC: U.S. Dept. of Health, Education, and Welfare, Public Health Service, 1978.

Maccoby, M. *The gamesman.* New York: Simon & Schuster, 1976.

McGrath, J. Stress and behavior in organizations. Pp. 1351–1395 in M. Dunnette (Ed.), *Handbook of industrial and organizational psychology.* Chicago, IL: Rand McNally, 1976.

Machlowitz, M. *Workaholics. Living with them, working with them.* New York: Mentor, 1980.

McKinley, D.G. *Social class and family life.* New York: The Free Press, 1964.

MacPherson, M. *The power lovers: An intimate look at politicians and their marriages.* New York: Putnam, 1975.

Miller, J., & Garrison, H.H. Sex roles: The division of labor at home and in the workplace. *Annual Review of Sociology,* 1982, *8,* 237–262.

Miller, J., Schooler, C., Kohn, M., & Miller, K. Women and work: The psychological effects of occupational conditions. *American Journal of Sociology,* 1979 (July), *85,* 66–94.

Moen, P. Continuities and discontinuities in women's labor force participation. In G.H. Elder, Jr. (Ed.), *Life course dynamics: 1960's to 1980's.* New York: Social Science Research Council, forthcoming.

Moen, P. The two-provider family: Problems and potentials. Pp. 13–43 in M.E. Lamb (Ed.),

Non-traditional families: Parenting and child development. Hillsdale, NJ: Erlbaum, 1982.

Mortimer, J.T. Occupational value socialization in business and professional families. *Sociology of Work and Occupations,* 1975 (February), *2,* 29–53.

Mortimer, J.T. Social class, work and the family: Some implications of the father's occupation for familial relations and sons' career decisions. *Journal of Marriage and the Family,* 1976 (May), *38,* 241–256.

Mortimer, J.T. Dual career families—A sociological perspective. Pp. 1–29 in S.S. Peterson, J.M. Richardson, & G.V. Kreuter (Eds.), *The two-career family: Issues and alternatives.* Washington, DC: University Press of America, 1978.

Mortimer, J.T. Occupation-family linkages as perceived by men in the early stages of professional and managerial careers. Pp. 99–117 in Helena Z. Lopata (Ed.), *Research in the interweave of social roles: Women and men, volume 1.* Greenwich, CT: JAI Press, 1980.

Mortimer, J.T., Hall, R., & Hill, R. Husbands' occupational attributes as constraints on wives' employment. *Sociology of Work and Occupations,* 1978 (August), *7,* 285–313.

Mortimer, J.T., & Kumka, D. A further examination of the 'occupational linkage hypothesis'. *Sociological Quarterly,* 1982 (Winter), *23,* 3–16.

Mortimer, J.T., & London, J. The varying linkages of work and family. Pp. 20–35 in P. Voydanoff (Ed.), *Work and the family: Changing Roles of Men and Women.* Palo Alto,, California: Mayfield, 1984.

Mortimer, J.T., & Lorence, J. Occupational experience and the self-concept: A longitudinal study. *Social Psychology Quarterly,* 1979 (December), *42,* 307–323. (a)

Mortimer, J.T., & Lorence, J. Work experience and occupational value socialization: A longitudinal study. *American Journal of Sociology,* 1979 (May), *84,* 1361–1385.

Mortimer, J.T., & Lorence, J. Self-concept stability and change from late adolescence to early adulthood. Pp. 5–42 in R.G. Simmons (Ed.), *Research in community and mental health,* Volume 2. Greenwich, CT: JAI Press, 1981.

Mortimer, J.T., Lorence, J., & Kumka, D. Work and family linkages in the transition to adulthood: A panel study of highly educated men. Special issue on "The Sociology of the Life Course." *Western Sociological Review,* 1982 (1), 13, 50–68.

Mortimer, J.T., Lorence, J., & Kumka, D. *Work, family, and personality: Transition to adulthood.* Forthcoming, Norwood, N.J.: Ablex Publishing Corporation.

National Commission on Working Women. *National Survey of Working Women: Perceptions, problems, and prospects.* Center for Women and Work, National Manpower Institute, Washington, DC, 1979.

National Commission on Working Women. A few facts about working women; Prime concerns about women in the '80s. Fact sheets in *Women at work.* Washington, DC: Center for women and work, National Manpower Institute, 1982.

Nye, F.I., & Hoffman, L.W. *The employed mother in America.* Chicago, IL: Rand McNally, 1963.

Oppenheimer, V.K. The life cycle squeeze. *Demography,* 1974 (May), *11,* 227–246.

Oppenheimer, V.K. The sex-labeling of jobs. Pp. 307–325 in M.T.S. Mednick, S.S. Tangri, & L.W. Hoffman (Eds.), Women and achievement. Washington, DC: Hemisphere Publishing, 1975.

Pahl, J.M., & Pahl, R.E. *Managers and their wives.* London, England: Allen Lane, 1971.

Papanek, H. Men, women and work: Reflections on the two-person career. *American Journal of Sociology,* 1973 (January), *78,* 852–872.

Parsons, T. The professions and social structure. *Social Forces,* 1939 (May), *17,* 457–467.

Piotrkowski, C.S. *Work and the family system.* New York: Free Press, 1978.

Pleck, J.H. The work-family role system. *Social Problems,* 1977 (April), *24,* 417–427.

Pleck, J.H., & Rustad, M. Husbands' and wives' time in family work and paid work in 1975–76 study of time use. Unpublished paper. Wellesley College for Research on Women, 1980.

Polit, Denise F. Nontraditional work schedules for women. Pp. 195–210 in K.W. Feinstein (Ed.), *Working women and families*. Beverly Hills, CA: Sage, 1979.

Poloma, M.M., & Garland, T.N. The myth of the egalitarian family: Familial roles and the professionally employed wife. Pp. 741–761 in A. Theodore (Ed.), *The professional woman*. Cambridge, MA: Schenkman Publishing, 1971.

Poloma, M.M., Pendleton, B.F., & Garland, T.N. Reconsidering the dual career marriage. *Journal of Family Issues,* 1981 (June), *2,* 205–224.

Quinn, R., & Staines, G. *Quality of employment survey: 1977*. Ann Arbor, MI: Survey Research Center, Institute for Social Research, University of Michigan, 1979.

Rainwater, L. Making the good life: Working-class family and life-styles. Pp. 204–229 in S.A. Levitan (Ed.), *Blue Collar Workers: A symposium on Middle America*. New York: McGraw-Hill, 1971.

Rapoport, R., & Rapoport, R.N. *Dual Career Families*. Harmondsworth, Middlesex: Penguin Books, 1971.

Regan, M.C., & Roland, H.E. University students: A change of expectations and aspirations over the decade. *Sociology of Education,* 1982 (October), *55,* 223–228.

Rice, D. *Dual career marriage: Conflict and treatment*. New York: Free Press, 1979.

Robinson, J.P., Athanasiou, R., & Head, K.B. *Measures of occupational attitudes and occupational characteristics*. Ann Arbor, MI: Survey Research Center, 1969.

Rosenfeld, R. Women's occupational careers: Individual and structural explanations. *Sociology of Work and Occupations,* 1979 (August), *6,* 283–311.

Rubin, L.B. *Worlds of pain: Life in the working-class family*. New York: Basic Books, 1976.

Rubin, L.B. *Women of a certain age: The midlife search for self*. New York: Harper Colophon Books, 1979.

Scanzoni, J. Resolution of occupational–conjugal role conflict in clergy marriages. *Journal of Marriage and the Family,* 1965 (August), *27,* 396–402.

Scanzoni, J. *Opportunity and the family*. New York: Free Press, 1970.

Scanzoni, J. *Sexual bargaining*. Englewood Cliffs, NJ: Prentice-Hall, 1972.

Scanzoni, J. Social processes and power in families. Pp. 295–316 in W.R. Burr, R. Hill, F.I. Nye, & I.L. Reiss (Eds.), *Contemporary theories about the family,* volume 1. New York: Free Press, 1979.

Schorr, A.L., & Moen, P. The single parent and public policy. *Social Policy,* 1979 (March/April), *10,* 15–21.

Sennett, R., & Cobb, J. *The hidden injuries of class*. New York: Vintage Books, 1972.

Severne, L. Psychosocial aspects of menopause: A survey of 922 Belgian women by the International Health Foundation. In A. Voda, M. Dinnerstein, & S. O'Donnell (Eds.), *Changing perspectives on menopause*. Austin, TX: University of Texas Press, 1982.

Sewell, W.H., Hauser, R.M., & Wolf, W.C. Sex, schooling and occupational status. *American Journal of Sociology,* 1980 (November), *86,* 551–583.

Sexton, P.C. *Women and work*. Washington, DC: U.S. Dept. of Labor, Employment and Training Administration, 1977.

Smith, R. The movement of women into the labor force. Pp. 1–29 in R. Smith (Ed.), *The subtle revolution: Women at work*. Washington, DC: Urban Institute, 1979.

Sorensen, G. *Gender Differences in the Effects of Employment on Health*. Unpublished Ph.D. dissertation. University of Minnesota: Minneapolis. August, 1983.

Spade, J.Z. Understanding the interaction of work and family in dual-worker families. Paper presented at the Annual Meeting of the Society for the Study of Social Problems. Toronto, August 1981.

Spenner, K.I. Occupational role characteristics and intergenerational transmission. *Sociology of Work and Occupations,* 1981 (February), *8,* 89–112.

Steinmetz, S.K. Occupational environment, child rearing, and dogmatism: Test of a linkage hypothesis. Presented at the American Sociological Association Annual Meeting, August 1972.

Steinmetz, S.K., & Straus, M.A. *Violence in the family.* New York: Harper and Row, 1974.

Stevenson, M.H. Wage differences between men and women: Economic theories. Pp. 89–107 in A.H. Stromberg & S. Harkness (Eds.), *Women working: theories and facts in perspective.* Palo Alto, CA: Mayfield Publishing, 1978.

Suls, J., & Mullen, B. Life events, perceived control, and illness: The role of uncertainty. *Journal of Human Stress,* 1981 (June), *30,* 30–33.

Tallman, I. *Socialization for social change: A comparative study of parent–adolescent relations in Mexico and the United States.* New York: Academic Press, 1983.

Tangri, S.S. Determinants of occupational role-innovation among college women. *Journal of Social Issues,* 1972, *28(2),* 177–200.

Taylor, M.G., & Hartley, S.F. The two-person career: A classic example. *Sociology of Work and Occupations,* 1975 (November), *2,* 354–372.

Treiman, D., & Terrell, K. Sex and the process of status attainment: A comparison of working women and men. *American Sociological Review,* 1975 (April), *40,* 174–200.

Turner, J.H. Entrepreneurial environments and the emergence of achievement motivation in adolescent males. *Sociometry,* 1970 (June), *33,* 147–165.

U.S. Census Bureau. Child support and alimony: 1978, Series P-23, No. 112. Washington, DC: U.S. Govt. Printing Office, 1981.

U.S. Commission on Civil Rights. *Unemployment and Underemployment among Blacks, Hispanics, and Women.* Clearinghouse Publication 74. Washington, DC. November 1982.

U.S. Department of Labor. Bureau of Labor Statistics. Report 631. Employment in perspective: Working women. Washington, DC, 1980. (a)

U.S. Department of Labor. Perspectives on working women: A databook. Bureau of Labor Statistics, Bulletin 2080. Washington, D.C.: U.S. Government Printing Office, 1980. (b)

Veninga, R.L., & Spradley, J.P. *The work/stress connection: How to cope with job burnout.* Boston: Little, Brown, 1981.

Vogel, S.R., Broverman, I.K., Broverman, D.M., Clarkson, F.E., & Rosenkrantz, P.S. Maternal Employment and perception of sex roles among college students. *Developmental Psychology,* 1970 (November), *3,* 384–391.

Walshok, M.L. Occupational values and family roles: Women in blue-collar and service occupations. Pp. 63–83 in K.W. Feinstein (Ed.), *Working women and families.* Beverly Hills, CA: Sage, 1979.

Whyte, W.H. *The organizational man.* New York: Doubleday, 1956.

Wilensky, H.L. Work, careers, and social integration. *International Social Science Journal,* 1960 (Fall), *12,* 543–560.

Young M., & Willmott, P. *The symmetrical family.* New York: Pantheon, 1973.

Chapter 6
PAID AND UNPAID WORK: CONTRADICTIONS IN AMERICAN WOMEN'S LIVES TODAY

*Nona Y. Glazer**

Portland State University

INTRODUCTION

"You've come a long way, baby!" Reality or media hype? A close look at the work and domestic lives of women in the United States today reveals that the answer is "both." Women's work lives have improved significantly over the last century. Women have gained many legal rights, including control over their own property and custody of minor children. Women have new freedom in marriage and greater control over their sexuality and reproduction. Married women are more likely to work for pay outside the home and thus have some degree of economic independence from their spouses.

Yet a contradiction exists. Many of women's new opportunities bring new obligations that are not easily met or must be taken on along with old obligations. Legal decisions, for example, assume that mothers and fathers can share equally in the financial cost of raising children after marital dissolution. These overlook the continued lower earnings of women compared to men, as well as the time and energy women give to child

* Nona Y. Glazer is currently (1982–1983) a Radcliffe Research Scholar at the Arthur and Elizabeth Schlesinger Library on the History of American Women, Radcliffe College, Harvard University. In 1984–85, she will be a National Science Foundation Professor at the University of California, San Francisco. She is professor of sociology and teaches also for the Women's Studies Certificate Program at Portland State University.

care. Also, the double day has been normalized. Women's average life work expectancy is now 25 years (Smith, 1982); over half of married women are in the labor force (Johnson, 1979). This means that women today expect to do paid employment outside the home, and yet they retain responsibility for domestic work. Housework and child care, as well as other myriad tasks, are socially assigned to women—employed or not— who do not have social solutions to the problems of the double day, but must work out personal solutions (Glazer, 1980a).

Many of the significant changes in women's lives resulted from the need of capitalism for female labor, rather than from expanded political rights. The flood of women into paid work during the 1960s and 1970s resulted from changing needs for labor, from the shift from manufacturing to clerical and service work (Edwards, Reich, & Weisskopf, 1978). Women (and men, too) have no legal right to employment and a reasonable wage but must adapt and adjust as best they can to the fluctuating needs of capitalism for women workers, and do so regardless of family needs (Glazer, Majka, Acker, & Bose, 1977). Indeed, after more than a 50-year struggle, American women still have been unable to win a basic political right—a constitutional amendment that would forbid discrimination on the basis of sex.

This chapter explores the theme of contradictions in women's lives in the United States. It asks questions about social life from the standpoint of women (Smith, 1977), rather than inserting women into traditional social science frameworks or ignoring women as too often still characterizes contemporary sociology (Committee of the Status of Women in Sociology, 1980). The view of women as "Other" in de Beauvoir's (1952) sense is abandoned, and women's daily domestic and work life is taken as a legitimate starting point for grasping many of women's contemporary problems. In addition, this chapter connects those everyday routines of women's lives (housework and child care, nurturing, paid work) to social relationships far removed from everyday personal experience—to the domination of contemporary life by monopoly capitalism.

In contemporary Western society, personal life is dominated by modern industrial capitalism, which as it emerged in the nineteenth century, pushed women (particularly married women) out of paid work outside the home and supported the development of an ideology of "private life" as a special female sphere (Cott, 1977; Welter, 1966). Within this sphere, women were to compensate men and their children for dramatic changes that affected the middle classes in the nineteenth century; in the twentieth century the working class, too, accepted the ideology of separate spheres, and women in working-class families were supposed to compensate their families for the low wages, poor working conditions, cycles of unemployment, poor housing, and political powerlessness that characterized working-class life (Zaretsky, 1976). (For a description of contemporary working-class family life, see Rubin, 1978).

Two factors must be examined in order to understand women's domestic lives and their activities outside the home: changes in ideology about family life and the actual effect of capitalism on people's daily lives. Since individuals must be able to meet certain material needs—for example, for food, shelter, basic health care—before being able to meet other human needs easily, it is important to understand how people subsist. Hence, my emphasis is on capitalism, the major economic form in the United States within which people work and consume.

Capitalism is a form of economic organization that emerged gradually between 1650 and 1850 (Jalee, 1977). In this economic system, wage labor is the main means by which those who do not own the means of production make a living. People (workers) sell their labor power for wages to those who own the means of production (tools, factories, land, banks, patents, newspapers, for example); the means of production are privately owned and run for private profit. In contrast, in socialist societies, there is no ownership of the major means of production. However, in both socialist and capitalist societies, most consumer goods (housing, autos, clothing, food) are privately owned, so that the difference between the economies has to do with the organization of production rather than the ownership of certain consumer goods. Furthermore, those who own and control the means of production, because of other people's material needs including the need for paid work, have enormous political as well as economic power over others (Miliband, 1978). The concentration of wealth permits a relatively small elite to have disproportionate power to define acceptable social values and to disseminate their beliefs through the mass media (Ewen, 1976) and through cultural institutions (Bowles & Gintis, 1976).

With this very brief, and hence simplified overview of the social and economic context within which family life occurs and within which women's family responsibilities have changed, along with their activities outside the household, the chapter will now examine (a) the dominant American ideology about women and the family; (b) women's experiences over the last 50 years in paid work; (c) the relationship between doing paid and unpaid work; (d) new unpaid work for women; and (e) the problems of the single-parent (mother-headed) household.

IDEOLOGY

Various ideologies support how most Americans view the family, women and capitalism. These ideologies are not separate from common understandings of how unpaid and paid work are related, nor from the solutions that are proposed to the problems of "the family."

Ideology has two facets: (a) the group or social class that promotes the particular beliefs about the social world and what is promoted; and (b) the group or social class that accepts that promoted ideology more or less uncritically. While many diverse ideologies are promoted in the United States and, indeed, people may even accept conflicting ideologies, social scientists can nevertheless discern and discuss dominant ideologies about women's family and work lives. Analyses of the mass media (television, magazines, movies, advertising, newspapers), of law, social theories, personal diaries and letters, ritual and ceremonies, and much more of everyday social life are among the social phenomena social scientists examine to determine what ideologies are current. Public opinion polls, in-depth interviews, observations, and oral histories are among the sources of data social scientists use to determine what ideologies seem to be currently accepted by people in society.

Here, I am concerned with what views of the social world (including how the social relationships between owner/boss and workers, between women and men, and between women and their families) are thought to be best organized, what is assumed to be women's natural responsibilities or at least most compatible with how the political economy is organized, how problems of combining paid and unpaid work are to be solved, and related questions. Beliefs about the rightness of social life (as it is currently organized) are promoted, most importantly, by those who have enormous amounts of economic wealth and political power and who seek to curb or dampen criticism of their control and to prevent social change that would lessen their wealth and power. Ideology is not organized necessarily by people who are attempting to fool those with less resources and power, though that may be the case with some frequency; rather, the ideology is accepted usually by those who seek to disseminate their beliefs through the mass media, cultural institutions (e.g., schools and research facilities), religious organizations, political parties, and other public and private groups. To the degree that women and men in the working class, employed women, and families with employed women accept the generally prevalent ideologies about gender, family life and working conditions, then the contradictory social relationships that often plague the lives of women who want to live in families are likely to be unexamined and to go unchallenged.

In spite of attempts during the last 15 years to persuade people that the term *family* covers a wide array of social relationships and households, many Americans think of the term as describing a nuclear family of husband, wife, and their minor children. In turn, the ideology privatizes the household, seeing it as isolated, a haven, a castle (Lasch, 1979). Many sociologists and other social scientists, practitioners and policymakers see the family as occupying a sphere that is separated from, for example, the workplace, politics, the community, political economy, civic life and the schools (Zaretsky, 1976).

Furthermore, some policymakers, social reformers, and religious leaders see the family as composed of social relations that preferably should be protected from the encroachments of "society." In turn, they may see "society" as an entity that though analytically it includes "the family," is still somehow external to the family. Ideology has an actual impact on family life. For example, in practice the ideology just described is used to justify lawcourts and police staying out of husband–wife conflicts, including wife battering, and child–parent conflicts, including physical and emotional abuse, unless these conditions are seen as extraordinary. In practice, it means also that the American state is seen as having a minimum obligation to support the individual and the family, and virtually no obligation to maximize human potential unless to do so would benefit capitalism.

Women

Ideologies that women's place is in the home and that women have only a secondary commitment to paid work continue to dominate how work is understood. In the paid workplace, women are still often understood to work for "extras" and hence to work for essentially frivolous reasons, even though most studies show that women do not work for personal pleasure and self-fulfillment. Rather, women, first and foremost, work because of financial need (Hayghe, 1981). The prevailing view that women do paid work for nonessential and noneconomic reasons makes it possible for policymakers, legislatures, New Right groups, and even women themselves to interpret the problems women encounter in doing paid jobs as resulting from their personal "choices" rather than as being social problems. Hence, the solutions usually proposed to problems women have in combining paid and unpaid work emphasize personal sacrifice and innovation (Glazer, 1980a). For example, *Working Woman* magazine advises, implicitly and explicitly, (a) that women should reorganize their lives to maximize efficient use of time and energy; (b) that women should forgo marriage and/or having children, though of course men are not told that in order to earn a living or pursue a career they must not marry or become parents; the advice also assumes (c) that women have high incomes and can buy substitutes for their own now absent labor in the home in the marketplace. In order for women, as distinct from men, to do paid work, women are basically told to take themselves as objects, to live on a highly scheduled basis and, often, to eliminate from their lives the personal pleasures of love, companionship, sex, and children.

This privatized view of the family is not consistently accepted by the state (Donzelot, 1980). The extension of rights to women has eroded aspects of the ideology of privacy. Women today can do paid work and have a credit standing independently of their spouses' preferences. The erosion of patriarchy in the family through the increase in the civil rights of women in relations to their spouses has provoked attacks by various groups on women's newly gained rights, for example, on abortion. The result is, ironically, that those groups arguing against abortion and contraception are actually also attacking the family as a private haven by working for the state regulation of reproduction and, by implication, of female sexuality.

Capitalism

Capitalism's needs and goals dominate in the formation of American policies on the family. Current ideology legitimates capitalism as the solution to many of women's problems by implying that the marketplace provides the goods and services needed and that the marketplace constitutes the solution rather than being itself a problem. Other situations are not even seen as problems. First, capitalism's continued existence as a dominant form, here and abroad, is the basis for legitimating most social decision-making. Of course, there are always ideologies that reject economic needs as primary, but not with the same degree of persuasion. Major social policies are shaped by how capitalists, who do not necessarily agree among themselves, understand their needs. For example, the interest payment deduction on home mortgage payments was not designed primarily to help families buy homes, but to increase the marketability of homes with the lure of tax reductions. The degree of accessibility to health care and higher education varies with capitalists' estimates of their needs for profit-making versus a healthy and educated (but not too well-educated) work force (Bowles & Gintis, 1976; Navarro, 1976). In times of economic expansion or war, when there is a need for female labor, the employment of wives and mothers is presented in the media and discussed by policymakers, etc., as having minimal disrupting consequences for the family. Though there will always be dissenting voices, this understanding gains wide currency. Governments may cooperate by promoting wage policies that encourage women's entrance into the workplace, for example, deliberately, by allowing the erosion of the so-called family wage by inflation to force women into the labor force (Holter, 1971). As the economy contracts, social scientists and other professionals "rediscover" the importance of a full-time mother for adequate childrearing.

Second, capitalism legitimates problem-solving through the use of the marketplace. Working wives and mothers are to solve what policymakers, foundation reports, and popular magazines label "their own personal problems" by turning to the marketplace. Employed women are supposed to find substitutes for the services and the goods that full-time housewives provide for their families by buying child care along with frozen beans since the American state has consistently refused to support more than token child care. By contrast with the United States, all socialist countries (and even other capitalist societies) provide or subsidize child care centers and/or provide family allowances (Kamerman, 1980).

Finally, the provision of goods and services such as child care, housekeeping services, holiday camps for children and parents, neighborhood facilities outside the market economy, and the redesigning of communities to support communal living arrangements that would eliminate the private character of housework and child care are attacked by capitalists as unfair competition and interference with capitalism. Moreover, Americans are encouraged by advertising and popular discussions of capitalism to believe that the market actually provides them with "choices" and, hence, overlook that market goods and services are designed to maximize profit. The ideology, ironically, makes it reasonable for people to have to select only from among the goods and services that private corporate executives have decided can be sold profitably, while eschewing ones that are not profitable. People are not entitled, usually, to goods and services, furthermore, unless they can buy them without government aid. The belief that social policy should be made to maximize human values, not profits, and give priority to human survival, not the survival of capitalism, is considered illegitimate and subversive in the dominant American ideology.

To summarize, the dominant ideologies that privatize the family, force women to do two jobs with little public support, and place the needs of capitalism before all others are the basis for social policies that reinforce contradictory demands on women—that they must do both paid work outside the home and unpaid work in the home.

PAID WORK

Since other chapters in this volume examine issues relating to the employment of women, this discussion will not examine women's paid work in any detail. However, the reader must understand the following to grasp the contradictions in women's lives: Women increasingly are paid workers for longer portions of their lives. The older employment patterns of most women—working before marriage and after their children were either in school or actually had left home—have been replaced by another pattern. Women leave the workplace for short periods of time to have children or carry out other family work, and sizeable proportions of mothers with preschool-age children regularly do paid work (Hayghe, 1982). Of course, divorced and widowed women, minority women, and immigrant women did not always follow the earlier patterns. Instead, these women worked "off the books," in their homes doing sweated labor, or taking what paid work they could outside the home, because their earnings were needed for family survival.

Women work, but they are concentrated in the sex-segregated sections of the job market. For example, in 1978 over 60% of women were employed in services, finance, insurance, real estate, and retail trades, where earnings were lower than in manufacturing, construction, and mining (Davis, 1980). In these industries, women work in so-called female work, as clerical workers, sales workers, and in service jobs. In the professions, women are concentrated in the so-called "semiprofessions," working as teachers, social workers, librarians, reporters, and nurses. Though professional schools have increasing proportions of women students, the professions of medicine and law still are dominated by men. The jobs that most women do can be characterized as low-wage work, with short advancement ladders, relatively minor fringe benefits (that is, relatively little in the way of vacations, pensions, training, etc.), subject to seasonal unemployment, and frequently part-time. The work is concentrated in what is called the secondary labor market, where work is routinized and heavily supervised (Blau & Jusenius, 1977; Edwards et al., 1978).

There is a sizable wage gap between the sexes that has not narrowed and, in fact, has increased. In the late 1950s, the wage gap was about 64¢ and increased so that by 1982, women were only earning 59¢ for every dollar men earned. While the wage gap between the sexes is often explained by the discontinuity of women's employment, a recent analysis concluded that only about one quarter of the difference in current average hourly wages ($8.00 for men and $5.29 for women) can be explained this way (Rytina, 1982).

Women's work (as well as men's) is subject to wage reductions through deskilling. Deskilling means that the work is changed by technology or the rationalization of the work process, so that old skills become obsolete but new ones are supposedly not demanded of workers: wages decrease accordingly (Braverman, 1974). For example, women and men sales clerks, valued and paid for selling skills (and sales records), have been replaced gradually by women cashiers. Cashiers supposedly need fewer skills than the clerks, since national advertising and the work of the consumers themselves substitute for selling skills, product knowledge, and even product location within a given store, and they are paid comparatively less than sales clerks (Glazer, 1984). Other sources of wage reductions include the flight of capital to cheaper female labor outside the United States and subsequent plant closures in textiles and electronics where women are the majority of workers. Women also are subject to technological unemployment, as the clerical and service work they do is automated. And, by a final irony, sex desegregation results often in men moving into managerial positions in the female professions. For example, while the vast majority of nurses are women, half of all male nurses are administrators (Grimm & Stern, 1974). In clerical work, management has displaced women with men in jobs that the company intends to phase out. By hiring men (rather than women), the company expects to have a higher attrition rate and relieve themselves of the obligation to retrain women who otherwise would be displaced workers (Hacker, 1978).

These data show that, at the very time in which women are increasingly expected, normatively and because of their social circumstances, to become regular, full-time workers, women's position in the workplace remains restricted and has even worsened in some areas.

An observation must be added about affirmative action. Affirmative action guidelines have been used against women. For example, Hacker (1978) reports that affirmative action guidelines have been met by hiring women for managerial positions in departments that the company plans to eliminate. In the current situation of cutbacks, there is little guarantee that affirmative action will protect women workers. It is likely that the "last hired, first fired" rule will prevail and eliminate many gains women made during the last decade.

PAID WORK AND UNPAID WORK

A major contradiction facing women is that they must now do paid work outside the home while still continuing to be responsible for unpaid housework and child care. The sex-segregated job market in capitalism assures that most women will earn less than men and that female earnings will rarely suffice for the purchase of goods and services that would be substitutes for the now absent work of the wife–mother. The state eschews most social programs that would help women with family responsibilities. The current American ideology generally supports the views of policy-makers, social theorists, and activists that women's ability to earn a living gives them both more power in the marital relationship and diminished responsibility in the home for domestic work: hence, in this view, the double day is not a problem for the employed woman.

Marital Power and Waged Work

Research does not consistently link the employment of the wife to an increase in her power in the family. Some studies show that employed wives gain in decision-making power, and others show no change. Still others suggest that wives may lose power when their former work is shifted to other family members. Unfortunately, many studies are also characterized by a naive view of power. Trivial and crucial decisions are mixed together, which may make decision-making seem more balanced or equal than it actually is. For example, studies may give equal weights to decisions to move the family or buy a car, and to decisions about children's bedtime hours and television program watching.

Wage Work and Housework

Wives' employment does not appear to change the gender division of labor in the household. Though an employed wife does less domestic labor than the nonemployed wife, her total working day is still longer than that of her husband. She remains responsible for the home; the hours of domestic labor decrease, because she buys substitutes for her own time and energy in the marketplace, children may do a bit more work, or some work simply does not get done. Only one time-budget study of a small sample shows some slight increase in the amount of time that husbands of employed wives reportedly spend at domestic labor compared to the husbands of nonemployed wives (Pleck & Lang, 1978). The pattern is this: under some circumstances, husbands will increase the time spent doing housework or child care. That amount of time is nominal and cannot be interpreted as husbands assuming equal responsibility with wives for housework and child care. Furthermore, the intent of couples to share equally in domestic work may not be realized after children are born. Even women trained in the professions take the responsibility for child care while their husbands focus on careers (Nadelson, Nofman, & Lowenstein, 1979).

In summary, the entrance of married women into paid work has not had the expected effect of markedly (a) increasing women's power in the marital relationship; (b) decreasing women's responsibilities in the home and increasing men's share of household work, at least to a degree that would be commensurate with the length of women's paid work day or their proportional contribution to family income.

The contradictory changes are apparent: More and more married women do paid work, but earn less on the average than men and without gaining power in the marital relationship or reducing their responsibilities in the home.

"Unemployment" in the Home: The Fictitious Account of Why Women Do Waged Work

Since some people, including social scientists, have argued that women's employment results from their release from household drudgery, changes in housework technologies are relevant to examining changes in women's lives.[1] Oppenheimer (1972) has examined the impact of technology, such as electric heat, lighting, refrigeration, and indoor plumbing in the household, on women's availability for paid work. She concludes that most major changes in household technology happened well before the recent increase in female employment. Oppenheimer also examined other social technological changes, such as municipal sewage plants, paved city streets, and the electrification of neighborhoods. Her data show that the basis for a decrease in the hours of housework preceded by many years women's employment increases. Furthermore, the municipal services that were necessary for reducing the terrible drudgery of housework (e.g., public waterworks, sewage systems, electrification, paved roads) were at first available only to the rich, by subscription, or through the support of the city (Strasser, 1982). On the contrary, it was, of course, the poorer women who first entered the work force as well as previously combining various ways of earning money in the household with the usual domestic responsibilities. The first employed married women had neither access to the necessary municipal services nor the money to purchase equipment that would have reduced their household work. Finally, capitalism's drive to create new social needs, and hence new markets for products, raised the housewife's standards of household cleanliness, increased the consumption of goods (clothing, houseware, furniture, play equipment) and hence, made more work for women (Ehrenreich & English, 1975). This new work replaced the old demands on women of the physically demanding work that predated modern appliances. For example, women spend more hours today doing laundry than they did two generations ago, though of course the work today is less physically demanding than it once was (Vanek, 1972).

Income in Old Age

As of 1980, pension plans for women had not kept pace with the increasing employment of women. The pension rules that require continuous employment mean a hardship for women whose employment is discontinuous. Interruptions in job service (even when regulations allow maternity leave, without loss of rights in a vested pension) may reduce women's pensions sharply, if leave is taken for long periods or before vesting. Since women do have an intermittent pattern of employment—shaped by caring for their families—this rule reduces pensions, because in spite of the recognition of women's rights in the Security Employee Retirement Income Act of 1974, the rules do not recognize the special family-connected employment patterns of women.

---

[1] For a review of the theoretical literature on unpaid domestic labor (housework, child care, nurturing, etc.) see Glazer-Malbin (1976, 1980). For a review of the literature on women's paid work, see Blumberg (1978). An excellent history of housework is Strasser (1982).

Death and divorce also have severe effects on women's income in old age. To give just a few examples, the Act of 1974 requires that (in most pensions) the worker automatically receives an annuity for his/her spouse upon the retiree's death, but the retiree may cancel that option without informing the spouse. Thus, a divorced wife can be excluded from a survivor annuity, even when an agreement had been made with the former spouse to provide such coverage. Divorced wives, regardless of the number of years of the marriage, have no right to pension money, unless the couple lives in a community property state or marital property state. However, even then, if the husband were to die before retirement, the surviving ex-wife might lose the survivor annuity.

Other problems for women include sex-based actuarial tables which give lower monthly pension benefits to women than to men, because women as a group live longer than men. The 1983 Supreme Court ruling forbids such practices in the future for government pension plans though private plans and all of the past contributions of women are unaffected.

NEW UNPAID WORK

Not all of women's work can be divided between waged work in the labor force or unwaged work in the household. Another category has emerged, unwaged work that is directly appropriated by firms and exploited by the state. Private firms and the government have reorganized various activities to draw increasingly upon the work of consumers (users, patients, customers, and clients) (Glazer, 1982). The reorganization results from attempts to eliminate waged workers and thereby increase profits or lower the state's cost in providing various services. For example, the organization of retail sales in the United States from 1912 to the present experienced a major change from a service-intensive to a self-service industry and a subsequent decline in the rate of wage increases (Schwartzmann, 1971). Both capitalist firms and state agencies have attempted to involve the customers and clients in such activities as recordkeeping work in the course of bill-paying. Some state agencies have tried to get women (as wives, mothers, and daughters) to do for free what was once done as state services. For example, under Medicare cost levels and the "average stay" estimates used by hospital Utilization Review Committees, the time between patient treatment and hospital discharge has decreased sharply, with relatives taking on the work of posthospital care that was once done in the hospital. Most recently, the self-help movement seems to have been co-opted by medical delivery systems and used as a philosophical basis for getting individuals to themselves perform services which the HMOs will no longer provide. For example, budget cuts for social service for the health care of the elderly mean that family members may have to provide services in the home that were once provided in the hospital, e.g., patients are returned to their homes earlier than in previous decades.

DIVORCE: NO NEED TO LIVE UNHAPPILY EVER AFTER

Divorce laws have changed over the last decades. Divorce rates have increased steadily, and women who divorce or are divorced no longer are stigmatized as they were 50 years ago. Similarly, a man who divorces, even to marry another woman immediately, seems relatively unstigmatized even by so obviously changing one wife for another, as serial polygamy becomes a part of American life. Some of the major results for women and for men are as follows.

Child Custody

Over the last several years a spate of films and stories has focused on the bravery of men who face raising children when death, or more likely, a runaway wife leaves them as the sole adult head of the household. Since the late nineteenth century, women have been awarded custody of children usually, a marked gain in their civil status. Until then, common law held that men, not women, had control of the offspring of marriage; and in the United States, though more so in Great Britain and on the European continent, women waged a long battle to win custody of their children. A reverse now seems to be the case, with men taking custody. However, that impression is false. In 1960, 1.2% of all children under 18 were living with their fathers only; by 1978, that had only increased to 1.6% of children. Among mother-only families, meanwhile, the percent of children had risen from 8.2 in 1960 to 17.6 in 1978. Thus, about 17% of all households in 1978 were headed by women only, compared to 1.8% by men only.

The single woman heading a household faces myriad financial and emotional responsibilities, as well as having to carry on the everyday routines of homemaking. Given the discrimination that women experience in the workplace, with resulting low wages and dead-end jobs with few fringe benefits, supporting a family becomes most difficult. Low levels of child support awards and irregular payments are the basis of some of the financial problems facing women who avail themselves of the new freedoms to leave unsatisfactory marriages (or who have been left by their husbands). Divorce for women and for children has severe and often permanent economic consequences (U.S. Dept. of Commerce, 1979). Most women do not receive child support payments from the father of their children. In 1975, only about 25% did, a level that has not fluctuated much this century.

In addition, the amount of child support payments is relatively small and is a small proportion of total family income. For half of women with child support, the payments are less than 10% of their income; and only 5% got more than half of their income from child support. Child support payments do keep some women from being at or below the poverty level (Mallan, 1975). An analysis of women who divorced between 1968 and 1975 showed that there was a drop in real family income that was all out of proportion to the drop in family needs. With the loss of a husband, women had an average drop of 18% in income needs compared to a 44% drop in real family income (Corcoran, 1976). If the contribution of labor that the man of the household makes to irregular housework—outdoor maintenance, repair jobs, some child care—is included, the loss to the family is even greater. Finally, in awarding child support payments and in considering the contributions that the custodial parent makes to the support of the child, the work that mothers do in maintaining the household is ignored. This housework and child care is invisible, free labor donated by women actually, to the fathers of their children as well as to their children.

CONCLUSIONS

The opening statement of this discussion was that women's lives are characterized by contradictory demands. This is because changes have occurred in work and family life without the development of supporting structures (discussed in this section) and so makes for difficult lives for women. The "freedoms" for women, thus, came into existence with an expansion of *non*freedoms for women. What this means is that many women have come to be a special underclass in society in which two jobs are expected and demanded of them. Women are forced to continue the unpaid domestic labor that allows capitalism to have a new labor force each generation and to have workers ready for work each day—but capitalism gets this domestic labor for free.

First, women's entrance into paid labor carries with it the freedoms to leave marriage, to bear children, and keep and raise them outside of marriage. But, women's labor as paid worker arises not from an ideology that says women are equal, with equal rights with men. The freedom comes from a need by capitalists for a labor force that is literate, pliable, and unable to refuse low-waged work. Oppenheimer (1972) has argued that women's entrance into paid labor did not follow changes in ideology about employment of women, but that changes in ideology came afterward. Hence, when the contraction of the economy results in a reduced need for women workers, we find a return to the promotion by some corporations, social theorists, policymakers, and others, and increased media attention to an ideology that would place women back in the home. The reemergence of this ideology as legitimate is evidenced in the serious consideration in 1982 by the United States Congress of the Family Protection Act. That Act would, for example, ban federal aid to all schools that did not teach the correctness of traditional (i.e., nineteenth century) gender relations. Second, the entrance of women into paid jobs provides both the need and the rationale for establishing women as entitled to the same civil rights as men. As women increasingly do paid work, it becomes increasingly incompatible with the capitalist conception of individual rights to deny contractual status to women. Hence, women are accorded credit rights, and married women gain the rights to their earnings, to selecting residences, to keeping their birth names. Abortion can be chosen without the consent of the father, and women can live with men without marrying. However, the new status also assigns a new set of responsibilities to women. Hence, women are now seen as less entitled to alimony than in earlier decades. It becomes easier to argue that women should share absolutely equally with men in financial contributions to child support, since women, too, can now earn outside the home. It is only an occasional woman who is knowledgeable enough to know that data on the wage differential between the sexes could be used in the law court to challenge such a specious argument.

One can argue that women bore the brunt of the expansion of capitalism in the mid-twentieth century by first being brought into waged work, kept in a marginal position within the capitalist economy, and susceptible to expulsion from work with each new economic crisis. What remains now is the contradiction: Women are entitled to various legal rights and new obligations, but lack the legal status and economic rights to enjoy an emancipated life. Furthermore, what is lacking for women and their families are supporting social arrangements that include both an ideological commitment to female equality that guides the designs of daily living, and a structural commitment that means that the designs, actually, not just hypothetically, contribute to making daily life more satisfying.

New social arrangements are needed that would ease the double day, but today few such arrangements exist, ones that might provide, for example, free or low-cost and desirable goods and services that substitute for the work women once did in the home. Such arrangements (infrastructures) are not developed ordinarily in a capitalist society unless they appear to be a source of profit for capitalism, while the quality of the goods and services provided under this kind of motivation may be shoddy indeed (e.g., as in fast food franchises, or in child care franchises) or be of limited use (e.g., flextime, which is convenient to some workers but which still means an extremely busy parent). Yet, we know that there are alternatives to overwork or shoddy goods and services, since some have been provided both in the United States and elsewhere: inexpensive, readily available child care, supervised by highly trained workers, and hot, nutritious meals to be picked up by parents along with their children (Kaiser shipyards, Portland, Oregon, during World War II); residence-located child care centers and residence-located attractive, low-cost communal dining (housing outside Stockholm, subsidized by an experimental and socially conscious Swedish builder until his death): the assembling without charge of grocery orders for employed women (in the "shopping bag system" in Cuba); and communal child care with intensive emotional involvement by parents (as in some Israeli kibbutzim) (Glazer et al., 1977). These programs are not necessarily ideal and might not suit American tastes, but are included here to illustrate alternatives to services designed to make a profit.

The current social arrangements for organizing everyday life are tied to capitalism's view of their needs for a labor force and to attempts to contain cyclical economic crises and various protests by the working-class and by women of various classes and minority groups. Women are today a large underclass. They are an underclass in two ways. Women are the majority of those who live at or below the poverty line and hold jobs that are the most subject to deskilling and to reduced wages. Women are the family underclass—increasingly the custodial partner, the sole adult responsible for raising the next generation. The state usually becomes interested in the father's relation to his children only for welfare children. In other cases, the pursuit of the transient father is perfunctory.

Several of the other chapters in this book center on the interpersonal social relationships that can be used to build trusting, active, well-developed children and hence, adults. I would not deny that interpersonal relationships are crucial to such goals. Without loving, warm, supportive relationships between children and their caretakers, there is little or no hope for a new generation of competent, loving, and creative adults. However, what one must recognize is that the complement of this ideal is a society that itself is not dedicated to business but also to people. It is difficult to imagine how women can be excellent mothers, raising a new generation which satisfies our ideals for the future, when daily, women struggle with impossible circumstances: poor housing, low wages, little respite from child care, violence, unemployment—the gamut of problems that plague contemporary capitalist societies. Many of the crises that women face in their personal lives arise from a society in which profits are first and children and their families last (Brandwein et al., 1974). The order must be changed.

REFERENCES

Baran, P.A., & Sweezy, P.M. *Monopoly capital.* New York: Monthly Review Press, 1966.

Blau, F., & Jusenius, C. Women and economic theory. In N. Glazer & H. Waehrer (Eds.), *Women in a man-made world* (2nd edition). Chicago: Rand McNally, 1977.

Blumberg, R.L. *Stratification: Social, economic and sexual inequality.* Dubuque, IA: Wm. C. Brown, 1978.

Bowles, S., & Gintis, H. *Schooling in capitalist America.* New York: Basic Books, 1976.

Brandwein, E., Brown, C.A., & Feldberg, R. Women and children last: The social situation of divorced mothers and their children. *Journal of Marriage and the Family,* 1974, *36,* 498–514.

Braverman, H. *Labor and monopoly capital: The degradation of work in the twentieth century.* New York: Monthly Review Press, 1974.

Committee of the Status of Women in Sociology. Sexist biases in sociological research: Problems and issues. *Footnotes,* 1980 (January: American Sociological Association).

Corcoran, M. The economic consequences of divorce. Women in Mid-Life Crisis Conference. Ithaca, NY: Cornell University, October, 1976.

Cott, N. *The bonds of true womanhood.* New Haven, CN: Yale University Press, 1977.

Davis, H. Employment gains of women by industry, 1968–78. *Monthly Labor Review,* 1980, *103,* 3–9.

de Beauvoir, S. *The second sex.* New York: Knopf, 1952.

Donzelot, J. *The policing of families.* New York: Pantheon, 1980.

Edwards, R., Reich, M., & Weisskopf, T.E. (Eds.), *The capitalist system* (2nd edition). Englewood Cliffs, NJ: Prentice-Hall, 1978.

Edwards, R.C. *Labor market segmentation papers.* Lexington, MA: Heath, 1975.

Ehrenreich, B., & English, D. The manufacture of housework. *Socialist revolution,* 1975, *5,* 5–40.

Ewen, S. *Captains of consciousness.* New York: McGraw Hill, 1976.

Glazer-Malbin, N. Housework: A review essay. *Signs,* 1976, *1,* 905–922.

Glazer, N., Majka, L., Acker, J., & Bose, C. The homemaker, the family and employment. *Hearings: American women workers in a full employment economy,* U.S. Congress, Joint Economic Committee, Subcommittee on Economic Growth and Stabilization, 95th Congress, 1977, 155–169.

Glazer, N. Overworking the working woman: The double day in a mass magazine. *Women's Studies International Quarterly,* 1980, *3,* 79–94. (a)

Glazer, N. Every woman needs three hands: Doing paid and unpaid work. In S.F. Berk (Ed.), *Woman and Household Labor.* Beverly Hills, CA: Sage, 1980. (b)

Glazer, N. The invisible intersection: Involuntary unpaid labor and women workers. *Radical Review of Political Economics,* 1984 (forthcoming), *16,* Spring. Special Issue on Women in the Economy.

Grimm, J.W., & Stern, R.H. Sex roles and internal labor market structures: The "female" semi-professions. *Social Problems,* 1974, *21,* 690–705.

Hacker, S. Sex stratification, technology and organizational change: A longitudinal analysis of AT&T. American Sociological Association meetings, San Francisco, CA, 1978.

Hayghe, H.H. Husbands and wives as earners: An analysis of family data. *Monthly Labor Review,* 1981, *104,* 46–53.

Hayghe, H.H. Marital and family patterns of workers, and update. *Monthly Labor Review,* 1982, *105,* 53–56.

Holter, H. Sex roles and social change. *Acta Sociologica,* 1971, *14,* 2–12.

Jalee, P. *How capitalism works.* New York: Monthly Review Press, 1977.

Johnson, B.L. Changes in marital and family characteristics of workers, 1970–78. *Monthly Labor Review,* 1979, *102,* 49–52.

Kamerman, S.B. Child care and family benefits: Policies in six industrialized countries. *Monthly Labor Review*, 1980, *103*, 23–28.

Kolko, G. *Wealth and power in America*. New York: Praeger, 1962.

Lasch, C. *Haven in a heartless world*. New York: Basic Books, 1979.

Mallan, L.B. Young widows and their children: A comparative report. *Social Security Bulletin*, 1975, *38*, 3–21.

Miliband, R. *The state in capitalist society*. New York: Basic Books, 1978.

Nadelson, C.C., Notman, M.T., & Lowenstein, P. The practice patterns, life styles, and stresses of women and men entering medicine. *Journal of the American Woman*, 1979, *34*, 400–406.

Navarro, V. *Medicine under capitalism*. New York: Prodist, 1976.

Oppenheimer, V.K. *The female labor force in the United States*. Westport, CN: Greenwood, 1972.

Pleck, J., & Lang, L. Married men: Work and family. In E. Corfman (Ed.), *Families today* (Vol. 1). NIMH Science Monographs (1). Washington, DC: U.S. Govt. Printing Office, 1978.

Rubin, L. *Worlds of pain*. New York: Basic Books, 1978.

Rytina, N.F. Earnings of men and women: A look at specific occupations. *Monthly Labor Review*, 1982, *105*, 25–31.

Schwartzmann, D. *The Decline of service in retail trades*. Washington: Washington State University, 1971.

Smith, D.E. Towards a sociology for women. In N. Glazer & H. Waehrer (Eds.), *Woman in a man-made world*. Chicago: Rand McNally, 1977.

Smith, S.J. New worklife estimates reflect changing profile of labor force. *Monthly Labor Review*, 1982, *105*, 15–20.

Strasser, S. *Never done: A history of American housework*. New York: Pantheon, 1982.

U.S. Department of Commerce. *Divorce, child custody, and child support*. Current Population Reports. Special Studies Series P–23, No. 84, 1979.

U.S. Department of Labor. *Women and private pension plans*. Washington, DC: U.S. Govt. Printing Office, 1980.

Vanek, J. Time spent in housework. *Scientific American*, 1974, *231*, 116–120.

Welter, B. The cult of true womanhood: 1820–1860. *American Quarterly*, 1966, *18*, 151–174.

Zaretsky, E. *Capitalism, the family and personal life*. New York: Harper & Row, 1976.

Chapter 7
Sexual Inequality: The High Cost of Leaving Parenting to Women

Daisy Quarm
University of Cincinnati

In every known society, there is a division of labor by sex. Although most roles vary widely from society to society, the care of very young children has been the universal responsibility of women. In our own society, at least until recently, the primary role of men was breadwinner and the primary role of women was homemaker and childrearer. The entrance of large numbers of women into the labor force is challenging this traditional division of labor. This chapter will examine the high cost of the traditional sex-gender system, the benefits of a more androgynous society, and the difficulties of the transition.

ATTITUDES TOWARD WOMEN'S WORK AND FAMILY ROLES

Between 1940 and 1980 women's labor force participation increased from 27.4 to 51.1%, largely because of the greater percentage of married women, often married women with children, who were working. By 1980, over 45% of married women with children under six were in the labor force. This dramatic change in women's roles was followed by dramatic changes in the attitudes of both men and women toward women's work and political roles. Since 1937 the percentage of both men and women favoring women working outside the home and holding public office has increased dramatically. Currently over three fourths of all Americans support women working and holding public office.

In 1937 only 27% of male and 40% of female respondents said they would vote for a qualified woman for president (Erskine, 1971). By 1978, 76% of men and 77% of women said they would vote for a qualified woman for president (Gallup, 1979). An even larger number, 88% of men and 89% of women, reported in 1975 that they would vote for a qualified woman for Congress (Gallup, 1978).

Similar changes in sex-role attitudes have occurred with regard to women working outside the home. When first asked by Gallup in 1937: "Do you approve of a married woman earning money in business or industry, if she has a husband capable of supporting her?" only 18% favored women working. In 1945 the percent favoring women working was still 18%, but by 1969, 55% were in favor and by 1976, 68% were in favor (Erskine, 1971; Gallup, 1978).

In spite of these dramatic changes, most Americans do not support equal roles for men and women. Most still view women's primary responsibility as home and family. Over 50% of both sexes agree that "it is more important for a wife to help her husband's career than to have one herself." Over 60% of both sexes agree that "it is much better for everyone involved, if the man is the achiever outside the home and the woman takes care of the home and family" (Quarm, forthcoming).

Moreover, not only do most people support a modified traditional specialization by sex in terms of family repsonsibilies, a large portion of the population supports sex segregation in the workplace. At least 60% of both men and women think that women would be better nurses than men, and at least 50% think that women would be better elementary school teachers and secretaries than men. Moreover, 50% of respondents think that men make better police officers, auto mechanics, and truck drivers. When asked, "For which of the following groups, if any, would you prefer to deal with a man?" 45% said that they preferred to deal with a male lawyer, 53% preferred a male doctor (general practitioner), and 45% preferred a male dentist (Gallup, 1978).

Although opposition to women working and holding political office is now espoused by only a small minority of both men and women, a majority of both sexes still feel that a woman's primary responsibility is to her home and family. It is acceptable for women to work, as long as they can still handle their reproductive roles as well. Also, although most people agree with general statements that women should have equal employment opportunities with men, they cling to traditional stereotypes about the jobs that women and men can perform. They still support very different roles for men and women. In other words, most people believe that women can have productive roles in the paid labor force, but only so long as they are compatible with the sexual division of reproductive roles.

BENEFITS AND COSTS OF TRADITIONAL SEX ROLES

The most frequently mentioned benefit of traditional sex roles by both sociologists and the general public is that they provide childrearing for the young and physical and emotional support for other family members:

> In our opinion the fundamental explanation of the allocation of the roles between the biological sexes lies in the fact that the bearing and early nursing of children establish a strong presumptive primacy of the relation of mother to the small child and this in turn establishes a presumption that the man, who is exempted from these biological functions, should specialize in the alternative instrumental direction.
>
> However the allocation may have come about in the course of bio-social evolution, there can be little doubt about the ways in which differentiation plays into the structure and functioning of the family as we know it. It is our suggestion that the recent change in the American family itself and in its relation to the rest of the society which we have taken as our point of departure, is far from implying an erasure of the differentiation of sex roles; in many respects it reinforces and clarifies it. In the first place, the articulation between family and occupational system in our society focuses the instrumental responsibility for a family very sharply on its one adult male member, and prevents its diffusion through the ramifications of an extended kinship system. Secondly, the isolation of the nuclear family in a complementary way focuses the responsibility of the mother role more sharply on the one adult woman, to a relatively high degree cutting her off from the help of adult sisters and other kins-women; furthermore, the fact of the absence of the husband–father from the home premises so much of the time means that she has to take primary responsibilty for the children. This responsibility is partly mitigated by reduction in the number of children and by aids to household management, but by no means to the point of emancipating the mother from it. Along with this goes, from the child's point of view, a probable intensification of the emotional significance of his parents as individuals, particularly and in the early stages, his mother, which, there is reason to believe, is important for our type of socialization. (Parsons, 1955, pp. 23–24)

Assigning the primary responsibility for the rearing of children to a single sex, the female, can have certain advantages even in technological societies. For example, in this volume Sroufe and Ward have pointed out the importance of high quality early care for the development of secure attachment by children. Having mothers remain at home with their children during their earlier years of life is one way of attempting to accomplish this goal.

However, the sexual division of child care responsibilities has spawned a complex sex-gender system with consequences far beyond childrearing. The relationship between the sex-gender system and these consequences is not obvious, and indeed many who advocate mothers as the primary childrearers would express strenuous opposition to these consequences of the sex-gender system. Nevertheless, this section will demonstrate that many social problems, such as rape, wife abuse, women's high rates of mental illness and poverty, the double day, and inexpressive men, are consequences of the sex-gender system, and only by eradicating the sex-gender system can they be changed.

Poverty of Women and Children

One of the most direct extensions of women's specialization in the care of very young children is the sexual differentiation of other social roles concerning work and non-work activities. Women's work roles, in turn, have a direct effect on the economic well-being of many women and children.

On the average, women earn only about 60 cents for every dollar earned by men, and women's low salaries often result in poverty. Of all people living below the poverty line in the U.S., 78% are women or children (U.S. Bureau of the Census, 1983). The low salary scale for women has been justified by the argument that women's wages were merely supplementing those of the primary wage earners. Although never true of all women workers, this supposition is even less credible today because of the increased frequency of marital disruption. The number of children in single-parent families grew from one out of nine children in 1970 to one out of five in 1980. By 1981, 45% of all female single-parent households with children under 18 were living below the poverty line, and 60% of all black female single-parent households with children under 18 were living in poverty (U.S. Bureau of the Census, 1983).

Clearly, women's specialization in the rearing of children has spawned a sexual division between housework and paid work and within the paid labor market itself that has resulted in high rates of poverty for women and their children, especially in female-headed families. Women's specialization in caring for children has been encouraged by the claim that good care in the first few years of a child's life is essential for the welfare of the child and society. Women are asked to perform this vital function for society and yet, when, because of the sexual division of labor, mothers find themselves without sufficient economic resources to support their families, society does not provide for them adequately. The average monthly AFDC payment between July and September of 1981 was only $99 per person (U.S. Department of Health and Human Services, 1982); therefore, many families receiving public assistance that year were left living below the official poverty line ($9,287 for a family of four) after receiving benefits (U.S. Bureau of the Census, 1983). About one-half of all children living in families with a female head, no husband present, were living in poverty, compared with 11 percent of children living in married-couple families (U.S. Bureau of the Census, 1983), indicating that our society is not meeting the needs of large numbers of women and children.

The Double Day

Although women increased their labor force participation dramatically between 1940 and 1980, there have been no such dramatic increases in men's participation in housework and child care. Vanek (1974) compared time spent in housework between 1924 and 1968, and Stafford and Duncan (1977) examined change between 1965 and 1976. Both reported that although employed women do less housework than non-employed women, men's contribution to housework has changed very little. Vanek (1974) found that husbands of both employed and non-employed women do about 7–10 hours of housework per week. A smaller study by Pleck (1979) reported that husbands of employed wives estimate that they spend a few hours more on housework than husbands of non-employed wives. This difference is still small, and Hartman (1981: 381) suggests that this finding may be due to the fact that husbands of employed wives think they are doing more housework because they are participating more often.

The fact that many women have changed their productive roles without men changing their reproductive roles is placing an enormous burden on many women. Vanek (1974) estimated that working women with small children work an average of 99 hours per week, when paid work and home work are combined. Such a hectic work schedule is costly to women, both in terms of emotional stress and lack of time for personal relaxation.

Mental Illness

Mental illness is one indicator of well-being. If the psychological costs of the sex-gender system were higher for women than for men, women should exhibit higher rates of mental illness than men. This is exactly what we find. The rates of mental illness, especially depression, are higher for women than for men, and they are higher for married women than never-married women. Interestingly enough, the mental illness rates of never-married men are higher than those of married men. It appears that marriage has detrimental effects on the mental health of women but positive effects on the mental health of men.

Just how is it that marriage can affect the mental health of men and women differently? Gove and Tudor (1973) have pointed out that marriage affects men and women differently, because the roles that they play are very different. Some of these differences are:

1. Most women are limited to a single role: homemaker (mother/wife). Most men have two roles—household head (husband/father) and worker. A man has two sources of gratification, family and work, while a woman has only one: her family. If one of the man's roles is unsatisfactory to him, he can concentrate on the other one.
2. A large number of women find that raising children and keeping house is frustrating. Guttentag and Salasin (1975) make a similar point when they emphasize that many women find homemaking stressful and that stress increases the likelihood of mental illness. Almost all wives end up being housewives. This is true even of working women—they do 26 hours of housework in the average week, and much of it is work that they don't find very appealing. Studies show that a generation ago only one third of high school women and one fifth of college women were interested in the domestic arts. The figures are probably even lower today. Also, in an interview study which I conducted, one of the questions that I asked was "Which household task do you enjoy doing most?" Over 20% of the respondents who were all female said, "NONE." The evidence suggests that many women do not find the housewife role rewarding. Two possible reasons are that the job itself has low status and that the job itself is monotonous, lonely, and demanding in terms of time (Oakley, 1974).
3. The housewife role allows women to brood over their troubles.
4. The housewife role is one of meeting other people's needs; therefore, it involves a great deal of uncertainty. It is characterized by adjusting to and preparing for contingencies. Many women find this uncertainty and lack of control frustrating. Guttentag and Salasin (1975) point out that we would expect high rates of depression among people who have a great number of stresses of life demands with which they must cope, and at the same time the fewest possible actual possibilities for mastery over them.
5. Working wives' jobs are not as good as those of men.

In short, the roles that married women play are more frustrating and less rewarding than those of men.

The situation of the single parent with young children is even more extreme. Ninety-seven percent of single-parent household heads are female. Their income is very low, even if they work. Guttentag and Salasin (1975) report that these women have very high rates of depression as do low-income married women with children, with low-status, low-paid jobs.

Both groups experience a high level of frustration, low rewards, and high powerlessness.

Generally, the relationship between work and mental health is positive. Even though most women do not have high status jobs (clerical, teaching, nursing, service), the rewards of many of these jobs outweigh the frustrations, perhaps because they increase women's feelings of control over their own lives.

Wife Beating

Although the rates of mental illness are higher for women than for men, men have greater difficulty in controlling aggression. Wife beating is but one of the forms that this inability to control aggression takes.

Wife beating is a method of social control used to control women. Although our culture seemingly disapproves of wife beating, the sex-gender system in our society actually encourages it, since the male role when carried to the extreme results in violence against women and the female role results in acceptance of that aggression.

One common misconception about batterers is that they are mentally ill. However, it is estimated that only 2 or 3% of all battering can be attributed to men who are psychotic or who suffer from brain damage which interferes with their ability to control aggression (Strauss, 1980). Some psychological studies based on small samples of special populations, such as batterers who are in jails or in treatment, have found high rates of mental illness among the men in their samples (Fawk, 1974), but since most batterers are not sentenced to jail or treatment, those that are are likely to be atypical. Therefore, findings based on jail or other institutionalized samples cannot be generalized to other batterers. The best available evidence suggests that batterers are no more likely to be mentally ill than are other members of the population.

Although most batterers are not mentally ill, they do seem to share several personality traits and cultural values and beliefs. Men who batter tend to be emotionally constricted and very dependent on women for nurturance and emotional support, but at the same time they hold antiwoman attitudes. David Adams and Isidore Penn (1981), two counselors who work with men who batter, have described how normative sex-role socialization encourages these characteristics in men.

Little boys are taught that to be a man is to not be a "sissy." Thus, rather than desired behavior being defined positively as something the child should do or be, undesirable behavior is indicated negatively as something the child should not do or be—particularly anything that is regarded as "sissy" (Hartley, 1974). Several consequences result from this type of socialization. First, little boys are taught to suppress characteristics attributed to females, especially the expression of emotions. The frequently heard adage, "Be a man; don't cry," epitomizes this message. One way to avoid expressing emotion is to actually curtail feeling emotions or at least one's awareness of one's emotions. Counselors of battering men report that batterers often fail to realize that their anger is a secondary reaction to hurt or fear, and many batterers even lack words to express their emotions.

Another consequence of this type of socialization is that men are especially wary of expressing their emotions to other men, and consequently become very dependent on women (often just one woman) for emotional support. Battering often erupts when a man is experiencing an emotional crisis that the woman, who is his sole source of emotional support, cannot solve. As McCormick (1980) explains:

> Most men do not feel comfortable with stoic emotional independence. It creates lonely and isolated people. After the "good times" of the corner gangs or the army are gone, men are left with few relationships that even hint at intimacy. When the woman they love is someone they feel they need to dominate, they are lonely indeed. This detached emotional life of men belies an internal festering that gives rise to rage, which often appears to be the dominant feeling in men. The rage is not only the result of mistreatment or hurt, it is also a deeper rage that is a response to the unmet need to share the feelings that he has. It is this rage that most people see as the cause of abuse. We must be clear that the rage is not a result of the woman's not meeting the man's needs. On the contrary, most men do not know how to ask for what they need. (p. 48)

A third consequence of socialization which requires boys to be hostile toward femininity is that it is difficult to be hostile toward femininity without being hostile toward females. According to Hartley (1974),

> Indeed a great many boys do give evidence of anxiety centered in the whole area of sex-connected role behaviors, an anxiety which frequently expresses itself in overstraining to be masculine, in virtual panic at being caught doing anything traditionally defined as feminine, and in hostility toward anything even hinting at "femininity," including females themselves. (p. 8)

This disdain for women is compounded by the fact that at the same time boys are taught to disdain everything that is "sissy," they are forced into a close relationship with the epitome of sissylike things, women (mothers and teachers) (Hartley, 1974). Moreover, they are also subordinates in this relationship in contradiction to the culturally prescribed relationship between the sexes. This situation breeds hostility toward women.

This type of sex-role socialization which encourages emotional constriction, heavy dependence on women (usually one woman) for emotional support, and hostility towards women is experienced to a greater or lesser extent by most men in our society, but most do not become batterers. Battering usually does not occur unless three other conditions are met: (1) a man must believe he has a right to beat a woman; (2) a man must believe that violence is a legitimate way of solving problems; and (3) a man must believe that he needs to maintain his dominant position vis-à-vis women (McCormick, 1980). Wife beating is an extreme attempt to achieve the socially approved pattern of interaction between the sexes: male dominance.

Rape

Rape is another act of male dominance, which although not approved of in our society, is fostered indirectly by society's sex-gender system. The socially approved sexual division of labor has fostered conceptions of masculinity and femininity which actually encourage rape. Two important aspects of the conception of masculinity in our society are sexual potency and dominance. Most people believe that males have a greater sexual need than females; to be a man is to be sexually potent. Also, our culture prescribes heterosexual relationships in which the male is aggressive and the female is passive. This norm covers actual sexual behavior and also those behaviors which lead up to it, such as asking for dates, paying for dates, even who calls whom on the telephone, and who initiates conversation at parties.

Herman (1979) has gone so far as to characterize our society as a "rape culture."

> In this country people are raised to believe that men are sexually active and aggressive while women are sexually passive and submissive. Since it is assumed men can't control their desires, every young woman is taught that she must be the responsible party in any sexual encounter. In such a society men and women are trained to believe that the sexual act involves domination. Normal heterosexual relations are pictured as consisting of an aggressive male forcing himself on a woman who seems to fear sex but unconsciously wants to be overpowered.

> So diffuse the aggressive-passive, dominant-submissive, me-Tarzan, you-Jane nature of the relationship between the sexes that in our culture there is a close association between violence and sexuality. Words that are slang sexual terms, for example, frequently accompany assaultive behavior or gestures. "Fuck-you" is meant as a brutal attack in verbal terms. In the popular culture, "James Bond alternately whips out his revolver and his cock, and though there is no known connection between the skills of a gun-fighter and love-making, pacifism seems suspiciously

effeminate." The imagery of sexual relations between males and famales in books, songs, advertising and films is frequently that of a sadoma-sochistic relationship thinly veiled by a romantic facade. Thus it is very difficult in our society to differentiate rape from "normal" heterosexual relations. Indeed our culture can be characterized as a rape culture be-cause the image of heterosexual intercourse is based on a rape model of sexuality. (p. 43)

Not only is rape fostered by our cultural conception of masulinity, but it appears that many men rape in order to prove their masculinity. Several pieces of evidence support this contention. First, adolescence is the period during which men are most insecure about their masculinity, and it is also the age group that experiences the highest arrest rates for forcible rape. Second, the incidence of group rape is very high; in one study, 43% of the cases were group rapes (Amir, 1971). Group rapes offer an even greater opportunity for the rapist to prove his masculinity, since he can prove it to others as well as to himself (Herman, 1979).

Many people falsely believe that all men would rape were there no laws and/or religious prohibitions against it. Rape is not natural or instinc-tive; it is learned. We know that rape is learned, because it does not occur with the same frequency in all cultures. For example, rape is very rare in hunting and gathering societies, which also happen to be societies in which sex roles are less differentiated and sexuality is not an act of power and domination.

FURTHER SUPPORT

The previous section has described some of the costs of the sex-gender system—the poverty of women and children, the double day, high rates of mental illness (especially depression) among women, woman battering, and rape. This section will provide further support for the connection between these consequences and the sex-gender system. This discussion will make use of the concept of social differential and of cross-cultural evidence.

Social Differentiation

We can think of men and women as being two different groups of people. Sociologists study interrelationships both within and between groups; thus, what they have learned about groups in general can help us understand the social relationships between men and women. One thing that is par-ticularly relevant to understanding the sex-gender system is a process called *social differentiation*.

There are four types or mechanisms of social differentiation: (a) symbolic differentiation; (b) physical (location) segregation and social segregation; (c) personality differentiation; and (d) functional or role differentiation.[1] In explaining each mechanism of social differentiation examples of sex differentiation will be used, but these same mechanisms operate for other groups such as age groups, social classes, religious groups, and even teenage gangs and sororities and fraternities.

Symbolic Differentiation. A symbol is anything that represents something else, anything that has meaning. A flag is an obvious example of a symbol; it is more than a pretty piece of cloth since it symbolizes "the republic for which it stands."

There are many examples of symbolic differentiation between the sexes. Males and females attach different symbols to their bodies, they speak differently, and they even move differently. For example, in our society, high-heeled shoes, ruffles, dresses and skirts, and certain colors (e.g., pink) are female symbols; neckties and pants are male symbols. Henley (1977) has pointed out that female symbols (skirts and high-heeled shoes) tend to inhibit freedom of movement, whereas male symbols (pants and flat shoes) tend to promote freedom of movement.

Women's language also differs from men's language. After reviewing the literature concerning vocabulary, pronunciation, grammar, sentence structure, and intonation, Richardson (1981) concluded, "Our language reinforces the idea that women and men have different abilities, personalities, and goals in life" (p. 31). For example, women are more likely to use intensifiers, e.g., so, such, quite, very ("This is so exciting"), tag questions ("It's hot, isn't it"), and intonational patterns, which are more polite and less definite than the males.

Richardson (1981) describes the consequences of sex differences in language as follows.

Women, then, are taught by the language they speak to appear weak, constrained, insecure, and dependent upon others. By using that language, women present themselves as persons not to be taken seriously, as persons whose opinions can be dismissed. Through the use of that style of speech, they perpetuate the stereotypes and, perhaps, even come to think of themselves as persons who are indecisive, incompetent, and silly. If they alter their speech patterns they are charged with being unfeminine or given the supposedly supreme compliment "You think like a man."

On the other hand, men are ridiculed if they talk like women. Their language constraints are the opposite—restricting them to seriousness of

---

[1] This formulation draws heavily on a lecture given by Karen Mason in a class on Gender Roles and Status, University of Michigan, 1973.

purpose, hard-hittingness, and decisiveness, whether they feel that way or not. Linguistically, it is difficult for them to express feelings of self-doubt or uncertainty. Indeed, their language style makes it difficult to emotively express practically any feeling except anger. We might, there-fore, hypothesize that the frequently noted lack of emotional expressivity in males (Deutscher, 1959; Balswick & Peek, 1971; Sheehy, 1976) is linked to the speech style that they are expected to adopt. While the emotional limitations of male speech do not in actuality turn off feelings, they do help men to repress their feelings and to see themselves as unemotional persons. (pp. 35–36)

Physical and Social Segregation. Because males and females must in-teract in order to reproduce, physical segregation cannot be as complete as the physical segregation between race and ethnic groups or social classes. Nevertheless, certain places are segregated by sex, for instance, public restrooms, private men's and women's clubs, and formerly, some public bars and social clubs. Segregation by sex often occurs at parties, family gatherings, and play groups. (See Borman and Frankel, Chap. 4, this volume, for a discussion of the consequences of sex-segregated play groups.)

In other societies sex segregation is more extensive than in our own. In some societies men and women do not eat together or walk side by side. *Purdah,* practiced in Middle Eastern societies, is an extreme example of sex segregation.

Although physical segregation of the sexes is not as extreme in our society as in some others, the consequences are serious. Friendship groups are frequently sex-segregated during childhood and adulthood. Whether by intentional exclusion or because men feel more comfortable with men, women are frequently excluded from informal friendship groups at work. Thus, women are often at a disadvantage when seeking to perform their jobs and gain promotions.

Personality Differentiation. In all known societies there is personality differentiation between the sexes, but the form that this differentiation takes varies from society to society. In our society, men are characterized as being more independent, objective, active, competitive, aggressive, and dominant; and women are characterized as being more dependent, sub-jective, passive, gentle, sensitive to the feelings of others, quiet, neat, emotional, and expressive (Broverman, Vogel, Broverman, Clarkson & Rosenkrantz, 1972). However, personality differences in our society are not always duplicated in other societies. For example, among the Tcham-buli the typical personality traits of men and women are the exact opposite of those in our society. Tchambuli women are more aggressive and dom-inant, whereas Tchambuli men are more passive, expressive, artistic, and nurturant (Mead, 1935).

Adult personality differences between the sexes are so pervasive that many have assumed they are innate. Three sources of evidence suggest that personality differences are learned rather than innate: the cross-cultural evidence already mentioned, studies of very young children, and studies of children whose sex was incorrectly labeled at birth. Literature reviews of studies of very young children find little evidence of personality differences in male and female children. There is no evidence that children under two differ in terms of dependency, empathy, sociability, nurturance, or emotionality (Maccoby & Jacklin, 1974; Tavris & Offir, 1977). There is some evidence that, on the average, males as young as two years are more aggressive than females, but it is possible that even this difference is learned.

Studies of children whose sex was incorrectly determined at birth corroborate that if any innate sex differences in predisposition exist, they are very weak. Ordinarily, when a baby is born, it is assigned a gender label which corresponds with the baby's physiological sex; however, there have been a number of cases in which the initial gender assignment has been incorrect. Studies of the mislabeled children show that they have developed the behavior patterns which correspond to their gender identities rather than their physiological sex (Money & Ehrhardt, 1972). In fact, once gender identity has been established, about the age of three, it is easier to change a child's external genitalia than their gender identity.

Current evidence suggests that personality differences between the sexes are due primarily to learning and the types of personality differences found between the sexes in our own society are not universal in all societies. Nevertheless, personality differentiation is an important component of the sex-gender system.

Functional Differentiation. Functional, or role, differentiation between the sexes occurs in all societies; however, the content of sex roles varies from society to society. For instance, in some societies, the women do all the fishing, whereas in other societies the men do all the fishing. The same goes for most other tasks. For instance, although women do the cooking, clothes-making, and food gathering in most societies, men do these tasks in a few (Murdock, 1935). While most roles are performed by both sexes in at least a few societies, there are one or two notable exceptions: (a) in all societies women have had the major responsibility for rearing very young children, and (b) in all societies where hunting has been the exclusive province of one sex only men have hunted large game and, until recently, only men had been involved extensively in war. Both of these exceptions have an obvious connection with lactation. The fact that only women lactate would explain women's specialization in the care of very young children, and suckling children is incompatible with most aspects of hunting large game and making war.

Although women have had primary responsibility for the care of young children in all societies and for the care of older children in most societies, in many societies women also contribute substantially to food production. Arnoff and Crano (1975) estimated that women's contribution to subsistence averaged 44% across the 862 societies in their study. Cross-cultural evidence suggests that the degree of women's involvement in productive roles varies widely and that women's involvement in production has been greatest in societies where productive roles compatible with childrearing were available to women (Blumberg, 1977). For example, in hunting and gathering societies, gathering and even the hunting of small game are compatible with women's childrearing roles, and in most of these societies women's contribution to production is substantial. By contrast, in agrarian societies in which fields are often located far from home, women's involvement in food production is less compatible with their childrearing roles; women's contribution to food production is minimal in agrarian societies. Blumberg also cites evidence from her own research on the Israeli kibbutzim which suggests that the long distances between the nurseries and fields discouraged mothers, especially breast-feeding mothers, from participating in agricultural production.

Evidence from other cultures suggests that women's involvement in production has varied widely, and that one of the major factors influencing their degree of involvement has been the compatibility of productive roles with women's reproductive roles. In societies in which women are involved in food production and control the product of their labor, social differentiation between the sexes is lower, and sexual inequality is minimal.

Within our own society, the degree of social differentiation between men and women has varied over time. Linda Gordon (1977) has described the changes occurring during the transition to industrial capitalism:

> Industrial production had begun profound changes in family structure. In agricultural and even commercial capitalist society, family enterprise had remained the unit of the entire economy. Whole families worked together under the authority of the husband/father; children, apprentices, servants, and wife were all assistants, differing in skill, experience, and authority, but all focusing their attention on the same problems. The economic unity of the family under its head represented to preindustrial people the natural microcosm of the political and economic organization of the whole society. Women were seen as inferior to men but not utterly different from them and not functioning in a different sphere. (p. 17)

As industrial capitalism developed, large numbers of men began to be employed away from their families. They were not only spatially separated from their families, but the increased functional differentiation between the sexes meant that men and women had different day-to-day problems and concerns. When women did work outside the home their jobs were usually sex-segregated. At this same time, a new ideology developed which emphasized that women were profoundly different from men. Thus, as the roles of men and women became more differentiated, the behavior and personality traits expected of men and women also became more different, including sexual behaviors and desires. The double standard, which already existed, was exacerbated.

Like the examples from other cultures, this example from American history suggests that women's specialization in the rearing of young children spawns other types of functional differentiation between the sexes and that a major determinant of women's participation in productive labor is the compatibility of these productive roles with their reproductive roles.

Consequences of Social Differentiation Between the Sexes

The mechanisms of social differentiation are helpful in establishing the connection between the sex-gender system and its negative consequences.

Poverty. Women's specialization in childrearing often results in poverty or low income for women, if they are without a breadwinner because of death, divorce, or never marrying. Childrearing responsibilities take most women out of the labor force for several years, discourage women from obtaining skills and training which would prepare them for high paying jobs, and create the expectation among employers that women are less committed workers than men.

Women's specialization in childrearing also affects the type of jobs women have when they do work and consequently their pay. Occupations are highly sex-segregated; different jobs acquire sex labels which are perpetuated over time. In her classic study of female labor force participation, Oppenheimer (1970) identified 17 occupations in which 70% or more of the workers were women in 1900. In 1950, there were 23 such occupations, and 46% of all women in the labor force were in these occupations. In 1981, more than two thirds of all working women were working as nurses, health workers, clerical workers, teachers, librarians, social workers, saleswomen, or service workers (U.S. Bureau of the Census, 1982). Many of the jobs sex-typed female are low paying jobs with at least moderate educational requirements. They also tend to be jobs which are consistent with roles and personality traits traditionally assigned to women.

Nancy Barrett (1979) described these characteristics as follows:

> First, women are rarely put in positions of authority. The assignment of male supervisors to a predominantly female work force limits women's upward mobility even in female-dominated occupations. In elementary and secondary schools, for example, two-thirds of the teachers are women, but only a third of the principals and other school administrators are women.
>
> Both white-collar and blue-collar jobs that women hold are stereo-

typed according to certain attributes commonly perceived as feminine. Jobs that require caring for others and nurturing small children are viewed as appropriately feminine, since these are tasks to which females are exposed from childhood.

Another characteristic of women's work assignments is that women are allowed only vicarious rather than direct achievements. The secretary who prepares her boss for business dealings, the nurse who assists the doctor in the operating room, and even the school teacher whose success lies in the achievements of her students exemplify indirect achievers. Society has long encouraged women to accept vicarious satisfactions. Girls have been taught to enjoy competitive sports as spectators or cheerleaders. Women have learned home economics with a view to pleasing husbands and raising healthy children.

Among blue-collar workers, too, sex-role attitudes affect job assignments. Women allegedly are better than men at tedious, repetitive tasks and at jobs requiring manual dexterity. Further, women are supposed to be more sensitive than men to loud noises and dirty places, and are presumed less able than men to work with heavy equipment (even though modern technology is such that most heavy equipment operates mechanically and physical strength often is not particularly important). As in the white-collar world, traditional sex roles dictate that blue-collar women should be supervised by men. (pp. 46–47)

Sex segregation in the labor market has serious consequences for women's economic well-being. One of the primary reasons that women earn less than men is because they are concentrated in predominantly female jobs, which tend to be low paying. The low salaries paid to workers in predominantly female jobs are not due to education or skill differences in jobs sex-typed male and female, as the following figures demonstrate:

Occupation	1981 Average Annual Income
Teacher's aide	$ 8,632
Truck driver	16,380
Secretary	11,908
Warehouse laborer	14,040
Prekindergarten & kindergarten teacher	13,728
Mail carrier	21,216
Registered nurse	17,212
Brick layer	20,852
Bank teller	9,776
Stock clerk	15,808

Functional and personality differentiation have the most obvious relationship to women's economic well-being, but symbolic, physical, and social segregation also contribute. Social segregation between the sexes often results in women being excluded from informal networks at work, which impedes their ability to perform their jobs and gain promotions. Physical segregation between the sexes discourages women from taking jobs in which they would be in traditionally male space, which includes all public space to some extent. Traditionally female jobs are much more likely to be in enclosed spaces such as schools, offices, or hospitals than are traditionally male jobs, which are often outside (bricklayer) or mobile (truck driver, mail carrier).

Symbolic differentiation also influences women's employment. For example, traditional female clothing (high heels, skirts, and delicate, difficult-to-wash clothing) is incompatible with traditionally male jobs requiring physical labor or getting dirty. As the income figures indicate, these jobs are usually much better paying than jobs sex-typed female. Women occupying managerial and professional jobs also face a dilemma in dressing. Because duplicating men's attire and wearing a suit would be inappropriate to their gender, women must walk a fine line between avoiding clothing which would draw attention to their sexuality and avoiding a masculine appearance.

Mental Illness. As the earlier section on mental illness described, factors which increase women's propensity for mental illness are their physical isolation in the home (physical segregation), the characteristics of housework (functional differentiation), the fact that homemakers have only one major role, whereas breadwinners have two (functional differentiation), and personalities which encourage the internalization of hostility (personality differentiation).

Wife Beating. Functional differentiation in our society has resulted in different roles for men and women, with females bearing the primary responsibility for childrearing and emotional support (the expressive functions) and males bearing the primary responsibility for the family's economic support (the instrumental function). Moreover, men are expected to be dominant over women. As the earlier section on wife beating describes, the socialization of males often results in emotional constriction, heavy dependency on women for nurturance and emotional support, and anti-woman attitudes—all of which are characteristics which facilitate battering.

Women have difficulty leaving the battering situation because (a) they possess personality traits encouraged by our society in women, such as passivity, dependency, and submissiveness, (personality differentiation),

· (b) they are economically dependent on the batterer (functional differentiation), and (c) they fear for their physical safety.

Who Will Rear the Children?

In the previous sections of this chapter some of the costs of the sex-gender system have been described and it has been argued that the fundamental basis of the sex-gender system is female responsibilty for the care of young children. Currently more and more women, like men, are choosing to invest in a role which is highly rewarded both socially and financially (work) and reducing their investment in a role which is poorly rewarded (parenting). More and more women are refusing to pay the price to be a parent of dropping completely out of the labor force and devoting themselves totally to childrearing.

Women's increased labor force participation has caused many to question the adequacy of the care the children of working mothers receive. Although current research on working mothers suggests that working does not have detrimental effects (Hoffman, 1974, 1977, 1979; Hoffman & Nye, 1974), this research is based on a population of women who, for the most part, have given their family roles priority over work roles. Women have dropped out of the labor force more frequently than men, worked fewer hours, and made job selections compatible with their family roles. By contrast, men have been more likely to expect their families to adjust to their work, even though men's work can also have negative effects on their families.

The rearing of children by at least one loving parent with adequate time, emotional energy, and economic resources to meet the child's needs is an ideal few would oppose, but a return to traditional sex roles will not provide such ideal conditions for childrearing. Even if large numbers of women stopped working, it is unlikely that the divorce rate would decline. The millions of children in single-parent households, almost always female-headed, would still be in a low income family with an emotionally strapped parent and inadequate day care. Millions of women who choose a traditional role and are then left without a breadwinner because of death or divorce would continue to face poverty because of low social security, pension, alimony, and child support payments.

Even in two-parent families women should not be presumed to have the major responsibility for caring for children, since the reproductive role of women is the fundamental basis of sex roles and sexual inequality. Women's specialization in childrearing has fostered differentiation between the sexes in terms of physical location, personality, symbols, and other work and family roles. Together these form an interrelated sex-gender system, and women's role as childrearer cannot be accurately assessed apart from the negative consequences of the sex-gender system—poverty of women and children, the double day, high mental illness rates for women, and male violence against women.

The alternative to returning to traditional sex roles is equal parenting by both sexes, government policies which facilitate parenting by both sexes, and an economic structure which gives human needs a higher priority. The workplace as it is presently structured does not give a high priority to family needs. Many women have chosen part-time work, work which corresponds to children's school schedules, or work which is sufficiently flexible to allow family needs to come first most of the time. Women's entrance into the workplace has highlighted the conflict between paid employment and family life. It also suggests a question which is seldom asked: Are there conflicts between men's work and the family? For many families, the answer is a resounding yes. Men's work often results in absences due to long hours, overtime, second, third, or rotating shifts, or frequent travel, and it often requires geographic mobility inconsistent with the well-being of the family (Mortimer & Sorensen, Chap. 5, this volume).

Sroufe and Ward (Chap. 1, this volume) have described the conditions necessary for the effective rearing of infants. Since the mother and not the father has traditionally filled the parenting role, the increased labor force participation of women is viewed as impinging on the needs of other family members, especially children. By contrast, the fact that the husband's work also impinges on family life is often overlooked.

A concern, either explicit or implicit, in most of the chapters of this book is the question, "Is there or isn't there a conflict between women's employment and motherhood?" In other words, are there costs to family members—men, women, and especially children—of women entering the workforce? The answer is yes, there are costs in many families. Women are experiencing the double day and some children may be receiving inadequate care. There are also potential benefits.

Although women's increased activity in the workplace and in traditionally male jobs could leave children the losers, with long hours in day care centers and unattentive parents, it has the potential to inspire workers to demand that employers pay more heed to the family needs of both male and female workers. The populace could decide paternity and maternity leaves, staying home with sick children, and day care were rights rather than privileges. They could demand that both the political and economic systems be restructured to give human needs a higher priority.

SUMMARY

This chapter began by examining women's and men's attitudes toward work and family roles. During recent years support for women working outside the home has increased dramatically among both sexes. Nevertheless, a majority of both sexes still support sex segregation in the labor market and a sexual division of labor at home.

The backlash against more equal roles for men and women has already begun. Affirmative action, reproductive rights, government supported day care, and even maternal–child health programs are under attack. A fundamental part of this attack is the promotion of an ideology that (a) women should be responsible for childrearing, and (b) women's work but not men's work affects family life.

As long as men do not participate in childrearing on an equal or nearly equal basis, we will have a society in which women and children get a smaller share of society's rewards. Women are going to experience lower pay, the double day, higher rates of mental illness (especially depressive disorders), rape, domestic abuse, and lack of emotional support from men. Children will also suffer from this arrangement because in two-parent families one parent will not be providing all the emotional support he could, and in single-parent families, in most cases, the single parent will be a woman who is strapped both emotionally and financially.

The fundamental basis of sex roles and sex inequality is the reproductive role of women. Even if the ideology that women should be primarily responsible for childrearing prevails, it is unlikely that women will abandon the workplace. Instead, they will continue to work for low wages in primarily female jobs, and bear the burden of long hours of housework and child care as well. The alternative is a society in which men do more housework and child care and become more emotionally supportive in their relationships with women, children, and other men, and a society in which both men and women demand that the workplace accommodate to the needs of children, women, and men, rather than vice versa.

REFERENCES

Adams, D., & Penn, I. Men in groups: The socialization and resocialization of men who batter. Paper presented at the Annual Meeting of the American Orthopsychiatric Association, April 1981.

Amir, M. *Patterns of Forcible Rape*, Chicago, IL: University of Chicago Press, 1971.

Arnoff, J., & Crano, W. D. A re-examination of the cross-cultural principles of task segregation and sex role differentiation in the family. *American Sociological Review*, 1975, *40*, 12–20.

Barrett, N. S. Women in the job market: Occupations, earnings and career opportunities. In R. Smith (Ed.), *The Subtle Revolution: Women at Work*. Washington, DC: Urban Institute, 1979.

Blumberg, R. L. Women and work around the world: A cross-cultural examination of sex division of labor and sex status. In A. Sargent (Ed.), *Beyond Sex Roles*. St. Paul, MN: West, 1977.

Broverman, I., Vogel, S. R., Broverman, D. M., Clarkson, F. E., Rosenkrantz, P. S. Sex role stereotypes: A current appraisal. *Journal of Social Issues*, 1972, *28*, 59–78.

Erskine, H. The polls: Women's roles, *Public Opinion Quarterly*, 1971, *34*, 275–290.

Fawk, G. Men who assault their wives. *Medicine, Science and the Law*, 1974 (July), *14*, 180–183.

Gallup, G. H. *The Gallup Poll: Public Opinion 1972–77*. Wilmington, DE: Scholarly Research, 1978.

Gallup, G. H. *The Gallup Poll: Public Opinion 1978*. Wilmington, DE: Scholarly Research, 1979.

Gordon, L. *Woman's Body, Woman's Right*. New York: Penguin Books, 1977.

Gove, W. R., & Tudor, J. F. Adult sex roles and mental illness. *American Journal of Sociology*, 1973, *78*, 812–835.

Guttentag, M., & Salasin, S. Women, men, and mental health. Paper presented at the Aspen Conference on Women, August 1975.

Hartley, R. Sex role pressure and the socialization of the male child. In J. Pleck and J. Sawyer (Eds.), *Men and Masculinity*. Englewood Cliffs, NJ: Prentice-Hall, 1974.

Hartman, H. The family as the locus of gender, class, and political struggle: The example of housework. *Signs*, 1981, *6*, 366–394.

Henley, N. *Body Politics: Power, Sex, and Nonverbal Communication*. Englewood Cliffs, NJ: Prentice-Hall, Inc., 1977.

Herman, D. The rape culture. In J. Freeman (Ed.), *Women: A Feminist Perspective*. 2 cd Ed. Palo Alto, CA: Mayfield, 1979.

Hoffman, L. W. Effects of maternal employment on the child: A review of the research. *Developmental Psychology*, 1974, *10*, 204–228.

Hoffman, L. W. Changes in family roles, socialization, and sex differences. *American Psychologist*, 1977, *32*, 644–657.

Hoffman, L. W. Maternal Employment: 1979. *American Psychologist*, 1979, *34*, 859–865.

Hoffman, L. & Nye, F. I. *Working Mothers: An evaluative review of the consequences for wife, husband, and child*. San Francisco, CA: Jossey-Bass 1979.

Maccoby, E. E., & Jacklin, C. N. *The Psychology of Sex Differences*. Stanford, CA: Stanford University Press, 1974.

McCormick, A. Men helping men stop women abuse. *State and Mind*, 1980, Summer, 46–50.

Mead, M. *Sex and Temperament in Three Primitive Societies*. New York: Dell, 1935.

Money, J., & Ehrhardt, A. A. *Man and Woman, Boy and Girl*. Baltimore, MD: The Johns Hopkins Press, 1972.

Murdock, G. P. Comparative data on the division of labor by sex. *Social Forces*, 1935, *15*, 551–553.

Oakley, A. *The Sociology of Housework*. New York: Pantheon, 1974.

Oppenheimer, V. K. *The Female Labor Force in the United States: Demographic and Economic Factors Governing Its Growth and Changing Composition*. Population Monograph Series, no. 5, Berkeley, CA: University of California, 1970.

Parsons, T. Sex roles and family structure. In T. Parsons & R. F. Bales, *Family, Socialization and the Interaction Process*. Glencoe, IL: Free Press, 1955.

Pleck, J. H. Men's family work: Three perspectives and some new data. *Family Coordinator*, 1979, *28*, 481–488.

Quarm, D. The effect of gender on sex role attitudes: An examination of the contradiction between college student studies and national public opinion polls. *Sociological Focus*, forthcoming.

Richardson, L. W. *The Dynamics of Sex and Gender*. Boston, MA: Houghton Mifflin, 1981.

Stafford, F., & Duncan, G. The use of time and technology by households in the United

States. Working paper. Ann Arbor, MI: University of Michigan, Institute for Social Research, 1977.

Strauss, M. A sociological perspective on the causes of family violence. In M. R. Green (Ed.), *Violence and the Family*. Boulder, CO: Westview Press, 1980.

Tavris, C., & Offir, C. *The Longest War: Sex Differences in Perspective*. New York: Harcourt Brace Jovanovich, 1977.

U.S. Bureau of the Census, Current Population Reports, Series P-60, No. 138, *Characteristics of the Population Below the Poverty Level: 1981*. Washington, DC: U.S. Government Printing Office, 1983.

U.S. Bureau of the Census. *Statistical Abstract of the United States: 1982–1983, 103rd Ed.* Washington, DC: U. S. Government Printing Office, 1982.

U.S. Department of Health and Human Services, Social Security Administration, *Quarterly Public Assistance Statistics, July–September 1981*. Washington, DC, 1982.

Vanek, J. Time spent in housework. *Scientific American*, 1974, *231* (14), 116–120.

III
CONTEMPORARY AMERICAN FAMILIES FACE THE FUTURE

Chapter 8
Conceptions of Kinship and the Family Reproduction Cycle*

Bernard Farber
Arizona State University

Despite the flood of writings on the family and social change, research is still sparse about the social residues of specific critical events (Farber, 1979a; Hill, 1979). Recent historical periods—such as the aftermath of World War II or the turbulent 1960s—have evidenced marked shifts in marriage, childbearing, and divorce statistics. Social commentators are often incautious, identifying these shifts as heralding basic revisions in family structure. Without careful analysis of the cohorts of people participating in the events which generate these statistics, these commentators immediately speculate—usually with dire predictions—about the future of the American family.

* The research reported in this paper was undertaken with grants from the National Science Foundation (with Morris Axelrod as co-principal investigator) and from the Provost's Research Incentive Program and Department of Sociology at Arizona State University (with Morris Axelrod, Florence Barkin, and Steven Dworkin as co-principal investigators). I am grateful for critical comments on the paper by Frederick Lindstrom, John M. Mogey, and Karen Smith of Arizona State University, and by my wife Rosanna Farber.

This chapter will follow a more deliberate path. It will concentrate upon a limited series of activities set into motion by the entrance into marriage. I shall examine ways in which people exhibiting a range of ideas about the structure of kinship ties have dealt with the timing of family events—such as marriage, childbearing, divorce, and remarriage. To some extent, I shall compare persons born in different decades—the 1930s, the 1940s, and the 1950s—not only with one another, but also with their parents. This comparison introduces an historical dimension into the analysis.

Social scientists have studied historical changes in family relationships by observing shifts in ages at which transitions in family-related roles and statuses have occurred. For example, the analysis by Modell, Furstenberg, and Hershberg (1976) of such transitions (i.e., exit from school, workforce entry, departure from family of origin, marriage, and establishment of a household) has shown that in the past century, "the period of youth has narrowed considerably, resulting in a more concentrated pattern of status changes" (Elder, 1978, p. S24). The authors interpret their findings as indicating a transfer in control over life course transitions away from the family of origin. More and more, they suggest, the contingencies of schooling and employment govern the timing of life course transitions. They conclude that social structural demands and constraints play a continually growing role in the timing of life course events. As a result, the impact of disruptions and dislocations in society upon one's life course will become ever more intense.

But studies of social change also show that new elements in a social system do not automatically have their way with existing institutional arrangements (Goode, 1970, pp. 22–26). Rather, the kinds of changes that institutions undergo likely involve some sort of compromise between the pressures introduced by the new elements and the existing norms dictated by the ongoing structures. Consequently, it is necessary in studying family change to delineate "categories of families *within* each cohort that are assumed to have relevance to the experiencing" and interpreting historical events (Elder, 1978, p. S24).

Kinship characteristics seem useful for establishing categories of families in studies of social change. Because ties with kin in modern society blend into ties with nonkin, the norms governing kinship have the task of defining the dimensions and boundaries of special obligations accorded to related persons. The existence of a diversity of kinship statuses permits much variation among groups in setting these boundaries. As a result, kinship norms are more sensitive to structural differences in society than are parental or marital bonds. Normative patterns of kinship seem to reflect a compromise among residential, economic, and religious forces (Farber,

1981). Hence, it seems appropriate to group families according to a kinship classification scheme.

The data upon which this chapter is based refer to two aspects of family life: (a) a classification of preferences, or normative patterns, in kinship ties, and (b) indicators of past experiences, that is, events that mark major transitions in family status. Two questions are addressed in the analysis. First, which modes of kinship organization are more vulnerable than others to pressures for change in the timing of life course events relevant to the family? Second, what implications do differences in vulnerability have for family policy?

The chapter is based on data from a household interview survey conducted in Phoenix, Arizona, in 1978. The analysis will involve three successive birth cohorts and their parents. The informants in the survey were all under 46 years of age and were married at that time or had been married. (The sampling techniques and field procedures are described in Farber, 1981.) The next sections present first the kinship classification scheme used in the analysis and then the conceptualization for dealing with life course transitions.

KINSHIP CLASSIFICATION SCHEME

The assessment of kinship in this research is based upon an analysis of cognitive kinship maps. This approach avoids the difficulty of trying to equate the quality of family and kinship ties among individuals who differ from one another in residential proximity to family members, configuration of living and/or of estranged family members, life course contingencies, and other situational factors. However, since the kinship mapping approach is one not ordinarily seen in family studies, it is necessary to describe the typology used and the research techniques applied.

Since resources may be limited and several relatives may have an equal need for them, societies develop sets of rules and justifications to designate which relatives have a greater claim to these resources. The establishment of a set of priorities results in the formation of cognitive maps of kinship distances (Atkins, 1974; Farber, 1979b, 1981; Murdock, 1949). These cognitive maps organize genealogical distances in order to locate kin according to their claims upon the individual. To be sure, superimposed upon these maps, one would find also variations in priorities based upon personal and social qualities of particular relatives (Schneider, 1968). But generally underlying these personal qualities, there exists for most people a hierarchy of priorities based on kinship status itself.

The cognitive maps of kinship priorities are formalized in measures of collaterality, which define the order in which kin succeed to decedents' estates and which delimit ranges of relatives considered too close to marry (Atkins, 1974; Farber, 1981). In Western civilization, despite great variations in economic and political systems, only a few such priority systems have sufficed to accommodate intestacy and incestuous marriage laws. These are the Parentela Orders model (with origins in ancient Judaism and classical Greece), the Civil Law model (whose source was the Twelve Tables of the early Roman Republic), and the Canon Law model, which appeared in the twelfth century codification of Church Law. More recently, proposals have been made to apply genetic relatedness (i.e., shared chromosomes) to inheritance and marriage laws. These different models emerged to meet the specific demands upon family and kinship in the particular social settings in which they originated. But although the original family systems have long since disappeared, the collaterality models have survived, and they seem to characterize the same basic principles in family organization as they did originally. As described in the *Mishnah* and the *Talmud,* the Parentela Orders model gives most emphasis to continuity of the family line; at the opposite extreme, consistent with Church writings, the Canon Law model is least oriented toward family perpetuation. The configuration of priorities (in terms of distances from Ego, the reference person) for the various measures of collaterality are shown in Table 1.

In recent research, a fifth model was discovered. This model emphasizes the individual's ancestral line and classifies kin according to whether they are children, grandchildren, great grandchildren, and so on of Ego's (i.e., the individual's) direct ancestors. The rank ordering of kin according to this model also appears in Table 1. Because the model is most prevalent among white Protestants of high educational and income levels (and with native-born parents and grandparents), it has been called the Standard American model (Farber, 1981 pp. 45–65).[1]

Although people are generally unaware of the priority patterns in religious writings, they tend to be overrepresented in the categories asso-

---

[1]The informants are asked to imagine that they are writing an intestacy law and to assign priorities among relatives in a series of paired comparisons for which the collaterality models differ. For example, Table 1 indicates that in the comparison between siblings and grandchildren of the descendants, (a) choosing siblings over grandchildren would be appropriate for the Standard American, Canon Law, and Genetic models; (b) equal claim would fit the Civil Law model; and (c) favoring grandchildren would be consistent with the Parentela Orders model. After answering nine such items, the respondents are then assigned to the category for which a majority of their responses appear. (If there is no majority, they are placed in a residual category.)

ciated with their own religion. More Catholics than might be expected fall into the Canon Law category, and Jews cluster in the Parentela Orders category. The more traditional the branch of Judaism, the greater is the tendency to conform to the Parentela Orders model of collaterality (Farber, 1979b, 1981). Moreover, like orthodoxy in Judaism, conformity to Neo-fundamentalist and Mormon doctrine is also associated with adherence to the Parentela Orders kinship model. Thus, factionalism or sectarianism in religion appears to be related to holding a Parentela Orders orientation in kinship.

The findings on kinship orientation can be extended to other social realms. Table 2 displays selected social characteristics of persons classified by kinship model. The table indicates that, in addition to religion, kinship orientation is related to socioeconomic status, intergenerational social mobility, and location of marital residence. Other relevant findings appear in an unpublished study, where the responses of Mexican-American university students to the *Who Am I?* (Twenty Questions) Test were analyzed to determine the degree to which the students regard family and kinship ties as central to their self-identity. The percentage of cases in each kinship category in which informants refer to themselves in terms of family and/or kinship as a collectivity (e.g., I am a member of a close family; I am close to all my relatives) is as follows: Forty-four percent in the Parentela Orders category apply a collective "family" or kinship terms as compared with 29% in the Standard American grouping and only 14% for persons with other kinship orientations.[2]

In general, the social characteristics associated with the series of kinship models are related to the structure of the models themselves. They

---

[2] The data for Mexican-American students were collected as part of a more extensive project dealing with language use among bilinguals at Arizona State University. The registrar supplied a list of all Hispanics registered during the fall semester, 1979. Of the 263 persons in the initial list, 149 were chosen by random sampling procedures for inclusion, and of these, 95 were ultimately interviewed during the spring semester, 1980. Since the study was restricted to bilingual, Mexican-American students, those who were not Mexican-American or who were monolingual were considered as ineligible for inclusion. For the eligible persons contacted, the response rate is about 80%.

The *Who Am I?* instrument (sometimes referred to as the Twenty Statements Test) is a form headed by the question "Who am I?" with a brief paragraph instructing the respondent to fill in the 20 blank spaces on the page with brief self-descriptions "as if you are writing them to yourself, not to somebody else" (Spitzer, Couch, & Stratton, n.d., p. 11). The reasoning is that the individual will apply to himself (or herself) those designations which are most characteristic of the way he (or she) usually thinks of himself (or herself). The answers thus provide a pattern of self-labels which reflects the salient aspects of the person's self conception.

Table 1.
Kinship Loci as Viewed from Ego's Perspective, as Computed by Parentela Orders, Standard American, Civil Law, Genetic, and Canon Law Measures

Type of Relative	Genealogical Distance from Ego[a]				
	Parentela Orders Measure (Rank order in distance from Ego)	Standard American Measure (Rank order in distance from Ego)	Civil Law Measure (Degrees distance from Ego)	Genetics Measure (Distance in biological relatedness)	Canon Law Measure (Degrees distant from Ego)
In Ascending Generations					
Parents	4	1	1	1	1
Grandparents	8[b]	2	2	2	2
Great Grandparents	12[b]	3	3	3	3
Aunts and Uncles	9	7	3	2	2
In Collateral Generation					
Siblings	5	6	2	1	1
First Cousins	10	12	4	3	2
Second Cousins	15[b]	18[b]	6	5	3
In Descending Generations					
Children	1	5[b]	1	1	1
Grandchildren	2	10[b]	2	2	2
Great Grandchildren	3	15[b]	3	3	3
Nieces and Nephews	6	11	3	2	2

[a]Formulae for measures are in Farber (1981, p. 191).
[b]Relatives in intervening ranks are not shown in table. Ranks include nineteen relatives genealogically close to Ego. (See Farber, 1981, p. 189.)

Table 2.
Social Characteristics of Persons Classified by Kinship Orientation[a]
(Phoenix Kinship Study)

Social Characteristics	Parentela Orders	Standard American	Civil Law	Genetic or Canon Law
Groups overrepresented				
Socioeconomic status	[b]	Upper middle class	Lower middle class	Blue collar
Major religions	Jewish	Protestant	Protestant	Catholic
Extent of intergenerational upward social mobility	High	High	Moderate	Low
Marital residence				
Are parents living in Arizona?	Most not	About half	About half	Most yes
Side favored	If any, husband's	Neither side favored	Neither side favored	Wife's side

[a]Table based on findings reported in Farber, 1981.
[b]No clear trend in data.

reflect variations in the emphasis upon line of descent as a principle in allocating priorities among kin. A componential analysis of collaterality measures by Farber (1981) reveals that both Parentela Orders and Standard American models stress line of descent as an organizing principle (albeit in different ways). The Civil Law approach does so to a lesser extent, and the Canon Law model not at all (with the Genetic model between the Civil Law and Canon Law positions). Given the historical backgrounds of these models, one would expect that emphasis on line of descent in kinship mapping would be related to the structure of family relationships.

The analysis in this chapter will examine how people who hold a Parentela Orders kinship orientation differ particularly from those with orientations that place little emphasis upon line of descent in the timing of transitions in familial statuses and roles. Suggestions will then be made of how these differences are relevant to problems in the development of effective family policies.

THE FAMILY REPRODUCTION CYCLE

Intuitively, the family life cycle seems to be a useful concept to describe changes in family relationships that have taken place in different societies and diverse historical eras. Although this concept has had heuristic value, its utility has been hampered for several reasons, among which are that (a) there is little agreement over the identification of its phases, (b) its links to sociological concepts and theories have been tenuous, and (c) usually the timing of events is based on cross-sectional data rather than the experiences of a cohort. Because of these deficiencies, it seems appropriate to redefine this concept in ways which may enhance its utility.

In the past, two kinds of definitions of the family life cycle have been proposed. One definition refers to the household group as the unit of analysis. Meyer Fortes (1958) describes the domestic group as the "group which must remain in operation over a stretch of time long enough to rear offspring to the stage of physical and social reproductivity if a society is to maintain itself. This is a cyclical process. . . . The domestic group as a unit retains the same form, but its members, and the activities which unite them, go through a regular sequence of changes during the cycle which culminates in the dissolution of the original unit and its replacement by one or more units of the same kind." (p. 2; see also Laslett, 1977). The second definition deals explicitly with the family of procreation as the unit of analysis. In this definition, the family life cycle begins with a couple's marriage and ends with their death (Glick, 1977, Hill, 1970). It, too, refers to the family group as connected through the household of the married couple. The focus in both definitions is upon the composition of the household over time and the role transitions that occur as the family of procreation produces members for the society, releases them to form their own families of procreation, and then fades away.

Both definitions of the family life cycle deal with the biological and social reproductive function of the family (or household) group at a particular time and place. Their focus, however, is upon the procreative family (or household) instead of upon the upcoming generation. For example, the timing of events is described in terms of parental ages rather than children's ages (Glick, 1977). However, the life cycle concept connotes something more. A cyclical process implies an ongoing phenomenon that consists of countless replications of events; it suggests that the family as a particular kind of institution (i.e., a something) renews itself generation after generation. As the concept has been applied in the past, there is no indication as to how the operation of the cycle in one generation affects its operation in the next generation. In brief, the traditional definitions neglect the mechanisms by which the cycle operates to reproduce family ties along lines of descent.

Keeping the idea of social and biological reproduction in mind, let us instead regard the family life cycle as the process by which Ego replicates the family-relevant statuses of his (or her) parents. Just as Ego's parents initiate the cycle as they are born into their families of orientation and move into their families of procreation, so Ego completes the cycle by reproducing that movement. From Ego's perspective, recycling the family refers to the status transitions taking place, beginning with the birth of the personnel who populate Ego's family of orientation (i.e., Ego's parents and siblings) and ending with the birth of Ego's children, the next generation in the family line. (Compare with Plath, 1980, and with Hagstead and Dixon, 1980.)

The concept of the family reproduction cycle leads the investigator to ask, in particular, whether an aberration in a life course transition (e.g., of age at marriage) in the parental generation is repeated in Ego's cohort. Variations in the timing and tempo of life course transitions may reflect crescive developments in the institutional structure of society (e.g., long-term growth in tertiary occupations, or changes in women's participation in the labor force). Others, however, represent readjustments to specific historical and personal events. One might profitably undertake systematic inquiry into the residual effects of these events upon the cycle of social and biological reproduction in the family in order to determine: (a) how persons with different kinds of kinship orientation vary in their family reproduction cycles; and (b) how historical events affect the family reproduction cycles differential among families classified by kinship orientation (e.g., the length of the cycle marriage timing, child spacing, dissolution of marriages, timing of remarriage, etc.).

DISCUSSION OF FINDINGS

The specific findings of the study are presented in the Appendix to this chapter. The data used are from a more extensive kinship survey undertaken in Phoenix, Arizona, in 1978. The informants, chosen by probability sampling techniques, were all age 45 or under and were either married at the time of the survey or had been previously married (Farber, 1981). The analysis deals with two issues: (a) how types of kinship mapping account for the variations in family reproduction cycles, and (b) how birth cohort influences the relationship between kinship and reproduction cycles.

The analyses regarding the connection between kinship mapping and reproduction cycles have yielded two distinct patterns of results. The first pattern pertains to the emphasis upon line of descent in kinship mapping. The findings falling into this pattern are:

1. For both Ego and Ego's parents, first births are delayed longer in families classified as Parentela Orders or Standard American than they are in families in the Civil Law, Genetic, or Canon Law categories.
2. The time span of the family reproduction cycle is longer for families in the Parentela Orders and Standard American groupings than it is in families in the Civil Law, Genetic, and Canon Law classes.

Both of these results on the time span of family reproduction cycles indicate a connection between the salience of line of descent and a delay in bringing children into the world. That is, people who conceive of family ties in terms of continuity over generations seem to take more time—to be more deliberate—in activities related to the family reproduction cycle.

The second pattern refers to findings which are similar for Parentela Orders and Civil Law mappings as opposed to Standard American, Genetic, and Canon Law orientations. There is a greater tendency in families in the Parentela Orders and Civil Law categories, as compared with others: (a) for parents of informants to remain married (a slight tendency) and to delay divorces until after the children marry; and (b) for the informants themselves when divorce does occur, to remarry in greater numbers and for these remarriages to take place soon after the divorce—within five years, and *not* to remain childless.

The findings in which the Parentela Orders and Civil Law groups are similar (as compared with the other kinship types) all suggest that these mappings express a strong salience of nuclear family ties. For individuals conforming to the Parentela Orders model, this salience apparently reflects a commitment to family continuity—one's secular immortality—as the results of previous investigations indicate (Farber, 1979b, 1981). For individuals conforming to the Civil Law model, the importance of nuclear family ties seems to be related to commitment to traditional norms and values. Past research has shown that persons with a Civil Law kinship orientation tend to be highly religious in outlook and frequent attenders of church services. They are overrepresented in Pietistic Protestant denominations and in stable working-class families (Farber, 1981). Although the Parentela Orders and Civil Law perspectives are based on different rationales, they converge in their support of stable nuclear-family ties.[3]

The second issue with which the research deals pertains to the influence of different birth cohorts on the relationship between kinship and reproduction cycles. In comparisons involving cohorts born in the 1930s, 1940s, and 1950s, one might have expected a linear trend in influence, reflecting the crescive changes that have occurred throughout this century. Instead, the data show that the family reproduction cycles of persons born in the 1940s differ from those of the 1930 and 1950 cohorts. The findings on the relationship between kin types and family reproduction cycles are quite similar for the 1930s and 1950s cohorts; it is the behavior of the 1940s cohort that must be explained. Relevant findings are that:

1. Without the results for Ego's parents, one would be tempted to interpret the 1940's cohort data only in the light of the 1960s, when that cohort attained adulthood. But the data also indicate that, particularly for the Parentela Orders and Standard American groups, the birth of the first child is delayed longer by both the 1940s cohort and their parents than it is for the 1930s and 1950s cohorts and their parents. This finding suggests that the turmoil in life styles in the Sixties had its roots at least a generation earlier. This interpretation is supported by the findings on divorce in the parental generation, namely, when the percentages of divorced parents are examined by Ego's birth cohort, the overall prevalence jumps considerably from the parents of the 1930s cohort (prevalence = 11.2%) to mothers and fathers of the 1940s cohort (prevalence = 21.9%), but increases at a slower rate among the parents of the 1950s cohort (prevalence = 27.6%).

2. Findings on divorce and childlessness in particular give evidence that the 1940s cohort was unusual: (a) variation in the prevalence of divorce shows large differences within the 1940s birth cohort; in this cohort, as compared with persons in the Civil Law category especially, those individuals with a Parentela Orders kinship map-

---

[3] There is a more technical explanation for the covergence between the Parentela Orders and Civil Law models in findings related to stable nuclear-family ties. That explanation is discussed in Farber (1982).

ping are vulnerable to divorce, and (b) as in the prevalence of divorce, the findings on childlessness bolster the view that the 1940s birth cohort is different; whereas variations in childlessness among kin types tend to be fairly small in the 1930s and 1950s birth cohorts, they are quite widespread in the 1940s cohort.

Considered together, the data suggest that the 1940s birth cohort was an unusual one. In the first place, parental child-spacing was especially long, and this tendency was repeated in Ego's generation. As a consequence, the span of the family reproduction cycles is particularly long in the 1940s cohort. As for interrupted family reproduction cycles, differences within the 1940s cohort appeared among the different kin types in divorce, remarriage, and childlessness. Families emphasizing the value of continuity were most affected. Thus, by family background and by the flow of historical events, the 1940s birth cohort seems to have been required to test familial loyalties and values in ways not demanded of other cohorts.[4]

POLICY IMPLICATIONS

The policy implications of the findings on the relationships between the kinship models and the family reproduction cycle are of two kinds: The first implication concerns the general connections between policymaking and social change; the second pertains to the potential role that kinship orientation and the family reproduction cycle can play in policy formulation.

---

[4] Various explanations have been proposed to account for the increase in divorce and in the delay of first births in recent decades. For example, Easterlin (1980 pp. 79–89) sees these increases as part of a cyclical process. Arguing on the basis of labor force supply and demand, he concludes that the declining birth rate from 1920 to 1940 produced a relatively small cohort of workers in the economic boom after World War II. The scarcity of youth "resounded wholly" to the benefit of young native Americans, who thereupon married earlier than previous cohorts, gave birth without delay, and tended to stay married. Easterlin then attributes the upturn in divorce and delays in childbirth in the 1970s to the economic squeeze generated by the large number of persons born in the post World War II baby boom. But Easterlin, like other economic determinists, posits a constant trend in divorce and spacing of births. Easterlin's interpretation is somewhat contradicted by the behavior of the 1940s cohort in this study. True, as he would predict, the 1930s cohort has few childless couples and a comparatively short delay in having a first child. Still, this cohort, unlike Easterlin's predictions, has a higher prevalence of divorced persons than later cohorts. In addition, the pattern of delay in the birth of first children for each cohort follows that of the parents (for every kinship type). Consequently, intergenerational transfer of hesitation patterns seems to be at least as important as generation size in accounting for childspacing and, to some extent, divorce.

Policy and Change

It has become commonplace for observers to regard the 1960s as a tempestuous era during which fundamental changes in norms of family life occurred. A view prevalent among youth in the 1960s was that the world was entering a postindustrial age in which traditional family norms and values were obsolete. With the demands placed on people in this period, the impression was that tensions mounted between husbands and wives, children were more often abused, and personal power replaced personal commitment. With the increase in family problems, surely the traditional norms were not working. The upcoming generation then saw its task as that of finding ways to keep "the burden of obsolete knowledge" about family life "from interfering with necessary changes" (Skolnick & Skolnick, 1971 p. 27).

The findings of this study, however, cast some doubt upon the observations of these critics of family life; the data suggest that it is even questionable whether the events of the 1960s have had any significant lasting effect on family life. Rather, the results on family reproduction cycles indicate that the birth cohort that reached maturity in the 1960s had parents who themselves seem to be different in role and status transitions from parents of earlier and later cohorts. Moreover, among the informants, the prevalence of disruptions in this cohort was not sustained in the succeeding one. These findings elicit the inference that the changes that occurred in the 1960s were more superficial than the commentators on the family thought that they had discerned. The ideas about kinship, which underpin family values, appear to be stable, despite the turmoil of the times.

Data not yet reported indicate that kinship orientations of the kind discussed in this study tend to be passed from parents to children. Given the stability of these kinship orientations, legislators and public administrators ought to refrain from introducing defensive family policies which assume that a radical transformation has occurred in domestic relations. Instead, deviations from secular trends may reflect only cohort differences in forces already present in family roots.

Kinship Types and Family Reproduction Cycles

The persistence of basic kinship orientations, even as social conditions change, does not imply, however, that family reproduction cycles are unaffected by social turmoil. Rather, the findings indicate that each kinship orientation influences family life differently. The existence of these diverse orientations underlines the pluralism of American society in ways which crosscut socioeconomic, religious, and ethnic diversity. If the differences among groups in their conceptions of kinship were superficial, one could indeed find a common ground as a basis for a coherent family policy—to create unity out of diversity. But if these differences represent fundamentally conflicting approaches to family and kinship, then, except on some very broad issues (e.g., monogamy, bilateral descent), attempts at formulating a coherent national family policy will face continuing opposition.

For policymakers, the findings of this study imply that any policy will have a differential effect on the timing and incidence of marriage, divorce, and parenthood according to kinship orientation. Given the potency of these kinship orientations, policymakers cannot assume that any particular policy will have a uniform influence even within socioeconomic, ethnic, and religious groups in the society. In fact, policies which presuppose a particular kind of relationship between employment status of women and their ideas about the timing or occurrence of marriage, divorce, and parenthood may create problems for those women whose kinship orientations diverge from those considered by the policymakers.

One might suggest that no uniform policy be established in American society. Yet, the legal structure pertaining to marriage, divorce, support provisions, and succession sometimes demands the creation of rules governing just treatment of the populace. Perhaps the most that can be hoped for is that legislators and judges, social welfare administrators and government officials keep in mind that a single family policy does not imply a single effect on all families.

REFERENCES

Atkins, J.R. On the fundamental consanguineal numbers and their structural basis. *American Ethnologist,* 1974, *1,* 1–31.

Easterlin, R.A. *Birth and fortune.* New York: Basic Books, 1980.

Elder, G.H., Jr. Approaches to social change and the family. *American Journal of Sociology,* 1978, *84,* s1–s38 (Supplement).

Farber, B. Family history as a moral science. *Sociology and Social Research,* 1979, *63,* 603–610. (a)

Farber, B. Kinship mapping among Jews in a midwestern city. *Social Forces,* 1979, *57,* 1107–1123. (b)

Farber, B. *Conceptions of kinship.* New York: Elsevier North Holland, 1981.

Farber, B. Kinship mapping and household strategies. Paper presented at annual meeting, American Sociological Association, August, 1982.

Fortes, M. Introduction. In J. Goody (Ed.), *The developmental cycle in domestic groups.* Cambridge, England: Cambridge University Press, 1958.

Glick, P.C. Updating the life cycle of the family. *Journal of Marriage and the Family,* 1977, *39,* 5–13.

Goode, W.J. World revolution and family patterns. New York: Free Press, 1970.

Hagstead, G.O., & Dixon, R.A. Lineages as units of analysis: New avenues for the study of individual and family careers. Paper prepared for NCFR Theory Construction and Research Workshop, August, 1980.

Hill, R. *Family development in three generations*. Cambridge, MA.: Schenkman, 1970.

Hill, R. Historical change in marriage and the family: Where do we go from here? *Sociology and Social Research,* 1979, *63,* 590–595.

Keesing, R.M. *Kin groups and social structure*. New York: Holt, Rinehart, & Winston, 1975.

Laslett, P. *Family life and illicit love in earlier generations*. New York: Cambridge University Press, 1977.

Modell, J. Changing risks, changing adaptations: American families in the nineteenth and twentieth centuries. In A.J. Lichtman & J.R. Challinor (Eds.), *Kins and communities: Families in America*. Washington, DC: Smithsonian Institution Press, 1979.

Modell, J., Furstenberg, F.F., Jr., & Hershberg, T. Social change and transitions to adulthood in historical perspective. *Journal of Family History,* 1976, *1,* 7–32.

Murdock, G.P. *Social structure*. New York: Macmillan, 1949.

Plath, D.W. Contours of consociation. In P. Baltes & O. Brim, Jr., (Eds.), *Life span development and behavior* (Vol. 3). New York: Academic Press, 1980.

Scheffler, H.W. Systems of kin classification: A structural typology. In P. Reining (Ed.), *Kinship studies in the Morgan centennial year*. Washington, DC: Anthropological Society of Washington, 1972.

Schneider, D.M. *American kinship, a cultural account*. Englewood Cliffs, NJ: Prentice Hall, 1968 (Second edition, University of Chicago Press, 1980).

Skolnick, A.S., & Skolnick, J.H. Rethinking the family. In A.S. Skolnick and J.H. Skolnick (Eds.), *Family in transition*. Boston, MA: Little, Brown, 1971.

Spitzer, S., Couch, C., & Stratton, J. *The assessment of self*. Iowa City, IA: Sernoll, n.d.

APPENDIX: SPECIFIC FINDINGS

The findings of the analysis of the Phoenix data are presented in two sections. The first section deals with results pertaining to the family reproduction cycles for all families studied, and the second section with the yield of the data for interrupted family reproduction cycles. In the second section, we shall see how divorce, remarriage, and childlessness are related to kinship orientations.

Family Reproduction Cycles

Table A describes the timing of basic events in the family reproduction cycles for individuals classified by their conformity to the different models of kinship mapping—Parentela Orders, Standard American, Civil Law, Genetic, and Canon Law. The table shows little distinction among kinship groups by age at marriage, either for Ego (i.e., the respondent) or for Ego's parents. If anything, the Civil Law, Genetic, and Canon Law groups evidence a discernable drop in marital age from the parents to their children; the decrease for women in the Civil Law group and for men in the Canon Law and Genetic category is over a year in age at marriage. But overall, there are no dramatic shifts.

Table A
Timing of Basic Events in the Family Reproduction Cycle, by Kinship Mapping
(Total Sample)

Basic Events in Family Reproduction Cycle	Timing of Events (Mean Number of Years)			
	Parentela Orders	Standard American	Civil Law	Canon and Genetic Law
Ego's parents' age at marriage				
Father	24.3	24.5	24.1	25.0
Mother	20.8	21.3	21.4	20.9
Number of years after parents' marriage that				
First child was born	2.9	2.4	1.9	1.8
Ego was born	6.3	5.9	5.5	5.6
Ego's age at first marriage				
Male Ego	24.4	24.9	23.8	23.7
Female Ego	21.6	20.5	19.5	20.9
Age difference between Ego and spouse				
Male Ego and wife	2.6	3.2	3.3	2.4
Female Ego and husband	−2.7	−3.5	−3.2	−2.5
Years after Ego's marriage that first child was born	2.0	1.7	1.5	1.4
Span of family reproduction cycle				
Male Ego	56.0	53.5	51.8	52.1
Female Ego	48.8	48.8	47.9	47.8
Number of cases	128	203	73	113

Families classified by kinship maps do, however, indicate considerable differences in the timing of the birth of first children. For Ego and parents, the rank ordering of the timing of first births follows a similar pattern with regard to kinship mapping. The Parentela Orders group exhibits the longest time span between marriage and the first birth for both generations, while those with a Genetic or Canon Law map of collaterality show the least time elapsing between marriage and the first child. In fact, these findings accord with the emphasis upon line of descent in conception of kinship ties, with Parentela Orders and Standard American exhibiting longer delays in first births than the other kinds of mapping.

How long after the parents' marriage was the respondent (i.e., Ego) born? The timing of Ego's own birth portrays the same picture of the role of kin categories as does that for first births. (Of course, sometimes Ego is the first child.) The timing of Ego's birth depends upon both the spacing of children and the birth order of Ego. This timing also expresses the period elapsing between marriage and the child of the average birth order. But despite the fact that when religion and socioeconomic status are controlled statistically, persons with a Parentela Orders mapping tend to have a large number of children and those with a Standard American mapping a small one, the timing effect is similar. (See Farber, 1981 pp. 146–154.) Both groups evidence a greater delay in the birth of the child of the average birth order than do those in the Civil Law, Genetic, and Canon Law categories. Hence, particularly in homes yielding a Parentela Orders orientation, children in families emphasizing line of descent in kinship mapping enter an environment in which the family reproduction cycle is proceeding at a slower pace than it is in families with other kinship orientations.

The time span of the family reproduction cycle provides a summary statement of the tempo of the cycle. The temporal boundaries of the cycle can be defined arbitrarily as extending from the birth of Ego's parents to the birth of Ego's children. The span of the cycle for any particular individual is then the period starting with the birth of the individual's parent of the same sex and ending with the birth of Ego's first child. At that point, the individual moves from the status of a person in the subordinate family generation to one in the superordinate generation—from the status of being oriented to the status of orienter. The tempo of the family reproduction cycle depends upon both the parents' and child's timing of marriage, the spacing and birth order of the child, and the timing of parenthood for child. A combination of delays in these events would affect the tempo of the cycle considerably.

In addition, Table A indicates the differences among kinship types in the span of the family reproduction cycle. The range in time span of the cycle for men is 56 years for the Parentela Orders to only 52 years for those with a Civil Law, Genetic, or Canon Law mapping. Differences in the cycle for women are quite small, from 49 years for Parentela Orders and Standard American groups to 48 years for the others. As a whole, however, the data reveal that, for both men and women, the tempo of the cycle is slower among persons whose kinship mapping emphasizes line of descent (i.e., Parentela Orders and Standard American) than among those whose mapping does not (i.e., Civil Law, Genetic, and Canon Law). Apparently, where line of descent is stressed, people are more deliberate in their decisions on the timing of parenthood.

Table A also demonstrates that the span of the family reproduction cycle depends more upon the timing and spacing of births than upon age at marriage. Although the range in the differences in time span of cycles among the kinship groups is four years, variations in marital age among the types in both parental and child generations are at most a single year. As a result, one would observe historical influences upon the cycle more readily in data on the timing of birth than on marriage information.

Table B reports for each cohort the number of years after marriage that Ego's and Ego's parents' first child was born. In the table, the data are classified by decade of Ego's birth and by kinship mapping. The figures in the table show that only among individuals with a Genetic or Canon Law map is there a steady decrease by decade in the time between marriage and the first birth for both Ego and Ego's parents. Particularly in the Parentela Orders and Standard American groups, the delay in first births for both Ego and parents is higher in the 1940s cohort than it is in the earlier or later ones. Hence, it appears that the people with a kinship mapping that emphasizes line of descent are more vulnerable to disturbances in the ordinary family reproduction cycle than are others. The findings below on interrupted family reproduction cycles will shed further light upon the ways in which the 1940s cohort differs from the others.

Interrupted Family Reproduction Cycles

Findings on interrupted family reproduction cycles are reported in Table C. As the table indicates, cycles in the Phoenix sample are interrupted by the divorce of Ego's parents, Ego's own marital breakup, or by the

Table B
Number of Years after Marriage that First Child Was born, for Ego and Parents, by Decade of Ego's Birth and Type of Kinship Map

Kinship Map	Mean Number of Years after Marriage (By Decade of Ego's Birth)			N
	1930s	1940s	1950s	
Parentela Orders				
Ego's parents first child born	2.3	3.7	2.2	
Ego's first child born	1.8	2.3	1.7	
N	54	57	16	127
Standard American				
Ego's parents' first child born	2.1	2.7	2.3	
Ego's first child born	1.3	2.0	1.4	
N	46	93	64	203
Civil Law				
Ego's parents' first child born	1.7	1.9	1.6	
Ego's first child born	1.6	1.2	1.6	
N	25	31	17	73
Genetic and Canon Law				
Ego's parents first child born	3.1	1.6	1.0	
Ego's first child born	2.0	1.4	1.1	
N	30	55	28	113
N in each cohort	155	236	125	516

Table C
Interrupted Family Reproduction Cycles, by Type of Kinship Map

| Kin of Interruption | Types of Kinship Mapping (Mean Number of Years or Percentage) | | | |
	Parentela Orders	Standard American	Civil Law	Genetic and Canon Law
Ego's parents divorce				
Percentage of parents in kinship category who divorced prior to Ego's marriage	13.6	19.6	17.6	20.7
Percentage of divorced parents who divorced after Ego married	22.7	2.6	20.0	0.0
Ego ever divorced				
Percentage of all persons in kinship category	35.1	33.7	28.4	45.6
Percentage remarried (1930s and 1940s cohorts)	57.1	46.0	76.5	41.3
N ever divorced	42	50	17	40
Mean number of years between divorce and remarriage	4.8 years	5.6 years	3.8 years	6.6 years
Childless couples				
Percentage of married persons in kinship category who are childless	9.4[a]	24.1[a]	11.9[a]	20.9[a]
N in kinship category	131	206	75	115

[a]Persons born before 1955 (for N's, see Table D)

failure of Ego to have children. For the families studied, death does not play a significant role in disturbing the cycle.

Let us first examine the Table C data for Ego's parents. The parental group most relevant to the interruption of Ego's family reproduction cycle consists of those parents who divorced prior to Ego's marriage. (Findings not reported here are that where the parents had divorced before the marriage of their children, sons especially tend to marry about a year younger than do sons from intact marriages.) The table reveals that kinship mapping is associated with the prevalence and timing of parental divorce. The per centage of parents divorcing before the marriage of their children is slightly larger for persons in the Standard American (19.6%) and the Genetic and Canon Law categories (20.7%) than for those in the Parentela Orders (13.6%) and Civil Law (17.6%) groups. However, for parents who delayed their divorces until after the children married, the trend is reversed, with about 20% of the divorces among parents in the Parentela Orders and Civil Law classifications and fewer than 2% in the Standard American, Canon Law, and Genetic groupings.

Data for divorced respondents are also reported in Table C. The pattern of findings among divorced respondents is different from that of their parents. The percentages reveal that divorce is most prevalent among individuals with a Canon Law or Genetic mapping (Farber, 1981). (As Table D will indicate, however, the variations in percentages for the other classes of kinship mapping are derived from cohort differences.) As for the length of disrupted marriages, those divorced individuals with a Standard American mapping (9.7 years) appear to hesitate to divorce longer than do others (about 8.6 years).

In the analysis of remarriage, since too few divorced persons in the 1950s cohort would have had a chance to remarry by 1978 (when the survey was undertaken), only individuals in the 1930s and 1940s cohorts are included. In Table C, the findings suggest a greater hesitation to marry again among respondents with Standard American, Genetic, and Canon Law mappings. A smaller percentage of persons with these mappings have remarried by 1978 (Standard American, 46.0%; Genetic and Canon Law, 41.3%), as compared with persons in the Parentela Orders (57.1%) or Civil Law (76.5%) categories. Among those who do remarry, Table C indicates that Standard American (5.6 years) and Genetic and Canon Law (6.6 years) respondents also take a longer time to wed again (Parentela Orders, 4.8 years; Civil Law, 3.8 years). Hence, particularly the results on remarriage (in support of those for divorce among parents) suggest that persons in Parentela Orders and Civil Law categories have a great commitment to marital and parental statuses than do those with Standard American, Genetic, and Canon Law mappings.

A similar conclusion derives from the findings on childless couples. According to Table C, the probability of childlessness is much higher for Standard American (24.1%) and Genetic and Canon Law (20.9%) persons than for people with a Parentela Orders (9.4%) or a Civil Law (11.9%) mapping. However, as in the case of divorce, differences among types of kinship mapping are markedly affected by birth cohort (as indicated in Table D).

Table D presents the findings on percentages of divorced persons and of childless couples by birth cohort and kinship category. With regard to

Table D
Interrupted Family Reproduction Cycles, by Decade of Ego's Birth and by Type of Kinship Map

Type of Kinship Map	Decade of EGO's Birth (Percentage Divorced or Childless)			
	1930s	1940s	1950s	N
Percentage of persons ever divorced				
Parentela Orders	35.2	37.3	25.0	
N	54	61	16	131
Standard American	41.3	32.6	24.6	
N	46	95	65	206
Civil Law	40.0	21.9	23.5	
N	25	33	17	75
Genetic or Canon Law	50.0	44.6	42.9	
N	30	56	28	114
Prevalence of Divorce among Parents of Ego	11.3	21.9	27.6	
N in cohort	155	245	126	
Percentage of married persons who are childless				
Parentela Orders	4.2	11.1	23.1[a]	
N	48	46	13	106
Standard American	7.1	25.3	39.0[a]	
N	42	83	41	166
Civil Law	4.2	3.6	40.0[a]	67
N	24	28	15	67
Genetic or Canon Law	0.0	23.9	36.4[a]	
N	23	46	22	91
N in cohort	115	202	91[a]	

[a]For persons born before 1955.

divorced persons, for each cohort, the holders of a Genetic or Canon Law mapping are the most vulnerable to divorce. Whereas uniformly the percentages of divorced persons in the other kinship categories decline from about 38% in the 1930s cohort to about 25% in the 1950s cohort, the prevalence of divorce in the Genetic and Canon Law category remains high, decreasing only from 50% for the 1930s cohort to 43% for the 1950s cohort.

Although the percentages in marital disruptions are fairly similar for the Parentela Orders, Standard American, and Civil Law respondents in each the 1930s and the 1950s birth cohorts, they differ from one another in the 1940s cohort. Among persons born in the 1940s, those with kinship maps emphasizing line of descent (particularly Parentela Orders) seem especially vulnerable to divorce. The percentage in the Civil Law category (21.9%) is clearly below that for Standard American persons (32.6%) and Parentela Orders respondents (37.3%).

In childlessness, as in divorce, the 1940s cohort produces differences among kin types that are not apparent in the 1930s and 1950s cohorts. The percentages of childlessness among the various kinship types are uniformly low for the 1930s cohort (0–7%) and uniformly high in the 1950s cohort (about 40%) (except for Parentela Orders). (Some of this difference between the 1930s and 1950s cohorts is undoubtedly attributable to differences in length of marriage.) But the 1940s cohort shows high percentages of childlessness in the Standard American (25.3%) and Genetic and Canon Law (23.9%) categories and low percentages among Parentela Orders (11.1%) and Civil Law (3.6%) respondents. Thus, the findings on childlessness add to those on parental and Ego's divorce in suggesting that those born in the 1940s decade (and their parents) show a pattern of family reproduction cycles different from those found for persons born in either the 1930s or the 1950s.

Chapter 9
Gender Roles and the State*

W. Norton Grubb
Lyndon B. Johnson School of Public Affairs
The University of Texas, Austin

Marvin Lazerson
Faculty of Education
University of British Columbia, Vancouver

The belief that families are in trouble has been persistent in American history. Colonial Americans expressed the "greatest trouble and grief about the rising generation," and brooded about "the great neglect in many parents and masters in training up their children in learning and labour." They sought to stabilize families through statutes enforcing parental responsibility and through public officials scrutinizing family life. In the early nineteenth century, especially between 1830 and 1860, alarm over family stability generated a profusion of guides to childrearing, often combined with calls for philanthropic and public efforts to "shore up" family life. Social reformers expressed similar concerns during the rest of the nineteenth century and into the twentieth century. It has often seemed that each generation has discovered in the "decline of the family" the source of its troubles and the motivation for public policies (Grubb & Lazerson, 1982, Chap. 1).

Since the conception of the American family has always been tied to its childrearing responsibilities, changes in childrearing arrangements have always been widely interpreted as threatening the family itself. The "crisis of domesticity" in the mid-nineteenth century involved reshaping roles for men and women at a time when the household economy was changing, when men's work was increasingly divorced from the home, and when

* This paper draws upon our book *Broken Promises: How Americans Fail Their Children* (New York: Basic Books, 1982), especially chapters 1 and 9. Julia Green Brody and Barbara Easton provided valuable comments on an earlier draft.

women's direct role in production was declining. The development of the domestic ideology—emphasizing maternal responsibility for children, separate spheres for men and women, and the private realm of the family separated from the public realm of employment and politics—established new conceptions of family and childrearing and allayed fears about the family's decline. With childrearing responsibilities assigned to women, the "family crisis" that developed during the Progressive Era reflected the expansion of paid labor for women, changing conceptions of what women might do. The Depression of the 1930s, another period of obvious "crisis," also caused great concern for traditional sex roles, as unemployment threatened to undermine the familial power of men. In each of these periods the change in women's work—in the home and outside—and the ideological and political constraints which shaped the changes have been central to the sense of families in "crisis."

Not surprisingly, the debate over the family has taken on a new intensity in the postwar period as women have dramatically increased their participation in paid employment. Since 1946, the movement of women (especially mothers) into the labor force and out of full-time family roles has challenged every aspect of the family, from everyday household duties to the balance of maternal and paternal responsibilities for children and the family's economic well-being. The changing roles of women and (to a lesser extent) of men have made the link between the "private" world of the family and the public world of work and politics explicit; they have revealed how much of what we take as personal is social in origin and scope. As the feminist movement has insisted, "the personal is political" and "the political is personal"; the individual negotiations of men and women in the aggregate amount to social changes, and in turn these negotiations and decisions are affected by political outcomes in areas like employment, child care, the availability of birth control, and abortion.

Maternal employment and expanding occupational options for women have therefore raised crucial questions about the relationship of the state to gender roles, since the efforts to expand occupational options for women and to reconcile paid employment with family responsibilities have made the roles of men and women an intense political issue. Although the range of politicized issues has expanded enormously in the last two decades, the trend parallels earlier feminist movements: women have always been forced to go outside the family to increase their power, both within the family and in society at large (DuBois, 1979; Easton, 1978; Gordon, 1979). In many ways the imbalance in power between men and women within the family has been the most resistant to change, lagging behind advances in the economic and political conditions of women; even now there is evidence that the internal dynamics of families have changed rather little, despite the enormous postwar expansion of employment for women and their greater political power. Small wonder, then, that women have always been better able to enhance their power by pressing on institutions outside the family, particularly political institutions.

Still another force influencing the tendency to politicize gender roles has been the search for a "family policy."[1] In the past, the concern in periods of family "crisis" with the presumed deterioration of childrearing has led to the creation of various children's institutions—like the schools, the welfare system, the juvenile court, and the more recent array of social services—on the assumption that creating public institutions external to families is the most appropriate way to help children. The interest in family policy during the 1970s and 1980s is, in many ways, a novel departure from this tendency. Even though much of the writing on family policy has been incoherent, vapid, or self-serving (Steiner, 1981), there remain at least two valid reasons for interest in supporting children by attending to conditions of their families. First, the expansion of the state has made it impossible to ignore the influences of the state on children through their families. Macroeconomic policy, the income tax structure, policies related to discrimination and other aspects of employment, and the staggering array of public programs all have consequences for children and their families, bewildering in their variety and often contradictory in their effects. As Alva Myrdal (1941) recognized four decades ago, state expansion has created an implicit family policy; the critical issue is whether that policy will be conscious, consistent, and principled, or whether it will remain unconscious, chaotic, and ambiguous in its effects on both children and their parents.

Second, the approach to family "crisis" of creating institutions for children while ignoring the conditions of their families has not worked very well. Distinguishing children from their parents, while simultaneously blaming parents for their children's problems, has had too many negative consequences; the stigma attached to children in compensatory education and the low levels of income support in AFDC are two of many examples. The hope that we can achieve equality of opportunity in an unequal society has been consistently thwarted by whites denying minorities equal access to schooling and middle-class parents vying to keep their children's schools superior. Class and racial biases make it nearly impossible to shape children's lives *de novo* in public institutions. Acknowledging just how inadequate children's institutions have been has led some liberals to promote a comprehensive family policy to address the structural inequalities of family life directly, since children's institutions cannot possibly work as

---

[1] On "family policy," see Kamerman and Kahn (1976), Giele (1979), Wallach (1981), Giraldo (1980), and Dempsey (1981). For a different view, see Grubb and Lazerson (1982), Chap. 9; for a critique see Steiner (1981).

they should if family life is ignored. In the search for a coherent family policy, efforts to address the roles of women and men have been central, since many of the problems which constitute the sense of "crisis"—the poverty rates of female-headed families, the increasing rates of divorce, the private and public negotiations about who will care for children when mothers work—are linked to changing gender roles.

Political activism in the past several decades has wrought one special change from earlier periods of family "crisis": the issues of changing gender roles are now clearly in the public realm, giving women access to state power previously denied them by the ideology of women's roles as "private" and familial. But the resort to the state has had ambiguous consequences: the power of the state to promote greater equality has also been the power to reverse the gains of women and to maintain traditional domestic patterns. In the debates of the postwar period—over birth control and abortion, the equalization of working conditions, pay, and opportunity, access to education and to credit, media exploitation and stereotyping— the issues are tremendously embattled and far from resolved; indeed, activism to use the state and to expand options for women has been met by a counterattack from the New Right using the same agencies of government. As we will see, the uncertain effects of state action in changing the status of women have several causes, but two have been especially powerful: the contradictory effects of capitalism in shaping the roles of men and women, and the continued link of women to the "private" system of childrearing, a link that generates serious questions about whether gains for women are detrimental to children and that continues to hamper public action.

THE CONTRARY FORCES OF CAPITALISM: THE PERPETUATION AND DISSOLUTION OF MALE DOMINANCE

The subordination of women to men obviously predated capitalism, existing in various forms in ancient and primitive as well as in modern societies. For contemporary Americans, the most significant precapitalist manifestation was the development of male-dominated families in Western Europe and North America between the sixteenth and nineteenth centuries, a family form bolstered by laws, an evangelical religion which stressed obedience to patriarchs, and male-dominated forms of ownership and access to occupations.[2] Capitalism gave male dominance a new eco-

---

[2] For a brief review of the anthropological literature, see Hartmann (1976) and Stone (1977). We often refer in this discussion to male dominance rather than the term "patriarchy" which many feminists prefer, since patriarchy denotes specific historical and religious roots of male dominance that are of little interest for our purposes.

nomic basis, partially transforming it from a religious and legal system of control into a system based on the impersonal operations of the market, which gave men greater power not only because of cultural and religious norms, but also because of their superior economic positions and the lack of economic options for most women. At the same time, the emergence of the domestic nuclear family, with the separation of public and private domains, further accentuated the status of the father as provider and circumscribed the possible roles of women. In the long run, however, other roles expanded under capitalism, especially the opportunities to engage in employment independently of husbands, and outlets for political expression. Ironically, then, even as capitalism placed relations between men and women on an economic basis and defined the family in a new way, subsequent developments provided the basis for an equality between men and women which was unthinkable in precapitalist societies.

In colonial America, the basis of male power was essentially legal and religious, not economic. The labor of women in the family-based colonial American economy of small farms and independent craft work could mean the difference between marginal subsistence and prosperity. Married women and widows both managed the household, producing nearly everything for domestic use, and cared for young children. Yet if women played important economic roles, men held by far the greater power. Husbands held legal title to property; the man was the family's political representative, while the Church confirmed his position as family patriarch in the image of God the Patriarch. Women had few alternatives to the marriages in which they were unavoidably subordinate. (See Cott, 1977, and Demos, 1970).

The decline of the household economy and the growth of wage labor in the eighteenth and early nineteenth centuries forced many young women out of their homes and into the labor market. Yet women rarely gained the independence men achieved, since they usually remained under some form of familial control: many women continued to work in their homes under the control of husbands and fathers, in cottage industries, and under the putting-out system. The early textile factories lodged unmarried female workers in dormitories under the supervision of mother-surrogates, to retain familial controls in new settings; sometimes they hired entire families, so that wives were still under their husbands' control. Many women who left home to work still viewed their responsibilities in familial terms, returning earnings to their families (Pleck, 1976). Even the kind of work reflected domestic ideals: domestic service was paid employment for women, explicitly linking employment to household activities.

Still, wage labor for women represented a threat to men as capitalists, workers, and husbands. Entrepreneurs found that the family's traditional rights with regard to work sometimes conflicted with their own authority, and they sought more direct controls over workers in place of indirect controls through the *pater familias*. Husbands complained about the independence (potential and actual) of their wives, and male workers sometimes fought to keep low-paid women out of the labor market. As a result, few economic opportunities for women existed during most of the nineteenth century, and wherever they worked women were usually segregated from men, in jobs of lower status and lower pay. Factory employment was viewed as a violation of feminine respectability and women's frail constitutions. Only middle-class occupations like school-teaching and nursing were open and respectable, since they were extensions of women's traditional roles as nurturers of the young and sick; but even here the tendency was to exclude married women from becoming a significant part of the wage labor force. When families needed income, they were more likely to send their children to work than wives or mothers.[3]

Married women as wage laborers threatened not only the power of husbands, but also the tasks of childrearing. As work and home became separated, the two roles of earning a living and rearing children could no longer be carried out simultaneously. The solution to combining the two tasks within the "private" family—the father working and the mother staying home full-time with her children—reflected the continuation of traditional childrearing responsibilities, but the "cult of domesticity" brought a new emphasis to traditional assumptions and made alternatives to full-time childrearing unthinkable. Of women, domesticity required disinterest in the outside world, selflessness and sacrifice, an acceptance of motherhood as self-fulfillment, and service to their husbands. Women's public role was to be limited to a moral example in a corrupt society. While domesticity had little applicability to working-class women in factories or to black women in slavery and on sharecropper farms, it urged women and men to think of paid employment for women as temporary and aberrant, opening the way for employers to treat women's wages as supplemental and women's work as peripheral (see especially Cott, 1977, and Douglas, 1977).

The definition of women's roles in domestic terms and the segregation of women in "women's work" continued, as the American economy developed and the range of occupations expanded. At the turn of the century, when corporate enterprises began to require more bookkeepers and secretaries, women were preferred because of their presumed dexterity and attention to detail, and because their lower wages were appropriate for their unskilled office work. The new clerical and retail occupations in turn

---

[3] On women's work in the nineteenth century, see Glasco (1977); Harevan (1977); Kessler-Harris (1967); Klacynska (1976); Kleinberg (1976); Bernard and Vinovskis (1977); Wood (1972).

gave women expanded opportunities in "suitable" work environments; women increased their representation from 25% of clerical positions to 42.1%, and from 18.5% of all white-collar jobs to 42.1%. But these employment patterns reinforced the occupational segregation by sex which had prevailed throughout the nineteenth century. In fact, this sexual division still holds nearly eight decades later; despite changes in the occupational structure and increases in women working, the extent of sexual segregation has remained relatively constant since 1900.[4]

The persistence of occupational segregation and wage differentials is testimony to powerful economic interests at work, as well as to the efforts of men in their own self-interest to exclude women from certain occupations. Employers have benefited from the lower wages they pay women workers, as their resistance to current legal efforts to equalize wages and occupational opportunities for women testifies. In addition, women have always served as a "reserve army" of labor, a pool of potential workers which can be easily drawn into the labor market in periods of high demand, and readily dismissed when demand slackens (Faber & Lowrey, 1973). Men as a group have also benefited from occupational discrimination, enjoying not only higher wages than women but also higher status in their work and better working conditions. Particularly through their control over unions and professional organizations, men have consistently resisted efforts by women to gain access to male-dominated occupations: skilled craftsmen, academics, and lawyers have all resisted the "intrusion" of women into their ranks, and have been forced only by legal challenges into special programs to open up occupations to women (Hartmann, 1976). The consequences of confining women to "women's work" have been devastating: lower earnings, averaging in the mid 1970s about 60% of men's, and fewer opportunities to work in the most creative and challenging positions.[5] The most enduring consequence of the sexual division of wage labor has been to give male dominance a new, economic basis. The inferior position of women in production has bound wom-

---

[4] *Historical Statistics of the United States,* Series D-182 to D-232; Gross (1968–69); *Economic Report* (1973, p. 155); Oppenheimer (1970). Occupational segregation is only the crudest form of gender segregation; other forms of segregation within occupations, particularly when women occupy lower positions and men have supervisory power, and segregation by firm, are more subtle. See, e.g., Blau (1977).

[5] This figure is for year-round, full-time workers; for all income recipients, the ratio in 1973 was 35% because women tend to work part time more than men *(1975 Handbook,* 1976, Women's Bureau (1976). Part of this difference is due to variation in the experience, education, and other qualifications of women and men; standardizing for these factors, Beller (1979) found an earnings ratio of 68%, virtually unchanged between 1967 and 1974. The enforcement of antidiscrimination status apparently offset the effect of lower experience of women just entering the labor force.

en into families, where men become the primary breadwinners and
women "specialize" in housework because of the difference in their
wages.

Despite its persistence, the relegation of women to "women's work"
is inconsistent with nineteenth century liberalism, especially with the conceptions underlying free labor markets. The labor market has been a system tending to break down the importance of ascriptive traits—rank, place
of birth, age, and even class background, race, and sex—in favor of productivity in the work force, even though other institutional and cultural
practices (like the cult of domesticity) have prevented labor markets from
operating freely. Where the logic of labor markets and cultural norms
have come in conflict—where needs have arisen for large numbers of new
workers, or where opportunities existed to hire women at lower wages
than would prevail for men—women have been hired, despite objections
that this would undermine family life and stunt the development of children. The expansion of the female labor force in office and factory work
in the early twentieth century provides one example. The emergency
caused by the expansion of the economy during World War II similarly
drew women into the labor market, overriding the convention that women
belonged in the home. The postwar period of relatively high growth stimulated increased employment of women, particularly given the high growth
rates of jobs defined as "women's work"—teaching, clerical, and service
occupations.[6]

At the same time that changes in employment have created new opportunities for women to work, other developments reinforced maternal
employment by pushing women out of the home. As corporations in the
early part of this century turned their attention to the home as a potential
market, they began to produce commodities—central heating, stoves
("gasless cookers"), refrigerators, vacuum cleaners, and canned foods—
which reduced the time necessary to maintain the home, making women
comparatively more valuable in the labor force earning the money necessary for running the home.[7] The role which the commodification of home
production played in pushing women into the labor force during the early
part of this century is unclear, because rising standards of cleanliness
prevented the amount of time spent in housework from decreasing (see
Hartmann, 1974; Hoffman & Nye, 1974, Chap. 2; and Vanek, 1970). But
since World War II, the income demands of running a household have
played a more obvious role in stimulating employment. The patterns of

---

[6] In calculating the growth rate of jobs considered to be "women's work," Oppenheimer
(1969) finds 1950–1960 to have been a decade of exceptionally high growth.

[7] For descriptions of the changes in home production during decades of the twentieth century
and the advertising campaigns which accompanied them, see Ewen (1973).

inflation have caused the costs of families with children to increase faster than the rate of inflation, and inflation has eroded real wages during the 1960s and 1970s.[8] As a consequence more wives were forced to work to prevent their families' living standards from being eroded.[9]

For most of this century, then, the roles of women have been subjected to the pulls and pushes of economic development. Two contradictory forces have been at work: The first—rooted in precapitalist conceptions of women's roles, patterns of male dominance, and the interests of capitalist institutions in discriminating against women—has tended to keep women's wages low, reinforced the patterns of occupational segregation, and left women subordinate to men. The second—stemming from conceptions of equality in labor markets and the labor requirements of a developing economy—has worked to undermine that subordination by increasing the demand for women workers. The power of old patriarchal norms, re-expressed in the domestic ideology, has prevented labor markets from operating freely and from incorporating women (especially married women), and during the twentieth century this ideology continued to justify various patterns of discrimination. But the power of economic development has been greater. The trend has been for greater women's participation in the labor force; the short-term reverses, in the attempts to eliminate women from the labor force during the Depression and right after World War II, were never effective for long. Another reason to suspect that employment gains will not be readily reversed, especially for mothers, involves the modeling effect of mothers working: the children of working women are more likely to accept maternal employment as legitimate, and their daughters are more likely to work themselves, compared to the children of nonworking women.[10] In this way the entry of women into the labor force—whether because of economic necessity, national emergency (like World War II), or economic demand—has been self-reinforcing, producing new generations less likely to adhere to the domestic ideology.

Because the development of capitalism has had contradictory con-

---

[8] The cost of a "higher budget" for an urban family of four increased 82% between spring, 1967, and autumn, 1976, while the Consumer Price Index increased 70%. On the erosion of real wages, see the Bureau of Labor Statistics, "Real Earnings in March 1979," which indicates earnings of production workers have declined in real terms since 1967.

[9] Because women who work for economic reasons also come to enjoy work as a release from family life, it is impossible to separate women who "want" to work from those who "need" to work. However, there are at least some indicators of economic necessity. In 1973, 42% of working women were single, widowed, divorced, or separated; an additional 29% were married to men earning less than $10,000 (1975 Handbook, 1976, Chart L, p. 124). Anecdotal evidence on the reasons for working comes from a variety of sources: see, e.g., Nye & Hoffman (1974); Rubin (1976, Chap. 9); and Lein (1974).

[10] For evidence on the modeling effect, see Hoffman and Nye (1974, Chap. 6). For a psychological perspective of mothering, see Chodorow (1977).

sequences for women, the liberal democratic state in this country has also taken contradictory and shifting positions. In its role of supporting the economic liberalism of the nineteenth century, the state has consistently supported those institutions and practices of entrepreneurial capitalism, including the sanctity of private capital and the dominance of markets and market incentives. But this in turn means that both sides in the debate over sex roles—both feminists and antifeminists—have been able to rely on capitalist ideology and practice to make their claims. Those who support the employment of women have been able to point to the ideology of individual freedom to thwart attempts to prevent the employment of women; in their efforts to obtain equal working conditions for women and men they have been able to rely on the ideology of merit, or "equal pay for equal work," which underlies capitalist labor markets. Those opposed to the employment of women and to equalizing occupation status and pay through state action have been able to point to the irrationality of having husbands support their wives' working when men earn so much more than women do. Both sides have, at different times, enjoyed politically powerful supporters: the efforts of women to move out of the home and into employment have been backed by firms needing women workers, while the efforts to eliminate employment differentials between men and women have been opposed by the same firms. Since both sides in the debates over the employment of women and men have been able to rely on capitalist ideology and power, the state's actions have been ambiguous, allowing the employment of women but failing to ensure equality between men and women.

THE AMBIGUITY OF WORK AND CHILDBEARING

The conflicting pressures on women have meant greater equality for women in an economic and social system in which they remain subordinate to men. In addition, the status of women as they have gained relatively greater economic power remains unclear because of a dilemma unique to women: work outside the home for women is invariably defined by its relationship to the "private" family. This link to the "private" family of the domestic ideal—the family set apart from the "public" worlds of work and politics—has in turn restricted the efforts of the state to develop those public measures that might in any way affect the familial responsibilities of women.

While the roles of wife and mother have traditionally given women meaning and status, the home has also been a trap for them, the locus of tasks which isolate them and drain them of energy. This contradicts the traditional understanding of the home as a refuge from work, and clarifies the extent to which the home as "haven in a heartless world" has been a peculiarly male view. Leaving the home thus takes on a special meaning for women, and work is a partial escape from the home and the isolation of the private family.

The pleasure many women find in employment, even when their jobs are menial and routine, testifies to the drudgery of being home-bound. One factory worker described her work in these terms:

> I really love going to work. I guess it's because it gets me away from home. It's not that I don't love my home; I do. But you get awfully tired of just keeping house and doing those housewifely things . . . You know, when I was home, I was getting in real trouble. I had that old housewife's syndrome, where you either crawl in bed after the kids go to school or sit and watch TV by the hour. I was just dying of boredom and the more bored I got, the less and less I did. On top of it I was getting fatter and fatter, too. I finally knew I had to do something about it, so I took this course in upholstery and got this job as an upholstery trimmer. (Rubin, 1976, p. 170)

Employed mothers also tend to have more positive images of themselves than do unemployed mothers. Their feelings of competence are enhanced through being valued by a larger circle of coworkers and customers, through being productive at tasks which are more permanent than cleaning and cooking (Nye & Hoffman, 1964, Chap. 9). The benefits to women at work also extend to family relationships, especially in the power and independence women gain within their families:

> I can't imagine not working. I like to get out of the house, and the money makes me feel more independent. Some men are funny. They think if you don't work, you ought to be home every day, like a drudge around the house, and that they can come home and just say, "Do this," and "Do that," and "Why is that dish in the sink?" When you work and make some money, it's different. It makes me feel more equal to him. He can't just tell me what to do. (Rubin, 1976, p. 175)

While women who work tend to remain subordinate to husbands in family and individual decision-making, they nonetheless have greater influence than those who do not work—especially in financial decisions (Bahr, 1976).

Yet the satisfactions with work and the increasing autonomy within families come at substantial cost, since working women continue to bear the main responsibilities for childrearing and homemaking. Theirs are the responsibilities for making child care arrangements, and theirs the anxiety when those arrangements fall apart. They bear the responsibility for a clean home, and shoulder the blame if television-spotless standards are not maintained (Nye & Hoffman, 1964, Chap. 2). Even those families where the husbands do take on additional household tasks, they tend to assume those which are relatively rewarding and more public—like the care of children—and leave the more repetitive and boring chores (cleaning and laundry) to their wives (Kotelchuck, 1976; Lein, 1974).

The strain for women is partly one of time, but it is also based on the conflict between the different kinds of responsibilities working women have. The ideological baggage surrounding maternal responsibilities—particularly the fear of working mothers that they are not providing their children with the emotional support necessary for healthy development—adds a measure of guilt to the physical strain. The consequence is that women are often pulled between two roles, finding satisfaction in both but feeling uncertain about each:

> Working is hard for me. When I work, I feel like I want to be doing a real good job, and I want to be absolutely responsible. Then, if the little one gets a cold, I feel like I should be home with her. That causes complications because whatever you do isn't right. You're either at work feeling like you should be home with your sick child, or you're at home feeling like you should be at work. (Rubin, 1976, p. 172)

The origins of this ambivalence are not difficult to discern. Nineteenth century domesticity assigned childrearing responsibilities exclusively to mothers. During the twentieth century, an increasingly elaborate structure of "scientific" thought and expert opinion has bolstered these older views. Psychoanalytic theory has stressed the importance of a single strong bond between mother and child and the devastating consequences to children of maternal deprivation. Child development researchers have raised their observations of childrearing dominated by mothers into normative prescriptions that only mothers could be effective parents, a clear nonsequitur. The methodological limitations of this work have been serious, especially the reliance on interviews and observations of mothers only, and the inability of researchers to investigate families in which sex roles are not traditionally defined. But these limitations never compromised the willingness of behavioral scientists and pediatricians to generalize their findings—essentially *descriptions* of traditional sex roles—into *normative* statements of what roles mothers ought to play and warnings of dire consequences for children if mothers left their children to work (see Kotelchuck, 1976, Lemasters, 1974, and Levine, 1976). As Dr. Spock (1947, 1958) told two generations of mothers:

> You can think of it this way: useful, well-adjusted citizens are the most valuable possessions a country has, and good mother care during the earliest childhood is the surest way to produce them. It doesn't make

sense to let mothers go to work making dresses in a factory or tapping typewriters in an office, and have them pay other people to do a poorer job of bringing up their own children.

Even the most recent generation of childrearing manuals has often rein-forced the old notion that there is nothing women can do as valuable as mothering. As Burton White (1975), author of a prominent childrearing manual, reexpressed the old sentiment:

> It is my hope that we will soon get to a point where raising a child in the home in the first few years of life will no longer be generally considered "mere mothering." I honestly cannot think of any task more exciting and more valuable that any of us do in our daily work than the task of providing an early education for one's own child under three years of age. The parent who takes the responsibility for structuring the experi-ences of the first three years of his child's life is at the same time taking on an important responsibility for helping to mold that child and helping to give that child's natural tendencies the best possible opportunities to flower. What could be more important and rewarding than this? Should this idea become more widely accepted, . . . we will find fewer families in conflict or dissatisfied about the woman's role. We will less frequently see a woman going back to something "more important" than child-raising as soon as possible in the child's first year of life. Finally, we are likely to find it acceptable and even desirable for men to assume more of the childrearing function on a regular basis. (pp. 255–256)

As familial practices have changed in the postwar period, the attention of developmental psychologists and social scientists has turned to a more balanced understanding of parental roles. While strong, continuous, and affectionate bonds between adults and children are basic to healthy de-velopment, the necessity of a single maternal bond no longer seems ten-able. The empirical evidence that two or more strong bonds are possible, that a strong role for the father in childrearing does not weaken the ma-ternal bond, that employment in itself does not undermine mother–child bonds, that men are as capable as women of loving and nurturing rela-tionships with their children, and that a strong paternal relationship creates richer possibilities for the child's development all stand in sharp contrast to earlier proclamations that the mother–child relationship should not be disturbed by anyone or any other activity (Clarke-Stewart, 1977; Lamb, 1976; Rutter, 1974).

Yet given the elaborate structure of thought that has developed, re-vising conceptions of what women's roles ought to be is not simple. Those wedded to traditional conceptions of family life and maternal roles still have the weight of some professional expertise to bolster their position. They can raise the specter of children deprived of care, denied the strong attachment necessary to healthy emotional and social development. This condemnation of working mothers partially explains the sense of crisis surrounding the increase in maternal employment: women who work are assumed to be neglecting their children. As long as working women continue to bear full (or nearly full) responsibilities for home and family, there is no way out of the tensions surrounding work and family. In trying to fulfill the expectations of their familial roles, they are hampered in their work and sometimes forced to take part-time work or less desirable jobs; childbearing hinders them from gaining superiority in their work and continuity in their work experiences (Mincer and Polachek, 1974). Conversely, their work roles hamper their familial roles, especially to the extent that work drains them of energy.

One response to this continuing dilemma has been to reduce the costs of dual roles in any way possible. One possibility has been the "private" solution of redividing family tasks, with men assuming their share of childrearing, cooking, and cleaning. The demands by working women that their husbands take over some of the household and childrearing duties have been part of the redivision of labor and status within the home; the other side of this struggle has been an equally constant effort to defend traditional male prerogatives. As one man described the struggles:

> She just doesn't know how to be a real wife, you know, feminine and really womanly. She doesn't know how to give respect because she's too independent. She feels that she's a working woman and she puts in almost as many hours as I do and brings home a pay check, so there's no one person above the other. She doesn't want there to be a king in this household. (Rubin, 1976, p. 176)

But these struggles over the redivision of labor have been "private," waged within the confines of the home. Even though the women's movement has made it clear how widespread these struggles are, it remains impossible to bring much social pressure to bear on these issues; they remain conflicts between individual men and individual women and—since power is unequally distributed to begin with—the result has been relatively little change in the division of household tasks.

Conditions outside the family complicate the attempts to redivide labor in the family so that men increase their childrearing and homemaking responsibilities. Wage discrimination almost invariably makes men's wages higher than women's. For mothers rather than fathers to work probably means a cut in earnings, making it rational, in this sense, for men to be full-time wage-earners, and making it costly for husbands to share childrearing responsibilities with their wives. The relative unavailability of decent part-time jobs provides an additional impediment to a redivision of labor.[11] Thus the efforts to redivide roles within the family have been forced to address public and political issues, including the attempts to reduce discrimination in employment and those to generate new part-time work and flexible schedules;[12] other efforts to reduce the impact of familial responsibilities on employment include the efforts to win maternity and paternity leave without loss of seniority. But these efforts have been resisted on two counts, both related to the limits of public intervention: such change would amount to intervening in the "private" family and upsetting familial roles; and they require intervening into "private" labor markets. As we will see in greater detail in the next section, the efforts to harness the power of the state in these battles—against employment discrimination, for example—have been strenuous for both of these reasons. As has been consistently true since the feminist movement before the Civil War, women have been forced outside their families to press for the conditions which might yield greater equality within families. But once in the arena of economic and political institutions, women have faced the same contradictory forces which have conditioned their subordination to men and the state's actions have therefore remained ambiguous.

The special link of women to childrearing and the "private" family has thus continued to be a powerful barrier to the individual freedoms arising out of economic liberalism. Although capitalism has generated pressures to move women out of the family into employment and thereby give them more options and more power, the conception of the family that arose with entrepreneurial capitalism—a private sphere, a refuge from the ravages of work, anticapitalist in its inner workings—and the special link of women to mothering have prevented the full force of economic liberalism from operating for women. The continuing assumption that families are private and should be as free from state intervention as possible has hampered efforts to use the power of the state on behalf of women— just as the efforts to improve the employment conditions of women have faltered because of political opposition to state interference with the prerogatives of "private" firms.

POLITICIZING GENDER ROLES AND THE AMBIGUOUS EFFECTS OF THE STATE

Many women have always recognized that public and political decisions shape gender roles and family functioning, and have turned to the state

---

[11] For a discussion of the difficulties men face in assuming full parental responsibilities, see Levine (1976). On the psychological impact which mothering by women and the lack of it by men have on sex roles, see Chodorow (1977).

[12] These proposals have become part of the standard liberal package of reforms; see, e.g., Keniston (1977, Chap. 6).

and public policies to challenge their subordinate status. In the nineteenth century, women actively supported temperance legislation, since alcoholism was a factor in poverty, desertion, and family violence. With few alternatives to marriage and valid fears about the dangers of childbirth, feminists led the fight for the state protection of birth control and abortion. In the Progressive Era, efforts to improve working conditions for women acknowledged that work outside the home affected familial obligations. The suffrage movement took women directly into the political arena, with the hope that equality at the polls would bring equality within the family (DuBois, 1979; Easton, 1978; Gordon, 1979). While it has been necessary to move outside the family in order to revise the roles of men and women, the expansion of the state in the 20th century and the widening influence of extrafamilial institutions has also made the political nature of the struggle over gender roles inevitable. As much as some may deplore the "invasion" of the family by the politicization of family issues, the alternative in the case of gender roles has been to keep the issues buried.

In the last two decades, the range of issues debated, litigated, and legislated has been immense. Efforts to reduce discrimination in employment have become institutionalized in the Equal Employment Opportunity Commission and in the right to sue discriminating employers privately. Discrimination in education, a source of crowding women into "women's work," has been attacked through Title IX of the Civil Rights Act. The discriminatory treatment of women in various public and private programs—in Social Security, in health insurance, in access to credit—has become a public issue. Increasing demand for child care has stimulated efforts to expand public subsidies. The mistreatment of women in the courts—the cavalier attitudes toward rape and wife abuse, for example—has come under attack, and court-ordered procedures in the area of child custody has weakened the presumption that only mothers should care for young children. Other issues intimately connected to rights within the family—divorce laws, and control over birth control, abortion, and sterilization—have similarly been opened to serious debate.

But the resort to the state has had ambiguous consequences; the power of the state to promote greater equality has also been the power to reverse the gains of women and to maintain traditional domestic patterns. The uncertain results of state action can be illustrated in three areas crucial to women and their families—employment, child care, and reproductive rights.

Employment policy has been torn between economic liberalism and the sanctity of private labor markets. Since labor markets have been justified in terms of rewarding productivity, obvious forms of employment discrimination have been an ideological embarrassment; the wide acceptance of "equal pay for equal work" reflects this fundamental concept of capitalist economics. The federal initiatives during the sixties and seventies to reduce pay and occupational differences between men and women have been able to draw on the ideology, but they have been hampered by the strenuous resistance of firms with simple economic interests at stake, invariably phrased ideologically as resistance to government meddling; the ineffective administrative structure of the Equal Employment Opportunity Commission, seemingly designed to prevent quick and effective action, reflects the ambiguity of federal interest. While an antidiscrimination policy has been established, its influence has been small and employment discrimination continues almost unabated.[13] Even these advances are being reversed, as President Reagan has reduced the scope of federal regulations and the ''intrusion'' of federal agencies into the workings of business.

The ambiguous nature of the state in the area of employment for women is also illustrated by the treatment of poor women and the development of the welfare system. At the turn of the century, the presence of poor women in the labor force presented a dilemma. Working women with children were presumed inadequate wives and mothers, but the only alternative to their working would have been legislation to make working illegal for women—an impossible intrusion into private labor markets— or some form of income supports to eliminate the need for mothers to work, a more direct intervention into the realm of private responsibilities than had been possible in the nineteenth century. The compromises that emerged through both organized charity and state intervention were typically contradictory. Some support was made available, through private philanthropy and through the mothers' pensions that developed after 1909, so that mothers might not work and could care for their children at home; but aid was always insufficient and given under degrading conditions so that poor women would continue to have to work. In the modern welfare system that developed from the mothers' pensions—the program of Aid to Dependent Children begun in 1935, and the current Aid to Families of Dependent Children—the conflict has continued between the cultural norms of domesticity, suggesting that mothers should be supported to rear their children at home, and the sanctity of economic independence and "free" labor markets making welfare programs an anathema. Income supports for mothers have expanded since the 1930s, but they have always been grudging, inadequate, and under attack; the moderate reduction in real welfare payments during the 1970s and the more devastating cuts of President Reagan are testimony to our inability to sustain a commitment

---

[13] See Beller (1979). Although Beller interprets her results as showing that federal efforts have had some impact on earnings differentials, her regression coefficients are statistically insignificant and therefore indicate the uncertainty of federal impact.

to poor children and their mothers. The logical alternative—to ensure jobs for women with adequate pay and status—has never been seriously pursued because such initiatives would infringe on private labor markets. Thus poor women have been especially susceptible to the inability of the state to address the inadequacies of capitalist labor markets.

The role of the state in child care has been similarly ambiguous. Child care by its nature violates not only conventional sex roles, but also the conventional conception of the "private" family: not only is the mother absent for part of the child's day, but childrearing can no longer be a purely private matter. As a result, government subsidies for child care have expanded under the pressure of increasing demand for child care, but only grudgingly. The dominant motivation behind federal funding of the 1960s and 1970s has been the desire to put welfare mothers to work and to provide compensatory education for lower-class children, rather than the liberation of women from home-bound roles. Public funding for child care as a way of expanding roles for women has still not drawn widespread support; the only source of public funding not tied to welfare concerns—the child care tax credit, which funds 20% to 30% of child care costs through the income tax system—does not begin to offset the wage differences between men and women or the high cost of child care. While there is more subsidized child care now than in the past, there is still relatively little and it remains expensive relative to women's wages; child care still suffers from the stigma of deviance rather than being considered a normal consequence of maternal employment. As a result, mothers are forced to make do with ramshackle arrangements of relatives, neighbors, and some paid care, while others arrange odd working schedules—nighttime and weekend work, for example—so that they need not use child care. The result is a strain for mothers and children alike (Lein, 1979; Bane, Lein, O'Donnell, Stueve, & Welles, 1979).

The sphere of reproductive rights—birth control, abortion, and sterilization abuse—has been the area most intimately connected to women's familial roles, and the most controversial. Since reproductive rights formally involve "private" behavior within families, we might expect the nineteenth century liberal state to have minimized its controls. Indeed, the right of women to contracept and to abort was generally accepted— if not publicly acknowledged—in the early nineteenth century; more accurately, it was not proscribed. But at the turn of the century, governmental control over both these areas of "private" decisions expanded. Fears that the white, Protestant, middle class was not reproducing itself, the growing divorce rate, and the increased independence of women as they entered the labor market, coalesced into legislation and propaganda which identified birth control with abortion and murder. As late as 1880, there were no American statutes on the subject of abortion; two decades later virtually every state and territory had made most abortions criminal offenses (Mohr, 1978). But as in debates over divorce, the defense of birth control and abortion took on a conservative cast: under the banner of "voluntary motherhood" supporters of reproductive rights argued that the elimination of unwanted children would strengthen the family by making mothers better parents. Only rarely were birth control and abortion justified in terms of women's autonomy or sexual emancipation.

Since then, access to contraception and abortion have been slow in coming, despite being goals of feminists throughout this century. The major advances for women came not through legislation, but through litigation; the dominant legal rationale has, ironically enough, been the traditional conservative ideology of the right of the family to privacy. *Griswold v. Connecticut* (1965) and *Eisenstadt v. Baird* (1968) prohibited government regulation of birth control; and *Roe v. Wade* (1973) seemed to put abortion beyond legislative control, with the Supreme Court arguing that state interference in woman's right to obtain an abortion was unconstitutional. In the wake of *Roe v. Wade,* two developments occurred with major consequences for women: a tremendous increase in the numbers of women seeking abortion, and an intense campaign to eliminate any public funding for abortion and then to secure a constitutional amendment to override the Court's decision. The efforts against abortion have been directed at all women, but their most formidable consequences have been against the most vulnerable women—poor women for whom the "right" of safe abortion is empty without subsidy. The refusal of all but a shrinking handful of states to continue subsidizing abortions with public money, and the growing effectiveness of political groups attacking politicians considered "soft" on abortion have testified to the power of the antifeminist position. The counterattack on the freedom to abort has drawn considerable strength from traditional conceptions of the family, especially the automatic connection of women to childbearing and childrearing.

In all three of these areas, the potential gains for *women*—equality in employment, more available child care, control over reproduction— are not necessarily gains for *children*. We can easily imagine conditions under which some children need full-time parenting or should not be in child care. Abortion is even more ambiguous: the unwanted child or its siblings might suffer if abortion did not take place, but the unborn child may have an interest in being born which conflicts with the mother's desire to abort. The potential tensions in these areas have been treated very differently by feminists and antifeminists, however. Those supporting expanded roles for women and those attempting to generate a coherent "family policy" have sought to eliminate or minimize the conflict between mothers and children. They have pressed, for example, to assure that decent jobs with stimulating working conditions are available to women, rather than stressful and degrading work which might affect family life; they have sued against employment discrimination, so that working mothers would not have to face the strains of poverty. They have tried to expand part-time work and flextime so that work schedules and family responsibilities can be congruent rather than antagonistic. In the area of child care, they have pressed for care of good quality, to allay the fears that child care might retard a child's development. In the difficult area of abortion, where even supporters admit to some qualms, feminists have tried to incorporate abortion into a broader program of reproductive issues addressed to both men and women, so that abortion does not become a substitute for contraception or an antidote for sexual irresponsibility but remains a last resort under extreme conditions (Joffe, 1981).

In contrast, antifeminists have made every effort to heighten the potential conflict between equality for women and the interests of children. Ironically, the policies they have espoused have often made matters worse for children as well as women, even as they have claimed to speak for children. Rather than finding ways to combine employment and child-rearing, antifeminists have insisted that part-time mothering is harmful to children, even though their insistence can do nothing to reduce the increasing numbers of mothers who work. Rather than pressure for an end to discrimination in employment and education, they have reasserted the old domestic ideals, an approach which only helps insure that the increasing fraction of women who do work suffer substandard wages, lower status, and poorer working conditions. Antifeminists have attacked child care, a position which does nothing for those millions of children who are in child care regardless of antifeminist opposition. Rather than downplay abortion issues, antifeminists have been strident in publicizing the most troubling aspects, acting as if those women who choose abortion do so gleefully without the serious reservations which almost all of them feel. These have been extreme reactions, but they have drawn upon a widely accepted link between women and full-time mothering which remains powerful despite a century of feminist efforts and constantly increasing rates of maternal employment. Those supporting this link have pressured the state to recognize only traditional roles for women. As one critic of the Equal Rights Amendment put it, the amendment undermined the domestic rights of women who "wish to be full-time wives and mothers"; the intended effect of ERA to expand choices for women was ignored. Only in welfare programs designed to force poor mothers into the work force has the tie between work and mothering been sundered by public policies—a measure of how little we are willing to pay for women to stay home and care for their children, at the same time that many public policies assume that mothers ought to be caring for their children full time.

The efforts to gain equality for women through state action have thus foundered on the most traditional assumptions about women's responsibilities. But they have also failed for another reason, one we encounter over and over again in social policy: the continuing assumption that families and labor markets are "private" and should be as free from state intervention as possible. Despite the overwhelming evidence that neither families nor labor markets are private, state involvement in them is still viewed as corrupting. The casual treatment of wife abuse provides one example, reflecting the convention that husband–wife relationships are private; another instance is the consistent unwillingness of the state to enforce the fiscal responsibilities of men who abandon their wives and children (except when welfare costs can be reduced). The efforts to improve the economic conditions of women (e.g., eliminating employment discrimination) have similarly faltered on the political opposition to state interference with the prerogatives of "private" firms. At the same time that growing employment for women has provided the economic basis for greater interdependence, the continued subordination of women to men in labor markets has retarded full equality between men and women. As long as those differences are seen to be rooted in "private" labor markets and in "private" family decisions, collective action on behalf of women through the state remains exceedingly difficult.

The resort to the state to develop more egalitarian gender roles has therefore been necessary, but ambiguous in its results. Public policies have lagged behind the employment of women, with detrimental consequences for both children and mothers. Expanded employment has made it possible for women to remain single or to leave unhappy marriages which they were earlier condemned to endure; but continuing gender discrimination in employment means that female-headed families are much more likely to be poor. The failure to fund child care has not reversed the influx of mothers into the labor force, but has instead forced women who must work and who still suffer low wages to make do with ramshackle arrangements, the use of relatives under inappropriate conditions, or poor quality care. The unwillingness of employers to take measures which would facilitate combining employment and parenthood—flextime, decent part-time work, maternal and paternal leaves—and the unwillingness of the state to promote such changes in employment conditions have placed working mothers under inordinate and unnecessary strain, which both they and their families may suffer.

Those who have tried to develop a coherent family policy have usually acknowledged the detrimental effects of unequal gender roles on women, family life, and children. They have then posed various policies—antidiscrimination measures, subsidized child care, the development of flextime and part-time work—to close the gap between men and women and ease the strains of maintaining employment and family life simultaneously.

If, like the call for full employment, these proposals sometimes seem naive, that is because they require more radical transformations than their authors envision. Eliminating employment discrimination requires public control over private institutions like firms, a direct attack against the dominance of nineteenth century liberal tenets. It further requires breaking the ideological link between women and childrearing responsibilities, which means new thinking about gender roles, as well as more social and paternal responsibility for children. Making employment and family life more compatible is similarly radical, since it requires that we recognize how false the ideological separation of home and work has been, and that we begin to accommodate employment to the requirements of personal life rather than leaving family life to be shaped by capitalist labor markets.

The struggle by women to undo their subordinate status raises basic issues about the relation between personal life and work life. Reshaping gender roles requires reshaping the relations between work and family life and parental responsibility. Such changes threaten the basic organization of capitalism as well as conventional relations between men and women; they cannot be accomplished without public and political action, involving the state and its potential power over the economy and the conditions of work. But efforts to use the state in such ways will remain frustrated unless we transform the limits on the state's ability to accomplish fundamental changes in a capitalist economy. Until we do, an appropriate policy which promotes expanded gender roles for women and a family policy which promotes the well-being of children will remain elusive.

REFERENCES

Bahr, S. Effects of power and division of labor within the family. In L. Hoffman & I. Nye, *Working mothers*. San Francisco, CA: Jossey-Bass, 1974.

Bane, M., Lein, L., O'Donnell, L., Stueve, C.A., & Welles, B. Child care in the United States. Family Policy Note No. 11, Joint Center for Urban Studies of M.I.T. and Harvard University, February 1979.

Beller, A. The impact of equal employment opportunity laws on the male/female earnings differential. In C. Lloyd, E. Andrews, & C. Gilroy (Eds.), *Women in the labor market*. New York: Columbia University Press, 1979.

Bernard, R.M., & Vinovskis, M. The female school teacher in Ante-Bellum Massachusetts. *Journal of Social History*, 1977, *10*, 332–345.

Blau, F. Sex segregation of workers by enterprise in clerical occupations. In R. Edwards, M. Reich, & D. Gordon (Eds.), *Labor market segmentation*. Lexington, MA: Heath, 1977.

Demos, J. *A little commonwealth: Family life in Plymouth colony*. New York: Oxford University Press, 1970.

Chodorow, N. *The reproduction of mothering*. Berkeley, CA: University of California Press, 1977.

Clarke-Stewart, A. *Child care in the family*. New York: Academic Press, 1977.

Congressional Budget Office. *Child care and preschool: Options for federal support.* Table 9, September 1978.

Cott, N.F. *The bonds of womanhood: Women's sphere in New England, 1780–1835.* New Haven, CN: Yale University Press, 1977.

Douglas, A. *The feminization of American culture.* New York: Knopf, 1977.

Demos, J. *A little commonwealth: Family life in Plymouth colony.* New York: Oxford University Press, 1970.

Dempsey, J. *The family and public policy.* Baltimore, MD: Paul Brookes, 1981.

DuBois, E. The nineteenth century women suffrage movement and the analysis of women's oppression. In Z. Eisenstein, *Capitalist patriarchy and the case for socialist feminism.* New York: Monthly Review Press, 1979.

Easton, B. Feminism and the contemporary family. *Socialist Review,* 1978, *8,* 11–36.

Economic Report of the President, 1973 (Washington, D.C.: U.S. Government Printing Office, 1973).

Ewen, S. *Captains of Consciousness.* New York: McGraw-Hill, 1976.

Faber, M., & Lowrey, H. Women: The new reserve army of the unemployed. In M. Blaxall and B. Reagan (Eds.), *Women and the workplace: The implications of occupational segregation.* Chicago, IL: University of Chicago Press, 1973.

Giele, J. Social policy and the family. *American Review of Sociology,* 1979, *5,* 275–302.

Giraldo, Z.I. *Public policy and the family.* Lexington, MA: Lexington Books, 1980.

Glasco, L. The life cycles and household structure of American ethnic groups: Irish, Germans, and native-born whites in Buffalo, New York, 1855. In T. Harevan (Ed.), *Family and kin in urban communities, 1700–1930.* New York: New Viewpoints, 1977.

Gross, E. Plus ça change . . .? The sexual structure of occupations over time. *Social Problems* 1968–69, *16,* 198–298.

Gordon, L. The struggle for reproductive freedom: Three stages of feminism. In Z. Eisenstein (Ed.), *Capitalist patriarchy and the case for socialist feminism.* New York: Monthly Review Press, 1979.

Grubb, W.N., & Lazerson, M. *Broken promises: How Americans fail their children.* New York: Basic Books, 1982.

Harevan, T. Family time and industrial time: Family and work in planned corporation town, 1900–1924. In T. Harevan (Ed.), *Family and kin in urban communities, 1700–1930.* New York: New Viewpoints, 1977.

Hartmann, H. Capitalism and women's work in the home, 1900–1930, unpublished dissertation. Yale University, 1974.

Hartmann, H. Capitalism and patriarchy. In M. Blaxall & B. Reagan, *Women and the workplace: The implication of occupational segregation.* Chicago, IL: University of Chicago Press, 1976.

Hoffman, L.W., & Nye, I. *Working mothers.* San Francisco, CA: Jossey-Bass, 1974.

Joffe, C. The abortion struggle. *Dissent,* 1981.

Kamerman, S., & Kahn, A. *Family policy: Government and families in fourteen countries.* New York: Columbia University Press, 1976.

Keniston, K. *All our children: The American family under pressure.* New York: Harcourt Brace Jovanovich, 1977.

Kessler-Harris, A. Stratifying by sex: Understanding the history of working women. In R. Edwards, M. Reich, & D. Gordon (Eds.), *Labor market segmentation.* Lexington, MA: Heath, 1967.

Klacynska, B. Why women work: A comparison of various groups—Philadelphia, 1910–1930. *Labor History,* 1976, *17,* 1973–87.

Kleinberg, S.J. Technology and women's work: The lives of working-class women in Pittsburgh, 1870–1900. *Labor History,* 1976, *17,* 58–72.

Kotelchuck, M. The infant's relationship to the father. In M. Lamb (Ed.), *The role of the father in child development*. New York: Wiley, 1976.

Lamb, M. *The role of the father in child development*. New York: Wiley, 1976.

Lein, L., & Associates. *Work and family life*. Cambridge, MA: Center for the Study of Public Policy, 1974.

Lein, L. Parental evaluation of child care alternatives. *Urban and Social Change Review*, 1979, 12–16.

Lemasters, E.E. *Parents in modern America*. Homewood, IL: Dorsey Press, 1974.

Levine, J. *Who will raise the children? New options for fathers (and mothers)*. New York: Lippincott, 1976.

Mincer, J. and Polachek, S., Family Investments in Human Capital: Earnings of Women in T. Schultz, Ed., *Economics of the Family* (Chicago: University of Chicago Press, 1974).

Mohr, J. *Abortion in America: The origins and evolution of national policy, 1800–1900*. New York: Oxford University Press, 1978.

Myrdal, A. *Nation and family*. Cambridge, MA: M.I.T. Press, 1968; original 1941.

Nye, I., and Hoffman, L., *Working Mothers* (San Francisco, Jossey-Bass, 1974).

Oppenheimer, V.K. *The female labor force in the United States, population Monograph Series No. 5*. Berkeley, CA: Institute of International Studies, University of California, 1970.

Pleck, E. Two worlds in one: Work and family. *Journal of Social History*, 1976, *10*, 178–195.

Rubin, L. Worlds of pain. New York: Basic Books, 1976.

Rutter, M. *The qualities of mothering: Maternal deprivation reassessed*. New York: J. Aronson, 1974.

Spock, B. *Baby and Child Care* (New York: Pocket Books, 1947, 1958).

Steiner, G. *The futility of family policy*. Washington, DC: The Brookings Institution, 1981.

Stone, L. *The family, sex, and marriage in England, 1500–1800*. New York: Harper & Row, 1977.

U.S. Bureau of the Census, *Historical Statistics of the United States, Colonial Times to 1970* (Washington, D.C.: U.S. Government Printing Office, 1975).

U.S. Department of Labor, *1975 Handbook on Women Workers* (Washington, D.C.: U.S. Government Printing Office, 1976).

Vanek, J. Time spent in housework. *Scientific American*, 1970, *231*, 116–120.

Wallach, H. *Approaches to child and family policy*. Boulder, CO: Westview Press, 1981.

White, B. *The first three years of life*. Englewood Cliffs, NJ: Prentice Hall, 1975.

Wood, A.D. The war within a war: Women nurses in the union army. *Civil War History*, 1972, *18*, 197–212.

Author Index

257

Subject Index

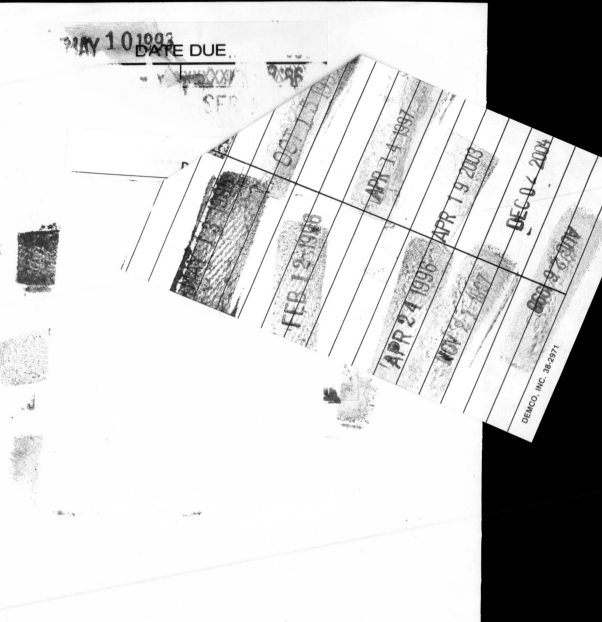